THE ABSORBED SELF

THE ABSORBED SELF

PRAGMATISM, PSYCHOLOGY AND AESTHETIC EXPERIENCE

Ciarán Benson

HARVESTER
WHEATSHEAF

New York   London   Toronto   Sydney   Tokyo   Singapore

First published 1993 by
Harvester Wheatsheaf
Campus 400, Maylands Avenue
Hemel Hempstead
Hertfordshire, HP2 7EZ
A division of
Simon & Schuster International Group

Typeset in 10pt Bembo
by Photoprint, Torquay, Devon

Printed and bound in Great Britain by
Biddles Ltd, Guildford and Kings Lynn

British Library Cataloguing in Publication Data

A catalogue record for this book is available from
the British Library

ISBN 0–7450–1395–3 (hbk)
ISBN 0–7450–1396–1 (pbk)

1 2 3 4 5   97 96 95 94 93

For Carmel

CONTENTS

PREFACE

There are 'bottom-up' and 'top-down' psychologies of art and of aesthetic experience. The first type starts with detailed analyses of how we see form and colour, for example, and leaves the experience of what it is like for me now to be looking at this painting by Spencer or that by Cézanne to another time or to another discipline. The advantages enjoyed by this first approach are largely advantages of the sort natural scientific disciplines enjoy, advantages of control, experimental analysis and verification. Its disadvantage has to do with the almost inevitable postponement of interest in the very complex processes of making or receiving art, and with the limitations of its languages of description and their range of application.

The 'top-down' psychologies start with trying to describe what these experiences of looking or listening or moving are like and with what influences them. If they have disadvantages in the eyes of experimentalists, then these have to do with the complexity of their concepts which elude experimental inquiry. Their advantages are many, however. They start, like folk psychologies, with the experiences to be studied and with the languages that describe these experiences. This has one particular advantage for a psychology of art which is that it both enables and invites collaboration with other interested disciplines such as philosophy, history and theories of criticism. Accordingly, the disciplines must develop some mutual understanding, and a *modus operandi* for investigating the complex problems associated with high-level experiences like the aesthetic.

This book is a contribution to the top-down psychology of aesthetic experience. However, languages of description are not neutral. Every descriptive language makes assumptions, and these help to shape what is then described. Psychologists often seem to be unaware of this and to be strangely blind to its consequences. Philosophy, on the other hand, is always preoccupied with assumptions. When it comes to sophisticated experiences like those of art, psychology will not get far without a partnership in philosophy. That partnership should be explicit and visible. To proceed without it is simply to proceed with an implicit philosophy that will help or hinder the inquiry, but will do so somewhere beyond the horizons of the investigator's critical awareness. My partnership in this book is with the pragmatic philosophy and aesthetics of John Dewey (1859–1952), and to a lesser extent with the work of William James (1842–1910), Charles Sanders Peirce (1839–1914) and George Herbert Mead (1863–1931). I choose pragmatism because I believe it has been unduly eclipsed by analytic and 'continental' traditions in philosophy, and by positivist traditions in psychology, and because I think it deserves a critical re-reading within the context of contemporary cultural theory. It also suits me to select it because it was always, and I believe continues to be, psychologically sympathetic. Philosophies like the phenomenology of Merleau-Ponty are also congenial. Because I have used notes extensively, I have woven the thoughts of other philosophers and psychologists into the main design supplied by pragmatism only where immediately relevant, and have otherwise allowed them to follow a parallel if subterranean path through these notes. Those who wish simply to read the text can do so, but those interested in wider connections and contexts will find them in the notes.

Aesthetic experience is far too complex a topic for one book. My focus is instead on one definitive phase of such experience. This is what I call aesthetic absorption, the experience of 'losing oneself' when looking at a picture or reading a novel, for example. Although it has been widely identified as a key part of aesthetic experience by psychologists, philosophers and artists of all sorts, it has not been investigated in any sustained way.[1] Given its acknowledged importance and interest, this is a curious omission from the theoretical literature on art. In identifying the absence of a satisfactory treatment and in making an initial attempt to fill it, my ambitions have been modest. These have been to make a case for its significance and to outline a description of it, bearing in mind the need for the assumptions of that description to be clear from the outset.

The two approaches to the psychology of art I mentioned above are not of course incompatible, but only incommensurate on occasion. So wherever it is pertinent I will utilize empirical findings, drawn mostly from early developmental psychology, to support my evolving description of aesthetic absorption. Within the topography of contemporary psychology, this book could be taken as an extended essay in cultural or interpretive psychology, as exemplified by Jerome Bruner or Rom Harré, as well as a contribution to the general psychology of aesthetic experience. In this respect, it emphasizes the need for a social–psychological theory of action and context, especially when addressing questions of art and experience. Within philosophical aesthetics, it is a re-reading of pragmatism (particularly of Dewey) on art and self with a view to describing the philosophically neglected topic of aesthetic absorption. In this sense it complements Richard Shusterman's recent revitalization of pragmatist aesthetics. It is also a response to Richard Wollheim's call to 're-psychologize' the theory of art. And within cultural studies, it is an argument for taking pragmatism and psychological studies more seriously and for seeing experiences of absorption as unexplored fusions of public and private interests.

As with all interdisciplinary investigations of complex phenomena, there is a price to be paid for travelling outside disciplinary boundaries. Specialists in one or other field may feel unhappy with the use to which their work is put or with the weight it is being made to carry. They may also experience treatments indebted to other disciplines as *longueurs*, or even as statements of the obvious. This is a common refrain amongst philosophers reading psychology and amongst psychologists reading philosophy. The purpose of the different types of chapter and argument may therefore need to be anticipated so that the attempt at an integrated description may be appreciated.

As a book dedicated to description, each chapter builds upon its predecessor. Chapter 1 is a brief introduction to the idea of aesthetic absorption as a central phase of what are called aesthetic experiences. Its purpose is to offer a general outline of what may be involved in being aesthetically absorbed. Chapter 2 then elaborates the pragmatic context, both philosophical and psychological, within which aesthetic experiences can be described and phases of 'being absorbed' analyzed. Much of this is concerned with problems of how to think of subject–object relations. Against this background, Chapter 3 plays a very specific role in the book's argument. Psychoanalysts are almost alone within the generic field of psychology in offering an explanation for aesthetic absorption. Their accounts use clinically-derived ideas of subject–object relations, boundaries and fusion. These ideas are challenged by more empirically-minded psychologists. I describe these issues and use the occasion to apply the ideas developed in Chapter 2 in a critique of these particular explanations of aesthetic absorption and to suggest the need to think in terms of the mutuality of subject–object constitution rather than in terms of subject–object differentiation. This then sets up the argument which I develop in Chapter 4.

I suspect that some psychologists may have difficulty with this chapter. However, I think that it serves a pivotal role in the unfolding description. Its purpose is to describe some of the key general features of absorption, notably the role of 'I/not-I' and of 'indexical/non-indexical thoughts'. These ideas will probably not be familiar to those unacquainted with the literature on the discursive psychology of self nor with the writings of its, as I argue, pragmatic predecessors. They lead me to explore those aspects of self often described as 'centredness'. There are different ways of being centred, and these are complexly and developmentally linked. It falls to Chapter 5 to show this, albeit in the most general terms.

I concentrate there on that dimension of self which is 'being centred in a field of experience'. I do this in order to spell out the idea that if there are different types of experiential field, and if there are different ways for self to be centred within such fields, then there are fascinating psychological questions to be asked about the transition/transformation of one form of centredness into another. In the context of my particular investigation, this alerted me to the need to outline what I call the process of 'recentring' and to suggest that within the psychology of aesthetic experiences of art, aesthetic absorption might usefully be described as involving the dynamics of recentring. Chapter 6 then offers an initial application of these ideas using pictures and narrative texts. It does this with the further question in mind of how it might be that aesthetic experiences of art could lead to changes of self. Finally, in the Postscript, I raise some general issues to do with self-absorption and with the involvement of the body when someone is aesthetically absorbed. Remembering this structure might help readers to be patient with what they may take to be my occasional long-windedness.

In tackling these neglected questions of self, art and experience I hope to fill a gap in the growing literature on development, psychology and art. Some investigators, such as Parsons (1987), have chosen to study talk about art from a cognitive-developmental perspective. Others have worked within psychoanalytical or within experimental traditions. Others still, such as Harvard's Project Zero, have contributed from within a semiotically influenced cognitive perspective.[2] I hope to suggest that discursive psychological and pragmatic philosophical viewpoints also have a special contribution to make to our understanding of the role of 'self' in complex aesthetic experiences.

There are a number of people to whom I am especially grateful for reading all or some of the chapters and often for not agreeing with me. These are Liberato Santoro, Dermot Moran, Seán Ó'Mathúna, Cyril Barrett, Gerry Gaden, Joe Dunne, Tom McGrath, Thomas Docherty, Rom Harré and Eduard Marbach. David Collins cast the cool eye of a friend on the text just when I needed it, and my editor Farrell Burnett has been splendidly supportive throughout. My final thanks are to Carmel who knows much more about these things than I do.

NOTES

1. See, for example, Diané Collinson's treatment of 'losing ourselves' or or '"being taken out" of ourselves' in Hanfling, 1992, pp. 174–6.
2. For a summary of Project Zero's work see the special 'Art, Mind and Education' issue of *The Journal of Aesthetic Education* (Smith, 1988). For a brief review of cognitive work on aesthetic development see Benson (1989a).

CHAPTER 1

————— · —————

BEING AESTHETICALLY ABSORBED

There was a child went forth every day,
  And the first object he looked upon and received with wonder or
                                                        pity or
  love or dread, that object he became,
  And that object became part of him for the day or a certain part of
                                                        the day
  or for many years or stretching cycles of years.
                                        (Walt Whitman)[1]

ON BEING AESTHETICALLY ABSORBED[2]

There is a famous line in T. S. Eliot's 'Four Quartets' where he speaks of

> music heard so deeply
> That it is not heard at all, but you are the music
> While the music lasts.[3]

What can this mean? How can you be the music, even if only while the music lasts? What is this 'you' and how can it be other than itself? These are some of the facets of aesthetic absorption I will explore in this book. Eliot is one of many who have marked the significant, if elusive, experience of becoming something other than oneself. In 'Among Schoolchildren' W. B. Yeats asks:

> O body swayed to music, O brightening glance,
> How can we know the dancer from the dance?[4]

And Wallace Stevens begins 'The House Was Quiet and the World Was Calm' like this:

> The house was quiet and the world was calm.

1

The reader became the book; and summer night
Was like the conscious being of the book.[5]

Each of these poetic descriptions is of a type of experience in which
selves are described as merging, fusing, uniting with, or simply
becoming something other than themselves.

Critics also use this category of absorption (etymologically
derived from the Latin *absorbere* meaning 'to suck in' or 'to
swallow'). Walter Benjamin, for example, notes that it can involve
a two-way dynamic: 'A man who concentrates before a work of art
is absorbed by it. . . . In contrast, the distracted mass absorbs the
work of art.'[6] In the general literature on art and experience
absorption is described as a 'breaking down the barriers' between
self and object, or as an 'outpouring' of the self 'into' the object.
Absorption is said to involve a 'self-elimination', a 'self-
forgetfulness' or simply a 'loss' such as a loss of subjective time-
sense, sense of place, bodily consciousness or awareness of feelings.
Edward Bullough writes of 'psychical distance' and of 'the utmost
decrease of Distance without its disappearance'.[7] Others write of
being completely attentive and engrossed, of being immersed or
lost in an activity, of being 'engulfed', and of being intensely
concentrated.[8] Terms such as entrancement, enchantment and
bewitchment are also used, with their connotations of pleasure,
wonder and delight.[9]

Analyses by connoisseurs of their own experiences of art are
another source of descriptions. Reflecting on his own long experience of looking at pictures, for example, Kenneth Clark identifies a
recurrent pattern he characterizes as impact, scrutiny, recollection
and renewal.[10] During the impact phase the picture is seen as a
whole. A general impression of the picture forms that depends on
the pictorial qualities of area and tone, shape and colour. This
precedes any identification of the subject of the picture. During the
next phase, that of scrutiny, critical powers come into play and he
finds himself looking for the central idea of the picture. Significantly, he observes that he cannot enjoy what he calls 'a purely
aesthetic relationship' with a picture for longer than he can enjoy
the smell of an orange, which is about two minutes. At this point,
his senses begin to tire, and he begins to utilize his recollections
from art history and criticism to answer questions about the
painting, the painter, the context of the work and so on. Mean-
while, he will find his receptive powers renewing themselves and

can notice 'a beautiful passage of drawing or colour which I should have overlooked had not an intellectual pretext kept my eye unconsciously engaged'.[11] He might then find himself looking at his own everyday world in a way that has been altered by his looking at the picture. In the language of John Dewey as we will shortly encounter it, Kenneth Clark's general impression of a picture, as formed during the impact phase, is the apprehension of the unifying quality or 'sense' of the work.

Clark does not use the phrase 'being absorbed' as part of his analysis, but the two minute duration of the purely aesthetic relationship, during the longer phases of scrutiny and impact, might be taken to describe the general location and duration of what I want to call aesthetic absorption, at least in so far as it relates to looking at pictures.[12] Being absorbed is a common element of experience as people engage in any interesting activity, when, as is often said, they are very 'involved' or 'caught up' in something. It is not clear that the quality of absorption characteristic of aesthetic experiences of art is different in kind from that in intellectual, religious or practical experience. Interesting as this problem is, however, it is not one that I will directly address in this book since my primary purpose will be to offer a description of aesthetic absorption.

Apart from passing references, psychologists and philosophers of art and of the aesthetic have largely bypassed this phenomenon, which lies at the heart of such experiences. Perhaps this is because descriptions of aesthetic absorption face a particular difficulty for reasons that Rudolf Arnheim identified. In reflecting upon what happens when 'the dynamics of the art product engulfs [sic] the self of the performer, creator, or beholder, that is, when the actor *becomes* Othello', Arnheim concludes that 'A psychology of the self does not yet exist that is subtle enough to describe the precise difference between situations in which the self acts as an autonomous perceiver of a dynamic state and those in which the self is the very center of such a state.'[13] In other words, an appropriate theory of self must be available to support any description of aesthetic absorption if it is to deal adequately with the transformation of the autonomous, detached perceiver of an art object into a subject intimately engaged with and centred in 'the world' of the art work.

Something more than a theory of self, however, is needed for a good description of absorption. We also need a theory of self–

other, or of subject–object, *relations*. Speaking at a poetry reading in Dublin, Seamus Heaney once described the process of listening to poetry as 'daydreaming in sympathy'. This is a fertile formulation for a philosophical psychology of aesthetic experience. In coupling daydreaming with being 'in sympathy', Heaney takes into account the mutual contributions of both the listener and the poem to the making of the experience. To describe this complex mutuality we need a theory of experience that does not oversimplify the relationships involved.

Psychological approaches to art and aesthetic experience all too often lack just such an underlying theory of experience. This is evident in psychological studies that are content to describe as 'responses' the encounters of selves (referred to as 'subjects') with works of art (described as 'objects' or, more revealingly, as 'stimuli'). What these approaches miss is the possibility that self and other mutually constitute each other for the duration of certain phases of their relationship. These analytic perspectives cannot cope with the idea that one can *be* the music while the music lasts. They miss the governing and initially undivided wholeness of the experience. They are, moreover, implicitly 'subjectivist'. Their tendency is to think in terms of a fixed subject called the self which does things more or less unilaterally. The idea that subject–object relations can be reciprocal eludes them or is actively denied.[14]

Subjectivist positions in psychologies and philosophies of art, as I am using the term here, overplay the role of self and downplay the role of the other in the dynamics of aesthetic and artistic experience. An illustration of this tendency in psychological aesthetics would be the 1981 study by David O'Hare.[15] In this study, aesthetic responses, so-called, to pictures and poems were analyzed. Using a repertory grid method (a technique derived from George Kelly's personal construct theory that involves eliciting the constructs people use to make sense of, or to 'construct', some aspects of their world), O'Hare shows how a sample of students construed certain pictures and poems that were presented to them. No mention at all is made of *what* pictures, for instance, the subjects were required to construe nor of whether these pictures were presented as originals, photographic prints, slides or whatever. Equally, it is felt unnecessary to say what poems were read to or by the subjects. In the psychological paradigm informing this study, and many like it, the particularity and unique qualities of the objects presented for attention merit no consideration at all, and the conception of· 'response' is wrenched from its context and made to stand unsteadily on its own.

The idea that the object of attention may also have a powerful role to play in the construction of the resulting experience has an exceptionally low profile within this paradigm. But the contrary position, which seeks to locate the determinants of aesthetic experience primarily within the object of experience, is equally problematic. Psychologists of art seem less likely to hold such a position, but some philosophers do. A 1979 paper by Kingsley Price, for instance, may be taken to typify this position.[16] Price argues that an experience cannot be understood in isolation from its object. Every experience, he argues, consists of some awareness and some object. The difference, then, between an aesthetic experience and any other type of experience, say a practical one, must lie either in the awareness or in the object. But according to Price, awareness is intrinsically transparent. We are never aware of awareness, only of that object of which we are aware. In the case of aesthetic experience, according to Price, what distinguishes it from other experiences must be its object. Aesthetic objects, and not some distinctive quality of experience, are what make for aesthetic experiences, according to this view.

The lineage of the position contrary to this, according to Price, runs from Locke and Kant, through Hegel to Dewey, and on to Monroe Beardsley. To these he attributes the idea that what makes an experience aesthetic is not an aesthetic object, but certain intrinsic traits of 'pure' experience. What Price offers here is, as we will shortly see, a rather typical misunderstanding of Dewey's concept of experience. This idea of 'pure' experience would make no sense to Dewey. For him experience is always concretely situated. It is experience of this person at this time in this place of this object. It is of course true that an aesthetic experience of a particular painting is in large part determined by the structure and unity of the particular painting (which is the point missed by psychological paradigms of the sort mentioned above). But it is also true that the person contributes to the nature of the experience of that painting. Dewey would point out that during the process of an actual aesthetic experience, the art object is an intrinsic part of the experience, as is the person. Both are necessary determinants of the integral experience. Experience is the superordinate term.

For a description of aesthetic absorption, therefore, we will need an adequate theory of self together with an appropriate theory of experience. But this will still not be enough. We will also need a description of specific types of experience, namely aesthetic experiences of art. This is because aesthetic absorption is not a 'stand alone' experience. It is a phase in the wider and more complex forms of aesthetic experience. Not all aestheticians are happy with' this idea of 'aesthetic experience' but their objections are not convincing.[17] Aesthetic experiences, however, and especially aesthetic experiences of art objects, are highly complex and difficult to describe. But the attempt must be made before we can explore the role of self and the dynamics of aesthetic absorption.

DESCRIBING AESTHETIC EXPERIENCES OF ART

In trying to offer a general description of aesthetic experience I will follow Nelson Goodman's example and speak of its 'symptoms' rather than try to tightly 'define' it.[18] Specific and detailed analyses of what is called aesthetic experience are scattered widely through the literature of aesthetics, criticism, psychology and autobiography. Drawing on some of these accounts Harold Osborne, in his *The Art of Appreciation*, offers a summary analysis of the characteristics of aesthetic experience.[19] Osborne describes 'appreciation' as a complex way of relating which

> is to be described in terms of taking up an aesthetic attitude to something rather than thinking analytically about it or responding to it emotionally or assessing its utility value or failing to notice it at all. Perhaps most basically of all to be aesthetically preoccupied with a thing is to apprehend it, to enter into growing awareness of it, in a special kind of way which will here be described as 'percipience'.[20]

The experiences associated with 'percipience' are sporadic, intensely memorable, and, in Osborne's view, capable of being developed. The examples he offers are Edward Bullough's famous description of being in a fog at sea, with its notion of 'psychical distance',[21] as well as Pepita Haezrahi's experience of a falling leaf in autumn.[22] One of the functions art has evolved to perform in our time is to invite and facilitate experiences like this. Only those who have such an experience without making any further use of it, however, remain within the aesthetic domain. Once they begin to analyze it, or to pursue it imaginatively, or to use it in any other way, they embark on a different kind of experience which may have its own legitimacy but which is not aesthetic.

Aesthetic experience involves a fixed, sustained attention of a non-instrumental sort to appearances in the here and now. Other aspects include the ideas of immediacy, ineffability, insight and fulfilment. I will touch on some of these other aspects only in so far as they can fill out a description of aesthetic absorption. 'Aesthetic interest', writes Osborne, 'leads to outward-turning forms of activity and inclines us typically to *absorption in the object presented for perception* [my emphasis] not to an inward dwelling upon our own moods and emotions. During aesthetic contemplation we are less rather than more conscious of our own feelings than usual.'[23] Osborne goes on to say that this absorption involves 'a loss of subjective time-sense, a loss of the sense of place and a loss of bodily consciousness' but never to the point where 'ego-consciousness' disappears. There always remains a 'residual aware-ness' of ourselves as spectators, listeners or readers. This, Osborne observes, is a logical requirement for aesthetic awareness and not a merely contingent fact. Like other writers on aesthetic experience, Osborne is indebted to John Dewey. Dewey's work, although very influential during his lifetime, quickly sank into relative obscurity after his death. Recently, however, his significance has begun to be re-examined.

Richard Shusterman is the most recent and persuasive advocate of re-reading what pragmatism has to say about art and aesthetic experience.[24] As would be the case for most contemporary aes-theticians, he came to pragmatic aesthetics after immersion in other traditions and with a liberating sense of surprise at the range and generosity of Dewey's aesthetics in particular. In essence, he locates pragmatist aesthetics as a desirable middle path between analytic aesthetics and poststructuralism. But whereas Shusterman's valu-able revitalization of Deweyan aesthetics unfolds at the general level of aesthetic theory and of its ideological and social relevance, my approach in this book will focus on that particular aspect of aesthetic experience I am calling aesthetic absorption. In discussing Dewey's analysis of aesthetic experience, Shusterman abstracts the following characteristics: that it is above all an immediate and directly fulfilling experience, that it 'involves the whole vital creature and sustains integretative [*sic*] unity in variety', that it is comparatively intense, that it is active and dynamic, that it is shaped through obstacles and resistances, and that it is 'an experience of satisfying form, where means and ends, subject and object, doing and undergoing, are integrated into a unity'.[25] My interest is specifically in this 'unity' of subject and object that I believe Dewey ranked in importance with immediacy when defining art as experience. My reading of Dewey and of other pragmatists like William James and C. S. Peirce is disciplined by this issue, and also by the belief that a developmental psychology of aesthetic experience, and especially of aesthetic absorption, is particularly well served by a pragmatist aesthetics. Consequently, the emphases in my reading of Dewey differ from Shusterman's, albeit in a complementary way.

NOTES

1. See Walt Whitman, 'There was a Child Went Forth', in Whitman, 1960, p. 138.
2. Throughout this book, I will use the word 'aesthetic' to describe the receiver's relationship with an art object, and the word 'artistic' to describe the maker's relationship. Receiver and maker are different roles that can be occupied by the same person.
3. See Eliot, 1969, p. 190.
4. See Yeats, 1970, p. 130.
5. See Wallace Stevens, 1972, p. 279.
6. See his 'The work of art in the age of mechanical reproduction', in Benjamin, 1979, p. 241.
7. See Bullough, 1957.
8. Peter Fuller speaks of 'engulfment'. See Eagleton and Fuller, 1983.
9. Bettleheim, 1982, and also Nell, 1988, especially Chapter 4 on 'Absorption and entrancement'. This offers an account of absorption in 'cognitive' terms, but one that does not tackle the complex phenomenon of aesthetic absorption as I understand it.
10. See Clark, 1960.
11. Ibid., p. 17.
12. It is likely that this varies with the constituting terms of the experience in question and could be longer with, say, a film or a book.
13. Arnheim, 1966, p. 318.
14. Gibson, 1979, does make a case for mutuality in perception. However, I think his welcome aspiration for an ecology of perception outstrips the thinking underpinning his approach. He pays practically no attention to the cultural and interpretive dimensions of perceiving in a social world, and his notion of the self is surprisingly simple. In effect, he identifies self with a notion of the body. For example:

> Information exists in a normal ambient array, therefore, to specify the nearness of the parts of the self to the point of observation – first the head, then the body, the limbs and the extremities. The experience of a central self in the head and a peripheral self in the body is not therefore a mysterious intuition or a philosophical abstraction but has a basis in optical information. (p. 114)

He says that 'Each *individual* sees a different self. Each person gets information about his or her body that differs from that obtained by any other person' (p. 115; emphasis in original) and that 'in fact he lives within his own skin' (p. 115). It seems to me that Gibson's conception of the mutual constitution of organism/self and environment/world is less radical or evident in his work than he thinks. He has a point when he says that the ostensibly separate realms of the subjective and objective 'are actually poles of attention' and that 'the dualism of observer and environment is unnecessary' (p. 116). But he himself seems to oscillate in and out of dualistic thinking. He objects to the subjective/objective distinction but utilizes the within/without construct. His discussion of the demonstratives 'here' and 'there' as being perceptible in terms of surface gradients further suggests this: 'These ranges of magnification and minification between limits link up the extremes of *here* and *out there*, the body and the world, and constitute another bridge between the subjective and the objective' (p. 121; emphasis in original). There is of course a central perceptual dimension to such indexicals that may anchor and help to originate later linguistic indexicals but they and their functions are not reducible to it. I will have much more to say about self and indexicals in later chapters.

15. O'Hare, 1981. For some further discussion of this see Benson, 1989a.
16. Price, 1979. This is indebted to Urmson's views on the aesthetic, and to questions attending aesthetic experience *per se*, without simultaneously attending to the objective aspects of that experience, which a Deweyan perspective would demand. Michael Mitias has answered this objection in detail (1982). He writes:

> Consequently, 'aesthetic-ness' is not, contrary to Price's charge, a simple quality which can be abstracted from 'experience' the way 'yellow' can be abstracted from a pumpkin, or which can be injected or imported into the experience, but a creatively formed reality achieved in the process of aesthetic perception. (p. 168)

See also Mitias, 1988a and 1988b.
17. Some analytic philosophers of art have objected to the concept of aesthetic experience. See, for example, Dickie, 1964 and 1965. For a recent discussion of this debate and for a defence of the concept of 'aesthetic experience' as a type of experience see Mitias, 1988a.
18. Goodman, 1976. There, Goodman makes this point:

> Repeated failure to find a neat formula for sorting experiences into aesthetic and nonaesthetic, in rough conformity with rough usage, suggests the need for a less simple-minded approach. Perhaps we should begin by examining the aesthetic relevance of the major characteristics of the several symbol processes involved in experience, and look for

aspects or symptoms, rather than for a crisp criterion. A symptom is neither a necessary nor a sufficient condition for, but merely tends in conjunction with other such symptoms to be present in, aesthetic experience. (p. 252)

Amongst the symptoms of aesthetic symbol systems and aesthetic functioning enumerated by Goodman himself are exemplification, relative repleteness, syntactic and semantic density, and multiple and complex reference. See also his 'On symptoms of the aesthetic', in Goodman, 1984, pp. 135–8. For an extension of this to aspects of ritual, see Israel Scheffler's 'Symbolic aspects of ritual 11: ritual and reference – five modes', in Scheffler, 1986, pp. 52–9. A similar strategy to the one I adopt here, and one which also draws on the work of Harold Osborne, is favoured by Pierre Bourdieu. See his 'Historical genesis of a pure aesthetic', in Shusterman, 1989, p. 159n6.

19. Osborne, 1970.
20. Ibid., pp. 18–19.
21. Edward Bullough's paper on '"Psychical distance" as a factor in art and an aesthetic principle' was first published in 1912, and is to be found in Wilkinson, 1957 or in Rader, 1979. Bullough's notion of 'psychical distance' is a renovation of the Kantian idea of disinterested contemplation. On this Dewey writes:

> Distance is a name for a participation so intimate and balanced that no particular impulse acts to make a person withdraw, a completeness of surrender in perception. The person who enjoys a storm at sea unites his impulses with the drama of rushing seas, roaring gale and plunging ship.

See Dewey, *Art as Experience*, 1958, p. 258. The most recent scholarly edition of *Art as Experience* is vol. 10 of *John Dewey: The Later Works* (1987), ed. Jo Ann Boydston. Throughout this book, however, my referencing will be to the 1958 edition.

22. Osborne, op. cit., p. 25. For this see Haezrahi, 1954, pp. 25, 35–6.
23. Op. cit., p. 31.
24. See Shusterman, 1992. He locates Dewey's relevance very well within the topography of modern aesthetic theories, and actively applies it to an analysis of contemporary popular music.
25. Ibid., pp. 55–6.

CHAPTER 2

_____ · _____

JOHN DEWEY, AESTHETIC
EXPERIENCE AND ABSORPTION

The painter, when he is really a painter, forms – or rather: he allows
form to arise. He has no intention, no direct one. He is glad to
contribute something to the self-forming work, this or that, adding an
accent to accents, directions to direction, in order to articulate, clarify,
order, to stress, emphasise, reduce in order to strengthen, activate,
suppress. He knows a great deal, but he only knows it _afterwards_.

(Paul Klee, 1930)[1]

DEWEY'S CONCEPT OF EXPERIENCE

Within English language aesthetics, there is some consensus that
John Dewey's _Art as Experience_, published in 1934, is probably the
most significant work on aesthetic experience in the twentieth
century. It has been called 'a work on experience in excelsis'.[2] As to
its place in the recent history of aesthetic thought, Monroe
Beardsley could write in 1966 – albeit controversially – that it was
'by widespread agreement, the most valuable work on aesthetics
written in English (and perhaps in any language) so far in our
century'.[3] In the language of the pragmatists, Dewey's aesthetics
was the consummation of, rather than the conclusion to, his
previous work. Despite the fact that explicit references to the
influence of Dewey in contemporary aesthetics are hard to come
by, the unacknowledged presence of his work is pervasive.[4] The
'enormous richness of suggestion' that Beardsley discerned in _Art as
Experience_ is far from exhausted. In the period since the publication
of _Art as Experience_, expositions of its ideas have not been lacking
and it is not my intention to add to them except in so far as is

11

necessary to contextualize Dewey's ideas concerning absorption and self.[5]

Dewey insists that

> the uniquely distinguishing feature of esthetic experience is exactly the fact that no such distinction of self and object exists in it, since it is esthetic in the degree in which organism and environment cooperate to institute an experience in which the two are so fully integrated that each disappears.[6]

Dewey thinks of absorption in terms of the self's surrender in the aesthetic construction of the object. Perception and its object progressively and mutually constitute each other within aesthetic experience. Such absorption is not exclusive to aesthetic experience. It is an ideal, according to Dewey, for all experience 'when the desires and urgencies of the self are completely engaged in what is objectively done.'[7] This understanding of absorption requires a conception of experience as constituted by the interactive relationship of self and object. Absorption is a quality of that relationship. In the experience of art, there is a 'rhythm of surrender and reflection'.[8] Absorption refers to the initial phase of the 'total overwhelming impression', a pre-reflective phase where the self gives itself over to the power of the object, exercising minimal control over the nature and direction of the experience. This, necessarily, is a brief experience and it may be succeeded by reflective experiences where answers are sought to questions of what, how and why concerning the previous phase. This reflective phase may lead to a return to the object and perhaps to a fuller and more elaborate experience. Hence Dewey's description of the process as a rhythm. For him, aesthetic absorption is a participative form of involvement in the formation of experience, where the self constructs the object and the object the self in mutually determinative ways.

In so far as John Dewey's philosophy was an attempt to refashion the idea of experience, it has failed to have any significant impact on the commonly held idea of experience. The result is that he is easily prone to misinterpretation, if not simply to incomprehension. This is further exacerbated by his writing style. In contrast to the vitality and sheer colour of his fellow pragmatist William James, Dewey's style exhibits, as Anthony Quinton observes, 'frequent turgidness and amorphousness'.[9] To others such as Israel Scheffler his writing is 'difficult and fine-textured'.[10] Each of these evaluations of his writing style is true. Dewey himself was aware of the obscurity with which his style confronted his readers, but felt that this difficulty was a necessary consequence of his attempt to deal formally and theoretically with 'the material of a maturing experience of contacts with realities'.[11] He felt obliged to avoid 'a specious lucidity and simplicity'. However, even the sympathetic William James was worried by Dewey's 'unchained formlessness of expression', as Jacques Barzun reminds us.[12]

Today, the Western vernacular concept of experience is of a subjectively circumscribed event, something that an individual has *of* something else, most likely in the past. But Dewey's idea of experience is much wider than this, and in key respects its opposite. At the very end of his life, having used his particular concept of experience as the keystone of his philosophical thinking, Dewey ruefully observed that the historical obstacles in the way of understanding his use of the idea of 'experience' were too great. Some such idea as 'culture', he felt, would have enabled him to be better understood.[13] Why he held so doggedly to this idea of experience is closely related to how he came to acquire it.

The roots of Dewey's concept of experience lie in a late nineteenth century post-Kantian tradition with a strong Hegelian emphasis on continuity and on overcoming the dualism of subject and object. This fundamental dualism of the internal and the external, of body and mind, was Descartes's legacy to Western philosophy. Kant exerted a particular influence on the thinking of both C. S. Peirce and John Dewey. Dewey, for example, completed his doctoral dissertation on *The Psychology of Kant* in 1884. However, in that same year Dewey published an article that foreshadowed his own theory of experience.[14] In it, Kant's recognition of the mutual dependence of conception and perception is the occasion for Dewey to emphasize the idea of knowledge as synthesis emerging from the dialectical relation of sense (thesis) and reason (antithesis). Even then, however, Dewey was finding the epistemological dualism of Kant problematic and was using elements of Hegelianism to achieve the unity of knower and known. He offers the image of the relationship of the parts to the whole of the organism as the best analogy for understanding the relationship of the Kantian categories to experience. An 'organic relation' obtains between subject and object; this relation is neither transcendental nor external but immanent, a higher unity constituted by the relation itself. In support of this idea, Hegel's dialectic allowed Dewey the following formulation: 'as Reason goes on manifesting its own nature through successive differences and unities, each lower category is not destroyed, but retained . . . at its proper value.'[15]

I think that one of Dewey's clearest presentations of his concept of experience is contained in a paper from 1917 called 'The need for a recovery of philosophy'.[16] Since his aesthetics is based on an interpretation of art *as* experience, it is worth spending some time at this stage clarifying his idea of experience and highlighting the underlying belief in the continuity of self with the physical and social world. He presents his view by contrasting it with opposing viewpoints. His main opposition is the subjectivist view that locates experience within individual consciousness and pays inadequate attention both to the situation, or context, and to the object of experience. He argues that the idea of experience must emerge from an examination of 'experience itself' and not from deductions of what it must be. Hume's separate sensations and ideas, for example, were a logical deduction from an a priori and unexamined concept of experience. Kant accepted this particularistic account of experience and corrected its empirical shortcomings by introducing a Reason that transcended experience and provided the necessary synthesis of the particulars. But Dewey, indebted as he now was to William James's analysis of the stream of thought (which I will consider below), could describe experience as 'a diversity of ceaseless changes connected in all kinds of ways, static and dynamic'.[17] From this point of view, Dewey felt that the empiricism of Hume and the rationalism of Kant become redundant since the rational solutions provided by Kant are unnecessary, given that the problems presented by Hume are false. They are false because the organization of experience is not particularistic as Hume's analyses of the origin of ideas led him to believe, but coherently organized as described by the psychological analyses of William James.

Following on from this, Dewey proposes five contrasts to define his concept of experience. These are contrasts between his idea of experience and what he takes to be the generally accepted understanding of experience. Where the conventional view considers experience to be primarily concerned with knowledge, Deweyan experience centres on the full relationship of a living being with its physical and social environment. This is a much more general and inclusive idea of experience than the one that identifies experiencing with knowing. A second difference concerns the generally held view of experience as a mainly subjective event. Dewey argues that it should be seen as part of a wider objective world that enters into people's actions and sufferings and is transformed by their reactions. And again, where the conventional view situates experience in the present but more predominantly in the past, so that the essence of experience is a reference to what has already taken place, Dewey stresses its connection with the future – its experimental projection into an indeterminate future. One view remembers the past as given, whereas the other anticipates the past as changeable. The fourth difference is that the conventional view stresses the particular and the discrete, and suspiciously views relations and connections as imports from outside experience. Dewey, on the other hand, highlights such relations, connections and continuities. He sees them as intrinsic to experience and as deriving from the intimate and open relationship a living being naturally has with its world. Finally, traditional empiricism contrasts experience and thought, reserving inference for the latter. For Dewey this is a false opposition since all conscious experience is intrinsically inferential.

These are the hallmarks of Dewey's concept of experience and they are directly related to what has been called his 'anti-intellectualism', his opposition to the idea that the map of knowing is the same as that of experience. Descartes is once again his primary opponent here. Dewey repeatedly attacks the Cartesian conception of the world for its duality of inner experience and outer reality, and for its legacy of related dualisms such as knower and known, mind and nature, subject and object, inner and outer life. Cartesianism's central distinction of subject and object, of inner and outer, is not, he maintains, a given part of experience. In the unanalyzed totality of pre-reflective experience, the 'two conjugate components' – to use Jerome Bruner's phrase[18] – of trying and undergoing, act and material, are one. Accordingly, the language of parts and of their relations emerges as a consequence of analytic reflection which in turn reads these distinctions back into the experience reflected upon. Cartesians begin with an already distinguished and separated subject and object, whereas Dewey insists that the integrity of pre-reflective experience is a given and must be the starting point for philosophy. Philosophy can then examine how and why reflective analyses make such distinctions within experience.

For Dewey, knowing is but one mode of human experience. Its contribution is to deepen, expand and integrate experience into a more fruitful and comprehensive form. At least four significant influences combine to form Dewey's epistemology. These are Peirce's anti-Cartesianism, Peirce's insistence that knowledge is socially grounded, William James's emphasis on knowledge as an active exploratory process, and the idea, argued by F. C. S. Schiller, that the conceptual instruments of human thought are human constructions. The result is Dewey's 'anti-intellectualism' which Anthony Quinton contrasts with the Cartesian tradition.[19] My particular interest in these contrasts is that they reveal some of the ways in which Dewey thinks of the human subject, and this is important for understanding the self-forgetfulness of aesthetic absorption.

To start with, Cartesianism wants to base all knowledge on absolutely certain premises. But Dewey argues that all human beliefs are open to error and correction. 'Warranted assertibility' rather than absolute certainty is the best that can be achieved. Because of this, Dewey characterizes himself as a theorist of inquiry rather than of knowledge. A second contrast concerns the degree to which the self is distanced from what it knows. Far from being the detached, contemplative spectator Descartes takes to be the knowing self, Dewey's inquirer or knower is an active experimenting being who participates in the world. Rational belief is the outcome of deliberate, experimental interaction by the subject with that world. The conceptual instruments of human knowing are constructed by ourselves as a consequence of trying to meet our needs and to fulfil our purposes. Connected with this idea of the self as a part of the world is the objection to the knowing subject as a Cartesian *res cogitans*, a pure mind or consciousness. The Deweyan subject is an intelligent incarnate being who is animated by primarily bodily purposes and who forms beliefs about the world through interacting with it. Finally, if the Cartesian knower lives in subjective isolation, the Deweyan inquirer is an intrinsically social being. Knowledge is a social product constructed of 'funded experience' upon which all may draw.[20] From these contrasts, Dewey's holistic perspective is quite evident. We can also see that the Deweyan subject or self is an incarnate social being who is immersed as a participant in the world, and who moves by active, fallible experimentation into a projected future.[21]

As I have emphasized, it is the idea of continuity that provides Dewey with the alternative to the dualistic notions he finds so pervasive in philosophy and psychology. This concept pervades his philosophy of experience and is especially important in his aesthetics.[22] Apart from the philosophical influence of Hegel, Dewey is indebted to Charles Darwin, William James and George Herbert Mead for his developed idea of continuity. Each of these applied the idea of continuity to a different aspect of experience. Darwin laid the basis for thinking of humankind as continuous with the natural world, William James argued for the continuity of the individual stream of consciousness, and George Herbert Mead developed ways of thinking about the continuity of self and society.

For Dewey, the complete 'situation' is the right starting point for any inquiry into experience. It is from a first consideration of 'the inclusive and the connected' that one should then proceed to consider the differentiations of that whole.[23] Those working in traditions in which the primary focus is on particulars, on the basis of which one works towards a notion of the whole constituted by these parts, are especially likely to be impatient with Dewey. Dewey argues that the given or 'the original datum, is always a qualitative whole'.[24] J. E. Tiles suggests that the reason why Dewey was so attracted to William James's description of infant experience ('a blooming, buzzing confusion') was that it epitomized the idea of progressive differentiation within an organic whole.[25] I will return to this question of how the infant's consciousness differentiates when I explore the development of that aspect of self that is its 'centredness' in Chapter 5. But at this point I want to review briefly the impact James's formulation of the stream of consciousness had on Dewey.

The Principles of Psychology was published in 1890 and straightaway established itself as a classic work of psychology.[26] James's formulation of the 'stream of thought' had an immediate and lasting effect on Dewey. James singled out five characteristics of this stream, the third of which was the proposition that 'within each personal consciousness, thought is sensibly continuous.'[27] By 'continuous' James meant 'without division'. There are 'interruptions' such as occur between sleeping and waking, or when a thought has no connection with preceding thoughts. Yet, notwithstanding this, the consciousnesses before and after such breaks still *feel* as though they belong together as part of the same self. The changes in the quality of consciousness from one moment to another are never absolutely abrupt. The continuous nature of subjective life requires the metaphor of the stream rather than that of the chain for its description. But there are 'sudden "contrasts in the quality" of the successive segments of the stream of thought' whose place in the continuity of consciousness must be accounted for.[28] It is the distinction between a thought and that of which it is a thought that ensures that the metaphor of the stream is not contradicted by such sudden breaks. Things referred to within the stream of thought may be discontinuous and discrete, but there is a 'large amount of affinity that may still remain between the thoughts by whose means they are cognized'.[29]

Change of subjective state may proceed at different rates. When slow, the person is aware of his or her thought in a stable restful way; when rapid, the awareness is of passage, of relation, of transition from the subjective state or between it and something else. According to James, we have immediate experience of the connections in consciousness. Language refers to such connections by prepositions and conjunctions. This idea that we have immediate experience of the connections in consciousness, rather than having all connections supplied afterwards by some sort of 'Reason', was to be a seminal idea in Dewey's account of the relations of cognitive to other modes of experience, and one that wins support from contemporary work on the development of consciousness in infants.[30]

In situations that become problematic, the connections in immediate non-cognitive experience can be thematized and can become objects of knowledge. The pace of the stream of thought is likened by James to a bird's life 'made of an alternation of flights and perchings'.[31] Dewey uses this image a number of times in his aesthetics. The rhythm of language manifests this by expressing every thought in a sentence and closing every sentence with a period. The 'perchings', or substantive parts of the stream of thought, are usually occupied by some kind of sensorial imagination that can be contemplated without it changing. On the other hand, the 'flights', or transitive parts of the stream, are occupied by thoughts of relations that may be static or dynamic and that usually obtain between the objects occupying the states of rest. The primary purpose of thinking, observes James, appears to be 'at all times the attainment of some other substantive part than the one from which we have just been dislodged. And we may say that the main use of the transitive parts is to lead us from one substantive conclusion to another.'[32] William James recognized the significance of the vague and the fleeting, the unnamed and hence the inadverted-to in experience. His influence enabled Dewey to think of relations as given parts of consciousness itself rather than as later additions by thought. James also moved Dewey towards a more biological conception of experience. As Gordon Allport put it, Dewey 'felt encouraged to abandon transcendental psychology for good and all in favour of a more earthy functionalism'.[33]

This Jamesian idea that connections are inherent parts of 'immediate non-cognitive experience' is a central feature of Dewey's philosophy of experience. But what can be said of primary, or precognitive or non-cognitive experience? Knowledge that, in Dewey's view, is always of relations, is existentially rooted in qualitative events. Were this not so, its subject matter would be 'algebraic ghosts, relations that do not relate'.[34] Knowledge always involves the *use* that is to be made of experienced events. Human beings' only way of controlling nature, according to Dewey, is to transform 'presence-in-experience' into 'presence-in-knowledge'.[35.] In this way Dewey endorses the Kantian view that perceptions are blind and conceptions empty when each is unsupported by the other. But unlike Kant, who thought of perception and conception as arising from different sources and so as requiring synthetic understanding to relate them, Dewey considers the difference between them to be a functional one. Perception locates and describes a problem whereas conception represents possible methods of solution. The 'facts' of a case are not to be taken as presented but rather as re-presented; they are not to be taken as qualitative but rather as symbolically formulated propositions.

While Dewey has much to say of the derived, refined, secondary objects of knowing experience, he has very little to say about 'primary' experience. This is simply because so little can be *said* of it. By 'direct' experience is meant experience of a particular object in all its qualitative individuality in the here and now. All direct experience is qualitative, and the role of reflection is to seek relations 'behind' immediately perceived qualities, without being bound to take account of the actual qualitative setting. For Dewey it is perfectly reasonable to talk of immediate experience which may be of an object or of an already mediated event. What he opposes is the idea of immediate *knowledge* since by definition all knowledge is necessarily mediated. But what more can be said of qualities? Dewey simply says that 'quality is quality, direct, immediate and undefinable'[36] and that the 'immediacy of existence is ineffable'.[37] Discourse and words can assist us in having experiences of things immediately by guiding us as to the ways of doing so; but they cannot adequately represent the directly available presence of things. As soon, however, as the quality is taken as a sign and related to other things, its immediate qualitativeness is superseded and it becomes an object of knowledge.

Like William James, Dewey is anxious to highlight the immediate, the transitory and the qualitatively unique since these had been relegated to relatively trivial status by the more dominant philosophical systems that had esteemed the general, the recurrent and the extensive. He aimed to redress the balance by arguing that 'the universal and stable are important because they are the instrumentalities, the efficacious conditions, of the occurrence of the unique, unstable and passing.'[38] Signs and symbols are more lasting than the events they signify. So it is that discourse engenders re-flection, re-collection and fore-sight. The symbolic enables the constitution and conquest of past and future time, but, to some extent at least, at the cost of present time. But this is not so for all symbols. Artistic symbols, and aesthetic experiences of them, become meaningful only for those who are capable of being fully co-present with them. The experience that emerges as a consequence of this relationship is the *work* of art. This is why Dewey can speak of art as experience. To explain this further, we must turn now to an examination of Dewey's aesthetics.

DEWEY'S THEORIES OF AESTHETIC EXPERIENCE

The distinctiveness of Dewey's philosophy of aesthetic experience can best be appreciated when it is contrasted with other aesthetic theories. Dewey is fundamentally naturalistic in his insistence that aesthetics be grounded in the activities and physicality of human being. This allows him to stress the way in which, for example, a bird's making of its nest is continuous with a person's making of, say, a painting. In sharp contrast, analytic aesthetics is firmly against attempts to situate aesthetics in a naturalistic context. If Deweyan aesthetics sees art as basically instrumental in serving and enhancing the vitality of selves as they relate to their worlds, analytic aesthetics tends to follow Kant and to stress the disinterestedness and non-instrumentality of art. For Dewey, however, this Kantian view results in 'a thoroughly anaemic conception of art'.[39] Dewey rejects all attempts to seal the aesthetic and art off from the rest of living. His explicit aim is to recover 'the continuity of esthetic experience with normal processes of living'.[40]

Whereas science, with its logical precision and rigorous methodology, is the paragon for analytic aesthetics, for Dewey artistic/ aesthetic experience is humanly richer and more fully engaging than scientific experience. Dewey understood the power and importance of science and dealt with it at length. But he did not feel that it was appropriate to seek in artistic and aesthetic experience the same sort of clarity that could be found in scientific experience. Artistic and aesthetic experience are richer forms of experience because, he argues, they have an immediacy and power to engage the person at all levels of being. Nonetheless, because of his insistent interest in finding the basic commonalities of all experiences, Dewey resists the differentiation of the scientific and the artistic/aesthetic and develops a theory that allows for scientific experience itself to be seen as aesthetic.

This attempt to seek the overlaps and continuities between apparently disparate forms of experience flies in the face of the distinction-making that characterizes so much analytic philosophy. Deweyan and analytic aesthetics also differ in their aims. Analytic aesthetics seeks to analyze and clarify established concepts and practices in the field of art. Deweyan aesthetics has its sights set more ambitiously and practically. It recognizes that 'Art' emerges from a socio-historical process and that this is ever-changing. The experiences that are artistic or aesthetic continually break the boundaries of aesthetic theory, and theory must recognize this. The ultimate purpose of aesthetics is to enhance the chances of having and of enjoying artistic and aesthetic experiences. Aesthetics, in this view, is not a detached procedure in the manner of 'objective' science, but is more like a participant in the process under observation. This is why Dewey opposes the isolationist tendencies of 'high art', and fights for an understanding of art as an integral, continuous part of everyday life.

Conceptions of 'art' as that which is found in museums have their roots, in Dewey's view, in the nationalism and imperialism that nourished the growth of such institutions.[41] Both art and our theories of art are powerfully conditioned by socio-economic and historical contexts. These emphases on context reveal a further contrast between Deweyan and analytic aesthetics. Analytic aesthetics focuses on the material object (the painting, the poem, the dance) as the work of art. Deweyan aesthetics, on the other hand, understands the *work* of art to be the experience that results from the transaction of the perceiving person's aesthetic relationship with the material object or event through which that object – which itself participates in the process – is created and re-created. These radically different conceptions of 'the work of art' – the one centred on the object/product, the other centred on a dynamic experiential process – form an essential difference between analytic and Deweyan aesthetics.

If one approaches Dewey from an analytic perspective, according to which experience is understood as being subjective (i.e. what it is like for the subject) and in which the 'work of art' is understood as being the art object/product, then undoubtedly his argument that art must be understood as experience will seem bizarre, if not downright obtuse. On the other hand, if one is unhappy with the idea of aesthetic experience as an isolated subject's experience of a discrete 'work of art', then Deweyan aesthetics, like contemporary continental aesthetics, offers an interesting alternative to the analytical philosophical approach. Better still, perhaps, it offers a wider field of interest within which the methods of analytic philosophy might be applied. It also offers a more dynamic description of aesthetic experience than that implicit in positivistic psychological aesthetics, which aims to study the individual's 'responses' to art objects. As I have already stressed, an adequate psychology of art demands a dynamic philosophy of experience to underpin it.

Dewey's aesthetics presents two accounts of aesthetic experience, one general and pertinent to many different types of experience, and one specific to experiences of art. The distinctive difference between instances of Dewey's general theory and his specific theory of the aesthetic in relation to the arts has to do with the materials of the experience. Dewey's concept of material is relational. The materials of experience are constituted by the transactions of the experiencing person and the experienced object or event. It is in this context that the strands or tendencies within an aesthetic experience of an art object can be understood.

At its best, says Dewey, human experience 'signifies complete interpenetration of self and the world of objects and events'.[42] There is a vast world beyond each person and 'any intense realization of its presence with and in us brings a peculiarly satisfying sense of unity in itself and with ourselves.'[43] Often this becomes clearest when the link is broken. The person may then experience disintegration since personal unity and fulfilment depend upon adequate relations with the world.[44] The incorporation of the art object into the work of art depends upon the active collaboration of the person.[45] For Dewey the 'work' of art is the experience that is the outcome of the interaction of self and art object. The work of art is not therefore the object, but the *process* of construction of a particular experience, an experience that is a joint production of the art object/event and the person who re-creates it. The form of such experience is an organized fusion of subject and object moving through an act of reciprocal doing and undergoing. And the occasion for good form in art is of the same type as for the aesthetic form or organization of other types of experience. What the arts characteristically do is to enact 'more deliberately and fully the conditions that effect this unity. Form may then be defined as the operation of forces that carry the experience of an event, object, scene, and situation to its own integral fulfillment.'[46]

It is in this notion of form, perhaps, that Dewey's distinctive formulation of art as experience can most clearly be grasped. This is an important and controversial idea. Some, like Monroe Beardsley, have dismissed this idea as 'cryptic', whereas others, like Richard Shusterman, identify it as 'perhaps Dewey's most central aesthetic theme: the privileging of aesthetic experience over the material object which ordinary, reified thinking identifies (and then commodifies and fetishizes) as the work of art'.[47] Dewey's deliberate transfer of emphasis from the art product as isolated, autonomous object to a more open, inclusive and dynamic conception of aesthetic experience anticipates much that is to be found in poststructuralist aesthetics.

As an example of how this idea may be critically applied, take the criticism Dewey makes of one of I. A. Richards's formulations. Richards had observed that we are used to saying that a picture is beautiful, rather than saying, as he thinks we should, that it causes an experience in us that is valuable in certain ways. Dewey objects to the dualism implied here, and in particular to the abstraction 'in us'. His argument is this:

> it is not the painting as a *picture* (that is the object in esthetic experience) that causes certain effects *in us*. The painting as a picture is *itself a total effect* brought about by the interaction of external and organic causes. . . . The *picture* is the integral outcome of their interaction with what the mind through the organism contributes.'[48]

In other words 'the picture' *is* the experience that results from the transaction of a person with the object that is 'the painting'. In experience, the painting becomes the picture and has its being neither in the object nor in the person but in the dynamic person–object relationship.[49] In all of Dewey's writings on experience, his pivotal preoccupation is with the dash in 'subject–object', or more generally with that in 'organism–world'. Once we have participated in the experience of the painting as a picture, we might then reflectively analyze the experience in order to determine how in fact we and the painting interacted to produce the experience. That is to say that the experience that is the outcome or conclusion of that interaction may, upon the instigation of reflection, become the starting point of an analysis. Here, as throughout his work, we find Dewey searching for the most precise way to convey his understanding of experience and, while retaining the word, trying radically to reformulate its meaning and consequences for critical analysis.

In general terms the work of art elicits and accentuates 'this quality of being a whole and of belonging to the larger, all-inclusive, whole which is the universe in which we live. This fact', suggests Dewey, 'is the explanation of that feeling of exquisite intelligibility and clarity we have in the presence of an object that is experienced with esthetic intensity.'[50] The intimate link between the aesthetic and the mystical in Dewey's thinking is evident here. Descriptions of mystical experiences, especially in the Buddhist traditions, bear many similarities to his notion of aesthetic experience.[51] Louis Arnaud Reid, the British philosopher, has analyzed similarities between aesthetic and mystical experiences. One point of resemblance is what is called the ineffability of both types of experience. 'What we know in art', he writes, 'cannot be told – except by presenting art to be experienced.'[52] Another similarity is the intense, concentrated attention or contemplation involved in both. There is also a breaking down of barriers between self and other, 'an outpouring of self into the object'.[53] But most important is the immediacy or directness of contact with what is given 'in contrast to commerce with the dialectic of symbols and concepts'.[54] Dewey makes the same point when he insists that 'what is not immediate is not esthetic.'[55]

William James had already identified these characteristics of what he called the 'mystical group' in his *The Varieties of Religious Experience*.[56] Such states of mind are ineffable in that they defy expression in words; are transient and cannot be sustained for long; involve a 'noetic quality' yielding insights beyond the reach of discursive thought; and, perhaps after a period of active preparation, the subject of such experience feels him- or herself as though 'held by a superior power'. Although James never identified an 'aesthetic group' of experiences, the similarities between his analysis of the mystical and the accounts of aesthetic experience given above are striking. His explanation of the attendant ineffability of such a state has to do with the immediacy or directness with which its quality is experienced. 'One must have musical ears to know the value of a symphony; one must have been in love one's self to understand a lover's state of mind.'[57] L. A. Reid makes no reference to James, nor indeed to Freud's notion of the 'oceanic feeling', to which I will return in the next chapter. Yet the similarities between the various accounts echo the link between the aesthetic and the mystical that is evident in Dewey's thought. Of special interest to us, however, is the identification of immediacy and of absorption as key aspects of both aesthetic and of mystical experiences.

An intellectual experience and an experience of art may share a similar organization of a kind that makes both aesthetic in the sense of Dewey's general theory of the aesthetic. But there is a stronger sense in which the experience of art is aesthetic. The material of intellectual experience is constituted by symbols that, because of their universality, abstraction and generally conventional rather than intrinsic relationship to what they signify, are not connected with the *qualities* of the realities to which they refer. A good artist, on the other hand, must master the exacting process of thinking in terms of the 'relations of qualities', qualities of things to be seen, heard, touched and so on.[58] Both types of material, and others, may constitute an experience that 'has a satisfying emotional quality because it possesses internal integration and fulfillment reached through ordered and organized movement. This artistic structure may be immediately felt. In so far, it is esthetic.'[59]

For Dewey, therefore, the experience of art may be aesthetic in two separate senses. It is aesthetic in the general sense if the 'organization' of the experience, as it develops in time, is of a specific kind. It is aesthetic in that sense specific to the arts if, in addition to its coherent organization, the 'materials' of the experience are of particular kinds and if they function in particular ways. It is important to stress that 'material' here does not simply mean physical constituents of art objects. Art, as experience, is a rhythmic unity of resistance, anticipation and resolution. It is not the art object on its own, nor the percipient subject on his or her own, nor simply both together. It resides in the dynamic relation of both, and it is that interactive relationship which is called the aesthetic experience of art. That experience is what the 'work' of art is, and that is what Dewey means when he proposes art as experience. In art work the factors that contribute to the rhythm and integrity of *an* experience (Dewey's colloquial phrase for a generally aesthetic experience), are 'lifted high above the threshold of perception and are made manifest for their own sake'.[60]

These are the ways in which Dewey wants the closely related ideas of experience, the aesthetic, art and the work of art to be understood. When plucked from the context of his extended presentation in *Art as Experience* – a presentation that systematically reformulates these commonly used terms in order to rehabilitate their non-dualistic meanings – Dewey's use of them runs a high risk of being misunderstood. His underlying preoccupation with experience as a series of dynamic interactional relationships is often lost when he is read by those unaware of his idiosyncratic redefinitions of common terms such as 'experience' or 'work of art'.

I can now return to the question of self. What is this 'self' that participates in aesthetic experiences of art? Recall Dewey's insistence that the uniquely distinguishing feature of aesthetic experience is that the distinction of self and object is erased and that they unite as parts or processes of a newly integrated experience. I took this to be a characterization of aesthetic absorption. But what does Dewey understand 'self' to be?

DEWEY'S CONCEPT OF SELF

I have already presented a negative description of what Dewey understands as the human subject. I said that Dewey's conception of the subject could best be described in terms of what it is not. It is not a detached, passive contemplative subject playing the role of a spectator; it is not an entity or pure mind constituted of some mental 'stuff' or *res cogitans*; nor is it subjectively isolated and detached from social life. Instead, human selves are intelligent, incarnate, active, experimenting, participating and social. Dewey's self is an active process and not an entity. His concept of experience is not of a subjectively or psychically circumscribed event. This is not to say that Dewey repudiates subjectivity. What he wants to emphasize is that the wider non-self world enters into the actions and sufferings of selves, and is transformed by their reactions. He wants subjectivity to be understood as residing in the interactional relations of self and the non-self world. In so far as Dewey, the later James, Peirce and Mead share a similar understanding of self, it is its nature as an interactional process that promises to be most helpful in understanding aesthetic absorption and the ways in which self can become other than itself. In later chapters, I will have more to say about the theories of self of C. S. Peirce, William James and G. H. Mead, each of whom influenced Dewey's thinking on the nature of the human subject. At this point, all I want to do is to make a few general points about Dewey's concept of self.

Mind and self are not synonyms for Dewey. Under the influence of Hegel's 'objective mind' (the idea that formative cultural institutions are mind objectified), Dewey attacks the idea of mind as ready-made and of subjectivity as some form of exclusively inward landscape. Minds must develop and differentiate from the larger whole of which they are a part, and so must selves. Dewey's conception of mind is far wider than that which identifies mind as an individual possession. What he offers is an 'emergent' theory of mind.[61] Novel qualities emerge as the organization of physical reality becomes more complex. Since the condition of living is a condition of continuous dialogue and adjustment by a living creature with its world, the qualities that constitute consciousness are qualities of reaction and of adjustment. As such, they are not exclusively qualities of bodily processes, but instead they inhere in the relations between the 'inside' and 'outside' of the organism.

With the development of language – understood in its widest sense as symbolic activity – there emerges a wide variety of activities that also become capable of being instruments. This is what, in Dewey's view, marks the emergence of mind, and especially of distinctively human mind. Against the idea, associated with Locke, that the function of language is to express or convey already existing thoughts, Dewey's claim is that it is language itself that makes thought possible, and with it such functions as reflection, foresight and recollection. But language, considered developmentally, must be understood as emerging from patterns of communication and from the coordination of interactions within social groups. These interpersonal patterns of communication – Wittgenstein's language games – precede the infant's observable development of symbolic functioning. The infant's language development seems to presuppose them. Furthermore, the meaning of language resides in use. Both Dewey and the later Wittgenstein 'rejected the notion that purely private experience could be what gives our words meaning: rather the reverse is the case, a publicly shared language is a condition of being able to refer to our inner states.'[62]

Language and self are, therefore, intimately connected. Dewey's broad conception of language is of a 'system of responses which incorporate the perspectives of others.'[63] Both mind and self, in his view, are best thought of as verbs rather than as nouns, as activities that develop out of active relations with the world and especially out of active social relations with other people.[64] This is for Dewey an empirically justified belief, and it is one I will actively consider in later chapters when I will use a broadly social constructivist theory of self to analyze aesthetic absorption, and to tease out some of what might be involved in the claim that aesthetic experiences of art can lead to changes of self.

Dewey is acutely aware of how the activities and functions that are mind and self are continuous with other non-linguistic and non-cognitive levels of interaction, and he highlights the primacy of contexts or situations in the constitution of experience.[65] This concept of 'situation' is one of the most important in his analytic lexicon. In line with his perennial insistence on the primacy of context in experience, Dewey insists on recognizing the constitutive power of relationships and on seeing them as part of what makes any object what it is. Objects – which he understands as being 'events with meanings'[66] – belong to wholes or contexts for which Dewey reserves the word 'situation'. Situations are 'wholes' which refer to the sum-total of all that is involved in the transactions of a living being with its environment at a particular time. Situations are unified by a single quality that pervades them, and that is directly felt by the living creature. This is what Dewey means by the *sense* of a situation. The parts that make up the whole which is the situation with its unifying sense, and which is directly felt by the participating organism, are the *significant* elements of that situation. As Tiles puts it, 'Sense/signification is the situation/object distinction in its subjective aspect, and this use of "object" is consistent with the definition of "objects" in *Experience and Nature* as "events with meanings".'[67]

As an example, take the idea of a situation having an emotional quality. When, for instance, a situation is characterized by a sense of anger it is as though everything is touched by the anger; there is the angry person, the objects and events about which he or she is angry, the context that houses the anger, and so on. It seems that anger pervades everything to do with it. The situation is unified by this quality of anger which is directly felt by its protagonist, the angry person. But that angry person is not aware of something called 'anger' which is causing him or her to be angry. The person's awareness is of the objects, events and circumstances that together compose this angry situation. Within the confines of this situation, 'anger' is as much a quality of the object of the anger as it is of its subject. In this example, the quality of anger is not an *object* of which the person is aware: but nonetheless it is immediately felt as a quality that is pervasively present in the situation, felt at a pre-cognitive level before perhaps becoming known for what it is at a cognitive level.[68] If, of course, the person began to reflect on this situation, perhaps worried because it has taken him or her by surprise, then in this new situation he or she can abstract out the anger as an object of thought the better to serve the function of understanding required by this new situation. There is thus a transformation of feeling from one situation to the next. This idea of a single quality unifying a situation has an important application in Dewey's aesthetics.

The notion that emotions are objective qualities of the interactions of self and other, and the further idea that the outcomes of these interactions are experiences with objective and subjective 'sides' or aspects, help to form an alternative conception to that which identifies experience as a primarily subjective phenomenon which happens in or to 'a self' when that self relates or responds to a separate object. Furthermore, these ideas of 'situation', 'sense', 'significance' and 'unifying quality' come together in Dewey's formulation of what he calls 'qualitative thought'. This idea of the 'qualitative' is central to his description of artistic and aesthetic experiences. But I have an additional interest in it that is worthwhile mentioning at this point. Later, in Chapter 4, I will examine and use William James's idea that the 'I' or knower *is* the 'passing' or 'present' thought. In anticipation of this, the question lying at the back of my next section on 'qualitative thought' is this: granting that there is validity in James's formulation of the knower *as* the present thought, what are the subjective implications when that passing thought happens to be the sort of qualitative thought Dewey sees as typifying the arts?

MEDIA AND IMMEDIACY: QUALITATIVE THINKING IN THE ARTS

Dewey insists that 'what is not immediate is not esthetic.'[69] An object becomes an aesthetic object 'when the material is so arranged and adapted that it serves immediately the enrichment of the immediate experience of the one whose attentive perception is directed to it.'[70] And again he says that the 'esthetic effect is found directly in sense-perception'.[71] More radically, he argues that, in the first pre-reflective phase, experience *is* the immediately given. Existences, according to Dewey, 'are not given to experience but their givenness *is* experience. But such immediate qualitative experience is not itself cognitive: it fulfills none of the logical ambitions of knowledge and of objects *qua* known.'[72] But what does this idea of 'immediacy' mean, as it is used to refer to aesthetic experience?

It is the 'medium' of an art that is the guarantor of the immediacy of its experience. Medium is for Dewey a means. But whereas some means are extrinsic to what is accomplished (such as boring work as a means for a wage), other means are intimately connected with their ends (such as occurs in the arts). Because, from one point of view, colours are the painting and tones are the music, it follows that 'esthetic effects belong intrinsically to their medium.'[73] In the arts, means are inseparable from ends; techniques and materials cannot be separated from that which they express and convey. While distinctions between form and content are valid for critical experiences of art, they are not present in aesthetic experiences where medium and meaning are fused and inseparable.[74] Whereas any sort of material is potentially available for use in art, it will only truly become a medium when 'it is used to express a meaning which is other than that which it is in virtue of its bare physical existence: the meaning not of what it physically is, but of what it expresses.'[75] As such, artistic media are for Dewey special languages with their own characteristics and possibilities.[76] And he emphasizes that 'sensitivity to a medium as a medium is the very heart of all artistic creation and esthetic perception.'[77]

With this in mind, one could describe the arts as being 'qualitative symbols', in order to convey the idea that they mean in and through the qualities of the materials that comprise them.[78] If the stuff of art is perceptible materials fused with artistic meaning, what is involved in the transformation of these physical materials into meaningful media, or qualitative symbols? I can attempt only a partial answer to this complex question here, but I can approach it from two directions. First, I will consider certain aspects of how qualities become meaningful, and then I can explore Dewey's ideas on what is involved in thinking in and of qualities.

In Dewey's view, the assumed distinction between sense and reason underlies many of the confusions that arise over how qualities (such as pigment colour, texture, luminosity, for example) become meaningful in art. The world in which we live is fundamentally qualitative. Qualities, as Dewey thinks of them, are uniquely and simply what they are, and as they are found in experience. They are said to be immediately felt or to be emotionally intuited or to be grasped directly and unreflectively. Even if verbal language can point out ways in which qualities can be had in experience, it cannot reduplicate them. The psychologist's fallacy, as James warned, involves reading back into unreflective experience distinctions that reflective experience has found helpful.

Although a reflective experience may follow and be closely connected with an unreflective one, it is not the same experience.

Dewey strenuously opposes ways of thinking that identify qualities as sensuous and meanings as ideational, and that separate the senses from reason. He sees these distinctions as deriving from rationalistic philosophies and psychologies which then go on to conceive of art as 'a cancellation of the separation' between sense and reason.[79] In this view, sense ordinarily conceals and distorts a 'rational substance' behind the appearances to which sense itself is assumed to be limited. It is not that Dewey is denying the utility of the sense–reason distinction: what he denies is that the distinction is given in experience. It functions validly in reflective experience when it 'lead[s] in the end to a perceptual experience in which the distinction is overcome – in which what were once conceptions become the inherent meanings of material mediated through sense.'[80]

Dewey would not want to say that only qualities apprehended through the senses in isolation can be directly experienced; nor would he hold that relations are extraneously added by association. His position on how 'connections' are experienced is directly indebted to William James. James had argued in *The Principles of Psychology* that relations such as 'if', 'and', and 'but' are apprehended directly in the stream of experience. They are not experienced as additions by some synthesizing reason. Furthermore, perceptible objects are not the only objects in experience that could be qualitative. Ideas also have their own immediate qualitative aspects or 'feels'. Should an idea lose this 'feel' then it becomes merely a stimulus to act in a certain way, an 'algebraic ghost'. It moves the understanding on to the next step in an intellectual process rather than itself enhancing experience by virtue of its own intrinsic qualities.

It is a mistake to think of qualities as autonomous or as 'pure'. All qualities are qualities *of* something. They are interrelated in such a way as intrinsically to define their objects, rather than to be thought of as additions to those objects. The enjoyment of qualities is always the enjoyment of the colour, sound or scent of objects. The colours of a painting are presented as those of, and for, whatever the painting expresses (although not necessarily of what it represents). And just as there can be no experience of 'pure' or 'simple' qualities (an insight that seems to have escaped some psychologists interested in 'experimental aesthetics'), it is also true that qualities are not limited to the range of a single sensory system. Since qualities are always experienced as qualities of objects, and since objects ('events with meanings') are present to the variety of senses in many ways, it is clear that even when pictorial colour is presented to the eye in that concentrated form appropriate to painting media, it also inexorably presents 'the resonances and transfers of value' exemplified by the meanings expressed, and the objects referred to.[81] Thinking of this from the side of the subject, it is a whole person who relates to the painting and not a visual system. The eyes or the ears are the channels through which the whole person participates in the experience that is the picture or the sonata or the poem.[82] Seeing, for example, the 'liquidity of water' carries with it the tactile sense of its temperature, texture and so on.[83] All the senses, in Dewey's view, 'are coordinated into a whole of vitality by their common relations to objects. It is the objects that lead an impassioned life.'[84] This echoes Cézanne's belief that 'Objects interpenetrate each other. They never cease to live. Imperceptibly they spread intimate reflections around them.'[85]

Whatever is being expressed in an art is concentrated and intensified in the qualities of that art's medium. And even if that medium is predominantly visual and two-dimensional, it can still carry qualities of depth, sound, touch or time. Whether the relationship between the art object and that which it expresses is conventional, or to do with some more direct and intrinsic connection, is a controversial question for contemporary aesthetics, but one I must leave open. The point I wish to make here is that the concentrated use of colour, say, to express meaning in painting, directly enhances the present experience of the spectator in a different way than does colour in ordinary non-art related experience. But there is a connection, and Dewey uses the idea of 'transferred values' to elaborate on the nature of the connection between non-artistic experiences, in which some element features, and artistic experiences in which a similar element takes on a new meaning.

The originator of this notion of 'transferred values', and the man to whom Dewey was deeply indebted for his knowledge of the visual arts, was Albert C. Barnes.[86] Barnes explained the meaning of 'transferred values' in this way: 'If an object has been part of an experience having emotional value, another object resembling the first may subsequently attract to itself at least a part of the original emotion.'[87] A learning theorist might see this as an instance of conditioning, but this is not how Barnes or Dewey thought of it. They thought in terms of the role of past experience in the interpretation of the present, a role played out in large part by imagination, the primary function of which is the fusion of past and present, 'the conscious adjustment of the new and the old'.[88] In the case of the arts, what is currently perceived is an object which has been deliberately and imaginatively made of materials the qualities of which are significant, and which embodies meanings immediately and coherently present in perception. Such adjustments are often accompanied by 'the emotional aura, the heat and glow, of our past sensations and feelings' which are brought to bear on present experience 'by an imaginative and metaphorical extension of meaning'.[89] There are in all of us, but especially in artists, a vast number of feelings ('in our minds in solution', as Barnes puts it). Artists can transfer the values associated with these feelings from one field of experience to another. Barnes and De Mazia argue that Matisse, for example, through his use of rosette patterns, tile motifs, stripes and bands, transfers values and feelings associated with outdoors, with spring and summer, with porcelain and clothes, flags and wallpaper, into his paintings. When such a transfer is successful we 'feel' it, as 'we feel in a Cézanne the qualities of a solidly constructed building; a Renoir picture of a girl recalls a rose in a garden in a morning in June. In short, there is scarcely an object or situation in life, or in art – the mirror of life – not fraught with emotional associations for which its objective qualities give no demonstrable ground.'[90]

Although Dewey was happy to borrow this idea of transferred values, he could be less satisfied with an explanation simply in terms of emotional associations. This is implicit in an important paper from 1930 called 'Qualitative thought' which contains some of the key ideas to be developed in *Art as Experience*, and reveals the significance of context for his philosophy of aesthetic experience.[91] The paper presents two related ideas. The first is 'that the immediate experience of quality, and of dominant and pervasive quality, is the background, the point of departure and the regulative principle of all thinking.'[92] The second idea is that 'Construction that is artistic is as much a case of genuine thought as that expressed in scientific and philosophical matters, and so is all genuine esthetic appreciation of art, since the latter must, in some way, to be vital, retrace the course of the creative process.'[93] If the arts are to be understood as qualitative symbols then we must ask what it is to think 'qualitatively', for that, it is claimed, is what both the makers and the receivers of the arts do. In both the artistic experience of making and the aesthetic experience of remaking, meanings are fused with qualities. Qualitative thinking is the sort of thinking that is done in qualities and the relations of qualities. Matisse, perhaps under the indirect influence of Bergson's thinking, also describes the relationship of artistic thought in similar terms. In his *Notes of a Painter* from 1908 he writes:

> But the thought of a painter must not be considered as separate from his pictorial means, for the thought is worth no more than its expression by the means, which must be more complete (and by complete I do not mean complicated) the deeper is his thought. I am unable to distinguish between the feeling I have about life and my translating it.[94]

Like Matisse, Braque also insisted that 'I don't paint things but their relations.'[95]

I have repeatedly emphasized Dewey's 'holism' and his stress on the need to take full account of the determining power of context in the shaping of experience. His use of the idea of a 'situation' with its characteristic 'sense' or 'pervasive quality' that is 'felt' at a generally pre-reflective level was discussed above. In applying this idea to art, Dewey's central idea is that both artists and enjoyers of art begin by directly and unreflectively apprehending the single, unifying, pervading quality of the work. This quality of the work can be understood as an instance of the 'sense' of a 'situation', one that evades naming or specific verbal description. This is a high order quality that unifies the other qualities of the work in a manner unique to itself, and that differentiates it from other works. One feels the presence of this pervasive quality as an immediate sense of relevance, 'our constant sense of things as belonging or not belonging'.[96]

An everyday example could be that of somebody describing a man to us. We follow this description easily because everything this person says agrees with what we know of the man in question. But then the person says something that surprises us, and we realize that up to that point we thought he was speaking of John Jones when in fact he was speaking of Tom Jones, whom we also know. Everything said up until then remains the same, but 'the significance, the color and the weight, of every detail is altered. For the quality that runs through them all, that gives meaning to each and binds them together, is transformed.'[97]

Take another example, this time from the arts. In 1952 Picasso painted a pair of pictures, *Peace* and *War* on the brick walls of an old chapel in Vallauris, France. *War* is done in oil mainly in blacks, purples, blues and reds. Its centrepiece is a horse-drawn chariot, with the horses trampling a book underfoot. In the chariot is a naked, devil-like warrior with a bloody stabbing sword in his right hand, and a vessel from which are released all manner of scorpions and crawly things in his left hand. Black silhouetted warriors fight in the background and on the earth beneath the traces are a pair of disembodied hands as though drowning in their black foil. What can be said of the quality unifying this mural? Picasso told Claude Roy about how he was thinking when he started *War*:

> What imposed itself first in my mind was the awkward and jolting course of one of those provincial hearses that one sees passing in the streets of little towns, so pitiful and screeching. I began to paint from the right side, and it's around this image that the rest of the painting was constructed.[98]

This simple statement presents an example of transferred values, of the functioning of imagination, and of the dominant regulating power of that central quality which has as its emblematic source the memory of seeing and hearing and feeling a provincial French, horse-drawn hearse passing through some little town. It is this quality that governs and regulates the meanings which make up *War*. But how does it do it?

Dewey was concerned to show how such quality could regulate meaning, but in terms of the power of 'wholes' rather than of parts. The explanation centres on the idea that experience begins with 'situations' and later proceeds to 'objects', rather than the other way around. In the work of art, as in situations generally, it is the quality of the whole that regulates its parts and that determines relevancy.[99] Dewey is well aware of the danger of reification when he says that this unifying quality of works of art is 'felt rather than thought'. We know that there is no ready-made, autonomous psychical entity called 'a feeling'. What 'feeling' and 'felt' refer to are relations of quality. Anger, as I observed in the earlier example of a 'situation', is a quality that resides in the relations between persons, things and contexts: and it is these qualities of things and persons in relation to us that we are aware of when angry, and not something called 'anger'. It is only during subsequent experience, that of reflective analysis, that anger is identified and conceived of as 'a feeling' or as 'an emotion'. The experience of 'being angry' temporally precedes and provides the existential grounds for the experience of 'anger' as an idea. Artistic and aesthetic thought begin with such unanalyzed 'wholes'.

Of aesthetic experiences of art Dewey observes that 'the total overwhelming impression comes first . . . an impact that precedes all definite recognition of what it is about.'[100] To say that artists and enjoyers of art think qualitatively is to say that they think in terms of the relations of quality available from the medium in question, and that they imaginatively fuse their own meanings with the qualities of that medium. This brings us back to the idea of 'association' as a basis for transferred values. What Dewey does is to reformulate the idea of association in the light of his analysis of the importance of contexts, and then he uses this reformulated idea of association to account for the operation of transferred values in art as described by Barnes.

Association is not caused by some original similarity or contiguity. Dewey turns this suggestion on its head and argues that association and contiguity can be apprehended only after an association exists. What is responded to in the first place is a context or situation within which the objects are related in space and time. But how can objects that were once part of a whole situation now be considered as two objects, the one suggesting the other? To this Dewey answers that there are an infinite number of things that are contiguous in space and time, and many things that are similar, but that what connects things are underlying qualities that determine relevance. Looking at a painting for the first time, a person might immediately say that it is a Goya, or by someone very influenced by Goya. Only afterwards might the grounds for this correct identification be sought by analysis. The practice of connoisseurship depends on high-level abilities like this. The point of this example is that it is the quality of the picture as a whole (remembering my earlier point that the picture is the experience that results from the joint relationship of a person with the painting) that is at work in the first instance, and it is this same quality that most reliably frames and guides later detailed analysis. An art expert who had no 'feel' for Goyas would be handicapped to a greater degree in his or her analysis of a Goya than one who had that particular 'feel'.

In the light of this analysis, the mechanism for the impact and operation of transferred values is not, in the first instance at least, that of association but is instead the immediate apprehension of the pervasive quality.[101] Dewey is no more precise than this in his description of 'pervasive quality', and this is probably because he cannot be. What is clear is that the function of pervasive qualities is organizational and that this function can be tested in particular instances of artistic and aesthetic experience. To be fair to Barnes, I should emphasize that it was emotional associations that he suggested as operating in the transfer of values. Bearing in mind the dangers of reification that lurk in words like anger, joy, sorrow and so on, one can say that 'emotion', while belonging to a self, is a quality of dynamic and complex experience. This is how Dewey conceived of it.

If we jump when we are suddenly frightened that is not because fright is an emotional state. The jump is a more or less automatic reflex. For it to become emotional there must be some concern on the part of a self for an object, or for the outcome of an event, such as the identification of a threatening animal and the accompanying desire to escape from it. In a situation like that, what 'fear' refers to is the emotional quality that permeates and controls the elements of the situation. Another experience may also be fearful, but not in the same way. There is no such thing as *the* emotion of fear, love or hate. Each experience will have its own unique qualities. This is why artists have the advantage over psychologists when dealing with emotion. They can fabricate a particular concrete situation that can be immediately apprehended so as to construct emotion. Dewey wants acts of artistic expression to be understood as the 'ordered use of objective conditions in order to give objective fulfillment to the emotion'.[102] The transfer of values from one experience to another (from seeing signs of death in spring daffodils to grasping a poem about transience, for example) occurs in acts of 'emotional identification' rather than acts of intellectual comparison.[103] In other words, such transfer involves, in the first instance, an immediate grasp of the unifying quality that pervades the situation in question. We could say that there is a feeling that something is somehow *like* something else, and that that feeling governs relevance in that particular situation.

This concentration on immediacy in artistic and aesthetic experience is balanced by Dewey's insistence that a form of thinking, qualitative thinking, is involved in artistic and aesthetic experience. Post-Deweyan studies in aesthetic experience have been dominated by ideas of art as symbol, and of aesthetic experience as cognitive and fundamentally interpretive. Semiotics, hermeneutics and analytical philosophy are the vibrant perspectives of contemporary aesthetics. There is little, however, to suggest that Dewey would have found these developments inimical to his thinking. But he would probably have found them too narrow given the scope of his idea of experience and of the continuities of experience.[104]

From this analysis of the immediacy of aesthetic experiences of art (understood as qualitative symbol), I could, for example, propose an empirical hypothesis that would help to distinguish aesthetic immediacy, as it is found in art, from the immediacy of early childhood experience, while at the same time acknowledging the developmental continuity between them. This hypothesis could take the following form: that there is a developmental psychological progression from the immediacy of sensorimotor knowing characteristic of the infant, through the development of symbolic mediation from around the end of the first year onwards, to the immediacy that characterizes aesthetic experiences of the mediations that are art. This latter immediacy I might hypothesize to be 'composite', and to be a later achievement that depends upon the satisfactory development of symbolization in its fullest sense. One implication of this hypothesis, if valid, would be that severely mentally handicapped people or pre-verbal infants or truly feral children or people brain-damaged in certain ways could not in principle experience art aesthetically, since such experience depends upon the mastery and high-level use of symbolization. This illustrative hypothesis brings us back to a type of continuity that is a key concern of this book, namely the continuity of early childhood experience and aesthetic absorption.

DEWEY ON THE ROOTS OF AESTHETIC ABSORPTION IN CHILDHOOD

Although the idea is never developed in Dewey's work, there is a clear recognition that aesthetic experience has its own developmental psychological history. Scattered throughout his aesthetics we find suggestive insights and intuitions concerning the roots of such experience. Early on, for example, we find him asserting that 'through the phases of perturbation and conflict, there abides *the deep-seated memory of an underlying harmony* [my emphasis] the sense of which haunts life like the sense of being founded on a rock.'[105] Santayana's 'hushed reverberations' are similarly rooted in such memories, but for the clearest statement Dewey relies on an extract from George Eliot's *The Mill on the Floss*:

> These familiar flowers, these well-remembered bird notes, this sky with its fitful brightness, these furrowed and grassy fields, each with a sort of personality given to it by the capricious hedge, such things as these are *the mother tongue of our imagination* [my emphasis], the language that is laden with all the subtle inextricable associations the fleeting hours of our childhood left behind them. Our delight in the sunshine on the deep-bladed grass today might be no more than the quaint perception of wearied souls, if it were not for the sunshine and grass of far-off years, which still live in us and transform our perception into love. [106]

Later, when discussing the idea of 'transferred values', Dewey reiterates George Eliot when he writes: '"Transferred values" of emotions experienced *from a childhood that cannot be consciously recovered* [my emphasis] belong to them. Speech is indeed the mother tongue.'[107] Dewey locates the origins of experiences that have a 'mystic aspect of acute surrender' (what I am now calling aesthetic absorption) in early relations with a person's surrounding world. It involves 'resonances of dispositions' which are acquired in those earlier relations, but which are now outside the range of conscious recovery and so cannot become the objects of intellectual thought.[108] The loss and recovery of union with the world are central themes pervading Dewey's thinking, and in this connection he accords a particularly important functional role to art.

Here again, we meet Dewey's preoccupation with questions of the continuity of experience. Dewey's sense of the continuities of culture and nature is radical. He sees the prefiguration of art in the processes of living itself. Something of artistic process can be learnt from watching a wren building a nest or a spider its web because in all such activities there is a dynamic organized transaction of creature and world. The distinctive feature of human beings is their consciousness of the relations found in nature with all that that entails. Just as the wren's building of its nest is an expansion of its life, so is people's making of art an expansion of their lives. But what people do in making art, and in appreciating and enjoying it, is to restore 'consciously, and thus on the plane of meaning, the union of sense, need, impulse and action characteristic of the live creature. The intervention of consciousness adds regulation, power of selection, and redisposition. Thus it varies the arts in ways without end.'[109]

As I understand him, Dewey does not mean by 'restoration' the simple reinstitution of an earlier state. States are transitory and open to relatively rapid change. Dewey's concern is with 'forces and structures that endure through change'.[110] His idea of continuity

> excludes complete rupture on one side and mere repetition of identities on the other: it precludes reduction of the 'higher' to the 'lower' just as it precludes complete breaks and gaps. The growth and development of any living organism from seed to maturity illustrates the meaning of continuity.[111]

The continuity of the less complex with the more complex is the primary postulate of Dewey's naturalistic theory of logic. So when Dewey writes of the restorative powers of art, he is referring not, I believe, to the restoration of states but to what one might call the restoration of forms of relationship. In the case of the developmental origins of aesthetic absorption this is a promising line of inquiry. The implication is that we should examine early forms of relating for possible prototypes of later more mature capacities for aesthetic absorption. This is precisely what certain psychoanalytic studies of aesthetic experience do, and for which they claim Dewey's support. In the next chapter, I will examine these ideas from a generally Deweyan perspective. However, it is worthwhile concluding this present chapter with a reiteration of Dewey's cautionary warnings.

Theories of art are strewn, he maintains, with the 'fossils of antiquated psychologies'.[112] He reminds us that experience is not 'something that occurs exclusively inside a self or mind or consciousness, something self-contained and sustaining only external relations to the objective scene in which it happens to be set'.[113] All experience is constituted by and resides in interaction. Reflective analysis can introduce distinctions into the 'psychological phase' of experience, distinctions such as sense, emotion, imagination, idea and so on. But these are not distinctions that are given experientially; they are 'different aspects and phases of a continuous, though varied interaction of self and environment'.[114] The arts, as experiences, remove conflicts between such 'divisions'. 'Hence', writes Dewey, 'the extraordinary ineptitude of a compartmentalized psychology to serve as an instrument for a theory of art.'[115] Psychoanalysis offers perhaps the only sustained account of aesthetic absorption in psychology. However, we need to ask whether that account is the offspring of just the sort of compartmentalized psychology Dewey explicitly warned against.

NOTES

1. Quoted in Norbert Lynton, *Klee* (New York: Castle Books, 1975), p. 49; emphasis in original.
2. Edman, 1967, p. 49.
3. Beardsley, 1966, p. 332. Beardsley's own aesthetics also grants a primacy to aesthetic experience, although not in quite the same way as Dewey. As to the validity of this evaluation of Dewey, John Fisher has observed that 'It is difficult to find Deweyans in aesthetics' and that 'one can only term the general attitude toward Dewey by professionals in aesthetics in recent years as largely disinterested.' He goes on to say that:

   > There is considerable sympathy for many of Dewey's more or less intuitive notions. Philosophers of art tend to say, 'He's right, now let me see if I can make an argument for what he says,' and suddenly his importance is minimized. (The philosophical world is heavily populated today with those of opposite talents, those who are soundly mistaken, but who possess incredibly powerful skills at provocative and persuasive argumentation.)

   But Fisher is quite confident in saying that 'The philosophy of aesthetic experience in English-language aesthetics is inescapably tied to *Art as Experience*.' For the source of these judgements see Fisher, 1989.
4. Susanne Langer's indebtedness to Dewey, for example, is evident throughout her work. Sometimes this is conceptual as when she writes of 'phases of the vital process', which for her is transpersonal in much the same way in which Dewey and Mead conceive of the act and the 'phases of experience': or when Dewey argues that the 'impression of life' we get from an art object has to do with our sense

of its having a 'career' or history (1958, p. 176), this is a similar intuition to Langer's analysis of organic form in art and to the idea that 'in an actual living form acts are made by and from other acts.' On this see Langer, 1976, p. 428 and Chapters 10 and 11. Furthermore, Langer's argument for the pre-scientific value of the arts for psychology, as in Langer, 1967, is distinctly Deweyan. Yet despite her avowal of indebtedness to Dewey generally, it is curious how she seems to misread his category of experience when she associates with him a psychologism that fails to take account of the autonomous qualities of the object. For this see Langer, 1953, pp. 36–7. Langer takes this mantle for herself (ibid., p. 39), with no acknowledgement that this respect for the constructive powers of the object was a clear part of Dewey's project also.

5. A representative list of commentaries on Dewey's aesthetics would include the following: Shearer (1935a and 1935b), Pepper (1939 and 1953), Zink (1943), Croce (1948), Ames (1953), Kaminsky (1957), Gauss (1960), Gotshalk (1964), Beardsley (1966), Edman (1967), Deledalle (1967), Morris (1970), Zeltner (1975), Kadish (1981), Alexander (1987), Burnett (1989), Fisher (1989), Tiles (1990), and Shusterman (1989 and 1992).

6. Dewey, 1958, p. 249.

7. Ibid., p. 240.

8. Ibid., p. 144.

9. Quinton, 1972, p. 2.

10. Scheffler, 1974, p. 189.

11. Dewey, 1981a, p. 5.

12. Barzun, 1984, p. 290.

13. Tiles, 1990, p. 4.

14. See Dewey, 1981b. This was Kant filtered through Hegel, and reveals the influence of one of Dewey's teachers, G. S. Morris. For a commentary on the influence of Morris on Dewey's early thought see Thayer, 1968. Dewey was 23 years old when, in 1882, he became a student of George Sylvester Morris (1840–1889). Morris had been taught in Berlin by Wilhelm Dilthey's teacher Friedrich Trendelenburg. Trendelenburg impressed Morris with the importance of Aristotle, Kant and Hegel, as well as with his conception of thought and being as 'organic'. He passed these influences, together with a critique of British empiricism, on to Dewey. Stylistically, he also bequeathed such Deweyan terms as 'vital', 'organic', 'dynamic', 'experimental' and 'instrumental'. For Morris philosophy became 'nothing but the examination of our whole and undivided experience, with a view to ascertaining its whole nature, its range and its content'. (Thayer, 1968, p. 470.) Dewey's lifework was an endorsement and elaboration of this conception of philosophy.

15. Dewey, 1981b, p. 23. Many of the key nineteenth century ideas on experience were to confederate in Dewey's philosophy of experience. The British neo-Hegelian philosopher Thomas Hill Green (1836–1882) in particular helped Dewey to develop the conceptual tools he

needed to reflect upon the ideas of Charles Darwin and William James. Green's sources were Aristotle, Kant, Fichte and Hegel. He highlighted the continuity of thought and things, of self and environment, of spirit and world.

16. Dewey, 1981c.
17. Ibid., p. 67.
18. Bruner, 1977, p. 20.
19. Quinton in Peters, 1977, p. 2.
20. For a similar contemporary idea, 'distributed knowing', see Bruner, 1990, p. 106. In a footnote to the chapter on 'Autobiography and self', Bruner says that the new 'interpretivist' trend he espouses in contemporary psychology can be traced back in some ways to G. H. Mead. However, he goes on to say that:

> In certain other respects, Mead was so wedded to the classic late-nineteenth-century view of the interaction of 'organism' and 'environment' that it is better, in my opinion, to consider him as a closing chapter on conceptualism in the late history of positivism than as an opening chapter in the new interpretivism. (p. 167)

Whether Bruner means this criticism to be extended to Dewey is not clear. Were he to do so, it could be said in Dewey's defence that he tries hard, especially in his aesthetics, to spell out the fluidity of the boundaries of organism and environment in a way that would not, I think, be incompatible with the idea of a 'distributed self' that Bruner is trying to develop within his cultural psychology. Dewey's concept of the environment is not of something separate and apart from the organism; it is in some ways an anticipation of the later ethological idea of the *Umwelt*. This is evident in his 1896 article (Dewey, 1981d). There he argued that a stimulus can only be a stimulus by virtue of that implicit response or interest of the organism that sensitizes it to those select features of the world that allow for the development of that response. Charles Morris later generalizes this to say that 'organism and environment are mutually determinative of each other,' and 'that what the organism is attentive to is by and large a function of its impulses seeking expression.' See Charles Morris's introduction to Mead, 1938, p. vii.

21. For a recent discussion of Dewey in relation to anti-foundationalism see Shusterman, 1992, especially Chapter 5.
22. Continuity, and especially individual and historical continuity, also plays an important role in Gadamer's thinking on art and the aesthetic. Gadamer's idea of continuity is underpinned by Hegel and Heidegger. See Robert Bernasconi's introduction to his edition of Gadamer's, *The Relevance of the Beautiful and Other Essays* (1986, p. xvi). One can also see the continuing influence of this idea in Bruner's recent work. What he calls the 'transactional contextualism' of, say, ethnomethodology in sociology and anthropology, or of Vygotsky's influence in psychology, requires a view of action as

> *situated*, that it be conceived of as continuous with a cultural world.

The realities that people constructed were *social* realities, negotiated
with others, distributed between them. The social world in which we
lived was neither 'in the head' nor 'out there' in some positivistic
aboriginal sense. (1990, p. 105; emphasis in original)

23. Tiles, 1990, p. 22.
24. Ibid.
25. Ibid.
26. The edition used throughout this present work is James, 1950.
27. Ibid., p. 237.
28. Ibid., p. 239.
29. Ibid., p. 240.
30. Maurer and Maurer, 1990, pp. 186–7. Also see Dewey, 1971, p. 533n.
31. James, 1950, p. 243.
32. Ibid. Natural language follows the contours of experience. Ideally, as James speculated, one would need a single interminable word to be true to this ever-changing stream. Amongst natural languages there are considerable differences in their abilities to capture this central quality of thought. Jacques Barzun believes, for example, that as languages drop inflections in the course of their development so they become more a shorthand than a contour map of thought. He argues that:

    highly inflected languages such as Greek and Latin fit thought more
    faithfully than French or English, because in their declensions and
    conjugations the words do not stay the same but change their endings
    so that 'the same but different' is rendered in tangible form.

    See Barzun, 1984, p. 44.
33. Allport, 1971, p. 267.
34. Dewey, 1971b, p. 74.
35. Dewey, 1981c, p. 85.
36. Dewey, 1971b, p. 93.
37. Ibid., p. 73.
38. Ibid., p. 97.
39. Dewey, 1958, p. 253.
40. Ibid., p. 10. This is a position Gadamer shares with Dewey. See Gadamer, 1986, p. xv.
41. Dewey, 1958, p. 8.
42. Ibid., p. 19. This could be a pragmatic precursor of Bruner's 'distributed self'.
43. Ibid., p. 195.
44. On this Dewey writes:

    Whenever the bond that binds the living creature to his environment is
    broken, there is nothing that holds together the various factors and
    phases of the self. Thought, emotion, sense, purpose, impulsion fall
    apart, and are assigned to different compartments of our being. For
    their unity is found in the cooperative roles they play in active and
    receptive relations to the environment. (ibid., p. 252).

45. The terms 'art object' and 'work of art' have a different meaning in phenomenological aesthetics than that which they will be given here.

46. Dewey, 1958, p. 137. On the conditions of the aesthetic form of the work of art, understood as experience jointly constructed by self and object, and extended over time, Dewey writes:

> There can be no movement toward a consummating close unless there is a progressive massing of values, a cumulative effect. This result cannot exist without conservation of the import of what has gone before. Moreover, to secure the needed continuity, the accumulated experience must be such as to create suspense and anticipation of resolution. Accumulation is at the same time preparation, as with each phase of the growth of a living embryo. Only that is carried on which is led up to; otherwise there is arrest and a break. For this reason consummation is relative; instead of occurring once for all at a given point, it is recurrent. The final end is anticipated by rhythmic pauses, while that end is final only in an external way. For as we turn from reading a poem or a novel or seeing a picture the effect presses forward in further experiences, even if only subconsciously. Such characteristics as continuity, cumulation, conservation, tension and anticipation are thus formal conditions of esthetic form. (pp. 137–8)

47. Shusterman, 1989, p. 65. On the judgement that Dewey's conception of the 'work' of art is cryptic, see Fisher, 1989, p. 58. Deweyan-type ideas are evident in one strand of recent literary criticism. Stanley E. Fish, in his reflections upon what the close sequential reading of literary texts involves, often comes very close to Dewey. For an example of this see Fish, 1980a. Also see Fish, 1980b. For a critique of Fish from within pragmatism, see Shusterman, 1992, pp. 59–61 and 106–14.

48. Dewey, 1958, pp. 250–1; emphasis in original.

49. Stanley E. Fish takes exactly the same idea from I. A. Richards to make the same point as Dewey: 'This is obviously a brief for a shift of analytical attention away from the work as an object to the response it draws, the experience it generates; but the shift is, in Richards's theory, preliminary to *severing* one from the other, whereas I would insist on their precise interaction.' See Fish, 1980a, p. 90 (emphasis in original).

50. Dewey, 1958, p. 195.

51. For Zen Buddhist ideas in particular see Suzuki, 1970 and 1957. See also Blyth, 1976, and especially vol. 1, 'Eastern culture', of his monumental four volume work on *Haiku* (1981). See also Gadamer's essay on 'Aesthetic and religious experience', in Gadamer, 1986, pp. 140–53.

52. Reid, 1969, p. 260.

53. Ibid., p. 261.

54. Ibid.

55. Dewey, 1958, p. 119.

56. James, 1908, pp. 380–2.

57. Ibid., p. 380.

58. Dewey, 1958, p. 46.

59. Ibid., p. 38.
60. Ibid., p. 57.
61. Tiles, 1990, p. 49.
62. Ibid., p. 98.
63. Ibid., p. 103.
64. See Dewey, 1958, where he says that 'Mind is primarily a verb. It denotes all the ways in which we deal consciously and expressly with the situations in which we find ourselves' (p. 263). For a contemporary reflection on this same idea see Sebeok, 1986, pp. 1–9.
65. For an parallel distinction between 'understanding' (which is taken to include that which grounds interpretation) and 'interpretation' (as understood in contemporary hermeneutic traditions) see Shusterman, 1992, Chapter 5.
66. Tiles, 1990, p. 63.
67. Ibid., p. 66. The concept of 'situation' was also developed by existentialists like Marcel, Sartre and Merleau-Ponty to describe the intricate relationships of self and society. See, for example, Kruks, 1990.
68. In Chapter 6, we will see that Richard Wollheim's ideas on 'simple'. and 'complex' projection, and on the 'expressive perception' of 'projective qualities' are close to Dewey's thinking here. Wollheim develops these ideas in his *Painting as an Art* (1987).
69. Dewey, 1958, p. 119.
70. Ibid., p. 116.
71. Ibid., p. 115.
72. See Dewey, 1938, p. 517. In some recent uses the term 'mediation' is not thought of as neutral but is instead understood to be capable of altering the things mediated through the forms that constitute the mediation. See, for example, Williams, 1981, p. 172. Williams identifies Adorno's use of the term as typical here. For Adorno, mediation is a direct and necessary activity between different kinds of activity and consciousness. Mediation is in the object itself, and not something between the object and something else. This is a position close to Dewey.
73. Dewey, 1958, p. 197.
74. In *Painting as an Art* (1957), Wollheim offers a psychological account of pictorial meaning and says this about medium and meaning: 'On such an account what a painting means rests upon the experience induced in an adequately sensitive, adequately informed, spectator by looking at the surface of the painting as the intentions of the artist led him to mark it' (p. 22).
75. Dewey, 1958, p. 201.
76. Ibid., p. 319.
77. Ibid., p. 199.
78. I intend 'qualitative symbol' to be understood in a much wider sense than did C. S. Peirce with his 'qualisign' by which he meant any sensory quality. A 'qualitative symbol' is a complex, deliberately fabricated sign whose qualities are imaginatively fused with mean-

ings. Peirce distinguished three basic sign types – icon, index and symbol. Icons contain some of the qualities of that signified; indices are in dynamic relationship with that signified, but in themselves say nothing; and symbols have agreed meanings. Elements of all three types may be found in art understood as qualitative sign. For a critical discussion of this, and especially of the idea of iconism, see Eco, 1977, especially Chapter 3.

79. Dewey, 1958, p. 258.
80. Ibid., p. 259.
81. Ibid., p. 121.
82. It is the failure to appreciate the significance of this point that emasculates the educational arguments advanced by some arts educators in favour of terms like 'visual education' as against 'art education'. This substitution of a notion of visual education or of 'visual literacy' for a more complete conception of 'art education' has been a powerful trend in art education since the 1960s.
83. For an account of the significance of synaesthesia in early human development see Maurer and Maurer, 1990.
84. Dewey, 1958, p. 126.
85. Quoted by John Berger in Berger and Mohr, 1989, p. 113.
86. Barnes was a wealthy American collector, author and founder of a museum of modern art in Philadelphia. He dedicated his *The Art in Painting* (1927) to Dewey 'whose conception of experience, of method, of education, inspired the work of which this book is a part', and to whom in turn Dewey dedicated *Art as Experience* in 1934. Dewey is clearly indebted to Barnes for his conception of form (ibid., pp. 202 and 117), for some of his examples on abstraction in art (pp. 93–4), and for the idea of transferred values (pp. 118–19). This last idea is developed in Chapter VI of Barnes and De Mazia, 1933. As a purchaser of modern art, Barnes's judgement was well regarded. See, for example Vollard, 1978.
87. Barnes and De Mazia, 1933, p. 40.
88. Dewey, 1958, p. 272.
89. Barnes and De Mazia, 1933, p. 30.
90. Ibid., pp. 30–1.
91. Dewey, 1930.
92. Ibid., p. 30. For an elaboration of this idea, but from a *Gestalt* psychological position, see Arnheim, 1969.
93. Dewey, 1930, pp. 31–2. This idea has a currency in a variety of traditions. See for example, Segal, 1955. For a more recent and more sophisticated treatment see Wollheim, 1980, especially 'Criticism as retrieval'.
94. See Flam, 1978, pp. 35–6 and 143 where, in his 1952 interview with Verdet, Matisse said: 'There is no separation between the thought and the creative act. They are completely one and the same.' For Henri Bergson on this, see his *Creative Evolution* (New York, 1911), p. 145.
95. See Brion-Guerry, 1977, p. 82 n.19, where Delacroix is also mentioned as saying that 'genius is the art of coordinating relations.'

96. Dewey, 1958, p. 194. In his 'Qualitative thought' (1930) Dewey wrote:

> Confusion and incoherence are always marks of lack of control by a single pervasive quality. The latter alone enables a person to keep track of what he is doing, saying, hearing, reading, in whatever explicitly appears. The underlying unity of qualitativeness regulates pertinence or relevancy and force of every distinction and relation; it guides selection and rejection and the manner of utilization of all explicit terms. (pp. 11–12)

Stanley Fish seems to be using a similar idea when he writes 'that I have usually found that what might be called the basic experience of a work (do *not* read basic meaning) occurs at every level.' See Fish, 1980a, p. 82. At this stage in the development of his theory of reading, Fish argues, in relation to sentence meaning, 'that what it does is what it means' and that 'It is an experience; it occurs; it does something; it makes us do something' (ibid., p. 77).

97. Dewey, 1930, pp. 8–9.
98. Roy, 1972, p. 157. See also John Berger's *The Success and Failure of Picasso* (1980a) from which this quote of Picasso's, supportive of Barnes's views on transferred values, is drawn:

> The artist is a receptacle for emotions that come from all over the place: from the sky, from the earth, from a scrap of paper, from a passing shape, from a spider's web. That is why we must not discriminate between things. Where things are concerned there are no class distinctions. (p. 100)

99. Dewey's thinking here bears many affinities to *Gestalt* psychology. In *Art as Experience*, for example, he writes: 'The recurrence of relations – not of elements – in different contexts, which constitutes transposition, is qualitative and hence is directly experienced in perception' (1958, p. 211). Again in his 'Qualitative thought' he writes:

> Were I to venture into speculative territory, I might apply this conception to the problem of 'thinking' in animals, and what the Gestalt psychologists call 'insight'. That total quality operates with animals and sometimes secures, as with monkeys, results like those which we obtain by reflective analysis cannot, it seems to me, be doubted. But that this operation of quality in effecting results then goes out into symbolization and analysis is quite another matter. (1930, p. 29n)

100. Dewey, 1958, p. 145. It is in this context that Dewey found himself agreeing with Bergson that intuition, one of the meanings of which has to do with apprehending the qualitativeness of a situation, precedes conception and goes deeper. Reflection and conceptualization originate in and elaborate prior intuitions.
101. Presumably, this would also be the starting point for a Deweyan account of metaphor formation.
102. Dewey, 1958, p. 78. In her formulation of the idea of art as the creation of forms expressive of human feeling, Susanne Langer can again be seen as being at least close, if not indebted, to Dewey.

103. Ibid., p. 76.
104. In much the same way, I suspect, as Wollheim does. See Wollheim, 1987, p. 44. This is not to say that semiotics is not highly relevant to the analysis of aesthetic experience. It is only to make the point that semiotic analysis is necessarily subservient to broader perspectives. Dewey, for example, repeatedly insists on the meaningfulness of the arts, and on artistic media as forms of language.
105. Dewey, 1958, p. 17.
106. Ibid., p. 18n.
107. Ibid., p. 240.
108. Ibid., pp. 28–9.
109. Ibid., p. 25. This is an elaborated description of what G. H. Mead called the manipulative phase of the act. It is on this recognition of the cultural development and transformation of the natural, with its underlying continuity, that Dewey bases his later description of his philosophy as a 'cultural naturalism'.
110. Ibid., p. 323. For a contemporary analysis of states and dispositions, and one to which I will refer later, see Wollheim, 1984.
111. Dewey, 1938, p. 23.
112. Dewey, 1958, p. 245.
113. Ibid., p. 246. On the idea of the 'externality of relations' see Mead, 1972, Chapter XV.
114. Dewey, 1958, p. 247.
115. Ibid., p. 248.

—————— · ——————

CHAPTER 3

PSYCHOANALYSIS AND THE INFANTILE ROOTS OF AESTHETIC ABSORPTION

How Childhood tries to reach us, and declares
that *we* were once what took it seriously.
We may have climbed beyond it a few stairs,
but it climbed too, and can mysteriously

emerge, when things we've placed beyond all doubt
suddenly make us hesitate and wonder.

(Rilke, 1918)[1]

FREUD AND THE OCEANIC FEELING

In December 1927, the French Nobel Prize-winning author Romain Rolland wrote to Freud about a feeling he described as *oceanic*.[2] Rolland was trying to describe a mystical, 'cosmic' emotion that he believed may be the source of religious sentiment. From his letters it is clear that Freud held Rolland in the highest regard even though Rolland's interests were quite different from his own. In July 1929 Freud wrote to Rolland:

> How remote from me are the worlds in which you move! To me mysticism is just as closed a book as music. I cannot imagine reading all the literature which, according to your letter, you have studied. And yet it is easier for you than for us to read the human soul!

Freud was 73 at this time and very conscious of death. His reference to his inability to appreciate music echoes his earlier confessions about the visual arts. 'I may say at once that I am no connoisseur in art, but simply a layman', he writes in 1914, and continues,

> I have often observed that the subject-matter of works of art has a stronger attraction for me than their formal and technical qualities,

51

though to the artist their value lies first and foremost in these latter. I am unable rightly to appreciate many of the methods used and the effects obtained in art.[4]

Not surprisingly, therefore, in classical psychoanalysis the primary interest is the attempt to relate the artist's own psychodynamics to the art object. This often entails a reduction of art, and of its significance, to individual psychodynamics and the artist's unconscious intentionality.[5]

Freud's personal experience of art is, by his own account, more intellectual than aesthetic. He says that his analytic turn of mind prevents him being moved by something, unless he can explain the effect on himself. Clearly there is no Deweyan 'surrender' here. Freud interprets the formal elements of art using the metaphor of the bribe. He writes:

> The writer softens the character of his egoistic day-dreams by altering and disguising it, and he bribes us by the purely formal — that is, aesthetic — yield of pleasure which he offers us in the presentation of his phantasies. We give the name incentive bonus or fore-pleasure to a yield of pleasure such as this, which is offered to us so as to make possible the release of still greater pleasure arising from deeper psychical sources.[6]

Freud said that Rolland's remarks about the oceanic feeling left him no peace, and he requested permission to explore an analytical version of this feeling. This he did in *Civilization and its Discontents* which was published in 1930.[7] Freud begins this book by again paying homage to his unnamed friend, Rolland, and then by describing the idea of the oceanic feeling which Rolland claimed never to be without and which he confirmed existed in others. 'It is a feeling which he would like to call a sensation of "eternity", a feeling as of something limitless, unbounded, as it were "oceanic".'[8] For Rolland, this feeling was a subjective phenomenon, but one from which, he believed, sprang the source of religious energy, which was then seized upon by the various institutional churches and religious systems. Even if one rejects all religious beliefs and illusions one can still justifiably call oneself religious on the basis of this feeling alone, according to Rolland. Freud could not discover this oceanic feeling in himself but he accepted the phenomenon as given and offered his own analytic reflections upon it. On this he wrote:

> From my own experience I could not convince myself of the

primary nature of such a feeling. But this gives me no right to deny that it does in fact occur in other people. The only question is whether it is being correctly interpreted and whether it ought to be regarded as the *fons et origo* of the whole need for religion.

Freud interprets this feeling to be that 'of an indissoluble bond, of being one with the external world as a whole'.[9]

What Freud does next, in keeping with his central interest in psychic archaeology, is to seek a developmental explanation for this feeling. Adults normally have a strong sense of their autonomy, a sense of their separateness from the not-self. But this is deceptive. One of the key projects of psychoanalysis is to show how, even within the individual, the autonomy of the ego is itself dependent upon unconscious processes. However, if for the moment one considers only the self's sense of separateness from the 'outside' world, there are many occasions when the boundaries between the self and the world change or even seem to disappear. An example of this would be the experience of falling in love where the lover has a very strong sense of 'being one' with the beloved. In more impersonal terms, there is a partial dissolution of the boundary between self and object. In the fields of psychopathology and of neurology there are also many examples of states where people's bodies, perceptions, thoughts or feelings can appear quite alien to them and are insistently interpreted as belonging to the external world. The neurologist Oliver Sachs, for example, describes his own experience when he damaged his leg: 'It wasn't "my" leg I was walking with, but a huge clumsy prosthesis (or hypothesis), a bizarre appendage . . . an absolutely ludicrous artificial leg.'[10]

The Freudian contention is that the boundaries between ego and object, between interior and exterior reality, between 'inside' and 'outside' are not constant and fixed. Instead, they are to be regarded as permeable, fluid and continually open to redefinition. Yet it is clear that normal adults' strong sense of the reality of the boundaries between themselves and the non-self world is different from that of children, since these boundaries are the outcome of a long and complex developmental process. Freud acknowledges that this developmental process cannot be demonstrated, but he believes that it can be 'constructed with a fair degree of probability'.[11]

In essence, Freud argues that the ego originally includes everything, and that only subsequently does it separate off an external world from itself. The ego-feeling of the adult 'is, therefore, only a shrunken residue of a much more inclusive – indeed, an all-embracing – feeling which corresponded to a more intimate bond between the ego and the world about it'.[12] It is precisely these sorts of feelings that have suggested to some psychoanalytical writers, as we shall see, that key aspects of aesthetic experience are rooted in the experiences of infants. But how did Freud himself try to explain this 'shrunken residue'?

Freud suggests that infants at the breast do not distinguish their own sensations from those that come from their mothers. Yet because some sources of excitation can provide sensations at any moment (these sources being their bodily organs), and yet other sources are elusive and only reappear when, for example, they cry or show distress, 'there is for the first time set over against the ego an "object" in the form of something which exists "outside" and which is only forced to appear by a special action.'[13]

Furthermore, the fact that infants frequently experience sensations of pain or unpleasure forces a differentiation between ego and sensation. There arises within the infant a tendency to project everything unpleasurable on to an 'outside' and threatening world. In time, the child learns to distinguish between what is internal and belonging to the ego, and what is external and emanating from the outside world. Assuming that there are many people in whose mental life this primary ego-feeling has persisted in some degree (and this is the source idea of the reavailability theories I will consider below), Freud observes that it would coexist with the narrower, more rigidly bounded, ego-feeling of the adult. But by contrast with the ego-feeling of the adult, 'the ideational contents appropriate to it would be precisely those of limitlessness and of a bond with the universe.'[14] This is to say that they would contain the same ideas as Romain Rolland's oceanic feeling.

This coexistence assumes 'that everything is somehow preserved and that in suitable circumstances . . . it can once more be brought to light.'[15] Such an analysis, applied as it is in this case to religious feeling and its institutionalization by churches, is essentially regressive. It accounts for the present in terms of the past, laying more stress on the infantile and early childhood origins of later adult psychic phenomena than on the progressive possibilities of such phenomena in the lives of adults as they unfold according to the requirements of present situations.[16] To be fair to Freud, he never claims to be concerned with the central questions of art and aesthetics. On the contrary, he states quite clearly in his essay on 'The "Uncanny"', for example, that psychoanalysts rarely feel impelled to study aesthetics, and when they do, they usually focus on some remote, neglected aspect of it.[17]

One school of psychoanalysis, object relations theory, did later become interested in aesthetic absorption and returned for its inspiration to Freud's account of the ontogenetic roots of the oceanic feeling. Classical Freudian thought bases itself on an instinct theory, and revolves around the person's need to reduce tension that is experienced as unpleasurable. In this view, the subject is seen as relatively isolated and biologically motivated. Object relations theory shifts the emphasis towards intersubjectivity, and is centrally concerned with the person's interpersonal relations and relations with the world. More precisely, it refers to mental representations of self and others.[18] The term 'object' refers to anything (another person, a part of a person, an inanimate object) towards which a person's action or desire is directed. This relationship with an object is not to be understood as a one-way affair. Just as a person constitutes his or her objects, so can the objects actively shape the person's actions. The process is a two-way interactive one. In practice, psychoanalysts of this persuasion are largely concerned with questions of phantasy, rather than with 'real' relations with others.

Ellen Spitz is one recent writer within this tradition whose thinking has contributed to an account of aesthetic absorption, and she in turn is indebted, amongst others, to Margaret Mahler and Donald Winnicott.[19] Object relational aesthetics is largely based on the idea that the prototype for developed aesthetic interaction is the aboriginal interaction between mother and infant. As Elizabeth Wright puts it: 'The medium of the artist becomes the mother's body; the separating out of the bodily self from the primal object is the central mode of experience. The creative act repeats the experience of separating from the mother.'[20]

The prototypical form of explanation for this psychoanalytic account is Freud's treatment of the 'oceanic feeling'. Freud approaches this feeling, as we have seen, in terms of early processes of individual psychological development, processes of 'fusion' with the world, and of the differentiation of 'inside' and 'outside'. Margaret Mahler elaborates these ideas, and it is to her that Ellen Spitz is especially indebted. Spitz describes aesthetic absorption as involving the reavailability, during moments of aesthetic absorption, of earlier infantile memories or states of fusion with the world, and she cites Dewey as one of her sources for this.

Dewey's intuitions concerning a deep-seated memory of an underlying harmony, and the idea of art-making as involving the reinstatement of a lost unity, are taken by Ellen Spitz to be, prima facie, psychoanalytic in tenor. Primitive harmony, its loss and a sense of loss, and the power of memory to shape and influence later life are central ideas in psychoanalytic theory. The related idea is that aesthetic absorption also involves a reliving or a partial reinstatement or the reavailability of particular aspects of what is taken to be the experience of infants. Ellen Spitz's account is valuable in so far as it highlights this neglected phase of aesthetic experience, and, in its shortcomings, her account indicates what the concerns of a more adequate description of aesthetic absorption should be.

INFANTILE 'FUSION', ELLEN SPITZ AND AESTHETIC ABSORPTION

Ellen Spitz argues that aesthetic absorption involves the reavailability from early infancy of experiences of being fused with or merged with the mother. Her claim is that:

> This symbiotic state of early infancy, prior to differentiation between inside and outside, 'I' and 'not-I', corresponds to the 'oceanic state' described by Freud, the 'original self' by Jung, the 'true self' by Winnicott, and the 'ideal state of self' described by Mahler. It is a pleasurable state dependent upon the active, almost complete adaptation by the mother to her infant's needs, which then creates within the child an illusion of magical omnipotence.[21]

She goes on to say that:

> The sense of fusion that the infant experiences with the 'all good' mother who exists as a part of self, and his accompanying sense of wellbeing and pleasure, are analogous to what some philosophers have identified as aesthetic pleasure, aesthetic emotion, the privileged moment, or the sense of beauty. [22]

Dewey, Socrates and Santayana are amongst those philosophers recruited by Ellen Spitz to underwrite the legitimacy of this analogy. For example, when Dewey says that the artist is especially concerned with 'the phase of experience in which union is achieved',[23] or with the 'moment of passage from disturbance into harmony that is of intensest life',[24] or that the creature is most alive and concentrated in those moments of 'fullest intercourse with the environment, in which sensuous material and relations are most completely merged',[25] Spitz interprets him in terms of Donald Winnicott's ideas on the transitional object.

I will consider Winnicott's ideas on this below, but first I want to ask what the phrase 'sense of fusion', which lies at the heart of Ellen Spitz's account of aesthetic absorption, might mean when it is used of the foetus or of the neonate. In particular I want to say something about the presuppositions that can govern the language describing such 'fusion'. My strategy will be to keep as close to empirical evidence as I can so as to disentangle defensible analogies from more fanciful ones. To present this as clearly as possible, I will contrast two opposing views on the possibility of 'fusion' in infancy, one from within psychoanalysis and the other from within an ethologically oriented developmental psychology.[26] Against the background of this contrast I will then evaluate the reavailability hypothesis of aesthetic absorption.

For the first nine, prenatal, months of life the child is related to its mother in the most intimate relationship it will ever have on a physical basis, more intimate than a mother will have with her child as she carries it before birth. Whereas the mother contains, the child is contained. We know a great deal about the physical development of the child in the womb, what stages it passes through, the sequence in which its organs appear, the development of its brain, the consequences for development of unfavourable uterine environments, and so on. But we know little about the psychological development of the prenatal child. This is partly because it is very difficult for us to imagine what that experience might entail, and partly because of the same difficulties – many of them to do with our available languages of description – that beset accounts of psychological development at later stages.

That psychological development must be an integral part of prenatal development is an under-researched proposition. However, substantive evidence for the possibility of such a prenatal psychological life has come from recent empirical work with infants. Until somewhat more than eight weeks the foetus floats passively in the amniotic fluid. By that time it has become capable of responding to touch. By the end of twelve weeks, spontaneous

movements of the head and legs may be observed. At sixteen
weeks, the first foetal movement can usually be felt by the mother.
A fairly complete ear has formed by this time. By twenty weeks,
the foetus is human-looking, and thumb-sucking can be observed.
By twenty-four weeks, the eyes are completely formed, but closed,
and the taste-buds are all formed. At this age the child is capable of
breathing if born prematurely. By twenty-eight weeks, the nervous system, blood and breathing systems are all well enough
developed to support life.[27]

What the impact is on the foetus's psychological life (assuming it
has one) of these sensory and motor capacities, is largely a matter of
speculation. Of central importance is the prenatal development of
the central nervous system. Trevarthen writes that 'the way the
human brain parts grow before birth suggests that the interacting
nerve-cells might make up and coordinate basic rules for object
perception, for purposeful movement patterns, and for motive
states, without benefit of experience.'[28] It is also his view that the
human brain is shaped for the acquisition of language long before it
hears a word, a view supported by the research synthesized by
Maurer and Maurer.[29]

The transition from the umbilically sustained floating world of
the womb to that of the newborn infant is a transition from limited
to limitless possibilities of experience. Rapid cortical development
is a response to and precondition of such experience. The world as
sensorily known has a major impact on the cortical development
of the neonate. Its role in the construction of the higher levels
of the brain includes giving 'the unfinished circuits of the cortex a
fresh set of criteria for selective retention of functional nerve
connections.'[30]

Concepts of fusion and of symbiosis are ubiquitous in descriptions of prenatal foetal being and in accounts of neonatal experience. The biological meaning of 'symbiosis' is 'the living together
of two dissimilar organisms, as in mutualism, commensalism,
amensalism, or parasitism'.[31] Psychologically, and especially psychoanalytically, the term is used to describe types of interdependent
relationship such as between mother and infant.[32] The psychoanalytic writer Margaret Mahler, on whom Ellen Spitz most heavily
relies, designates the early stage of psychological development,
during which the infant is wholly dependent on its mother, as a
time of symbiosis, 'a state of undifferentiation, of fusion in which

the "I" is not yet differentiated from the "not-I" and in which inside and outside are only gradually coming to be sensed as different'.[33] She goes on to say that 'The essential feature of symbiosis is hallucinatory or delusional, somatopsychic fusion with the representation of the mother and, in particular, the delusion of a common boundary of the two actually and physically separate individuals.'[34] She sees this stage as beginning around the third month of postnatal life. In her view, 'inner sensations' are the initial 'core' of the self, around which 'a sense of identity' later becomes established.[35] Mahler speaks of this symbiotic phase peaking in the third quarter of the first year and coinciding 'with the beginning of differentiation of the self from the symbiotic object'.[36] This is, she says, an 'intrapsychic process'. She speaks of the toddler's 'autonomous ego functions' expanding and centring on his/her 'developing self-concept'. This is what she calls the 'individuation–separation phase'.

More empirically oriented investigators of infant development dispute this at the level of evidence, whereas philosophers have difficulty with the idea of 'self' assumed by this analysis. Clearly there is an important conflict here about the nature of the infant mind, one that needs some resolution if we are to understand Ellen Spitz's analogically based assertion concerning 'the re-availability to us, during moments of creativity or responsiveness in the arts, of aspects of our preoedipal life, with its pleasurable sense of merging and union'.[37] I will first consider the conflict of evidence before turning to certain of the philosophical problems.

The ethological psychologist Colwyn Trevarthen is adamant that infants 'do not, at any stage, confuse themselves with objects "outside" nor do they fail to recognize that other persons are separate sources of motives and emotions'.[38] Whereas Mahler's separation–individuation theory is derived largely from clinical experience and theoretical reflection, Trevarthen's is based on ethological and experimental studies of infants in relation to their mothers and the immediate physical world. Trevarthen's evidence provides the clearest grounds for arbitrating on the nature of this apparent conflict between himself and Mahler.

Approaches to foetal and neonatal development like those of Trevarthen quite clearly privilege holistic, relational-type descriptions of infant–world situations over types of descriptions that tend to think atomistically in terms of 'a baby' relating to 'a mother', and vice versa. For example, after birth we know that subsequent brain development is closely tied to the level of stimulation received by the child, especially when that stimulation is tactile. But what regulates these stimuli? This requires an answer capable of describing a complex process of agency, rather than conceiving of infants at that early stage as quasi-autonomous agents. An ethological-type answer says that what regulates the stimuli so crucial to cortical development are the infant's movements and the mediating actions of the caretaker. But it goes further in attributing control of the *caretaker's* behaviour partially to the immature brain of the infant which commands the infant's emotional expression which in turn influences the likely responses of others. As Trevarthen puts it, 'the most precociously mature functions of a young child's brain are those that communicate needs, feelings and motives to other persons, and that lead them to present the world to the child in precisely regulated ways.'[39]

Underlying positions like this is the idea that human being is profoundly social. This idea is as central to developmental biology as it is to developmental psychology. Vygotsky insists upon the key significance of already competent human beings for the progressive construction of children's minds, through their being what Bruner later called 'vicarious consciousness' for the developing child.[40] This is also a basic idea for Trevarthen. Language and symbolic functioning are both the means and the milieu for the formation of the normal child's mind. Against this background what can be said about the idea of a prenatal psychological life? How can this help us to understand ideas of union, fusion and symbiosis, especially when they are psychologically applied in descriptions of infant minds? Is the psychoanalytic description of an initial, primordial union of mother and child followed by a 'separation' of 'self' from the 'outside world' – on which hinge Ellen Spitz's assertions about the relations of adult aesthetic absorption and infantile experience – consonant with contemporary research and theory on infancy?

This research supports the view that infants are born already competent in many sorts of ways. At birth, for instance, they are capable of orienting their heads, ears and eyes in the direction of a voice. They already demonstrate a capacity for linking looking and grasping, a type of capacity which is necessary for the development of a consciousness of objects as well as for the emergence of intentional actions.[41] The newborn also has a definite preference for its own mother's voice, having learned the vocal characteristics of that voice *in utero*. Indeed there is research that 3 day old infants show signs of recognizing the sounds of a story that was repeatedly read to them in the womb.[42] Such a learning capability suggests a prenatal psychological life, however rudimentary. Within two to three days after birth, the neonate learns the semblance of its mother's face. And certainly within the first month, babies are capable of imitating facial expressions.

By the second month the perceptual systems of the cerebral cortex, and especially the visual system, have developed, and the infant's smiling, cooing and hand gestures when spoken to indicate a growing responsiveness to others. Their capacities to imitate are also quickly established. Babies and mothers control their interchanges, their expressions and exchanges of mood. It is research findings such as these, and an ignorance of their existence or implications, that lead Trevarthen to identify 'a strange, culturally induced belief that a newborn cannot have awareness of persons as such'.[43] From a philosophical point of view, this is itself a questionable formulation if the emphasis is placed on 'persons as such', rather than on the type of 'awareness' involved.

The difficulty in coming to an understanding of the apparent conflict between the kind of view held by Margaret Mahler or Ellen Spitz and that held by Colwyn Trevarthen and others is partly philosophical, and requires a clarification of the presuppositions inherent in the languages of description they use.[44] But before turning to such philosophical issues I should also summarize the conclusions of research into the development of attachment in infancy, given its relevance for early self–other relationships.

The first precursors of emotional attachment in infants are not seen until 2 to 3 months, and firm attachments are only formed at around 8 months.[45] When the 2/3 month old infant comes to prefer interacting with its mother this is not because it has any idea that there is 'Mother'; it has to do with the fact that the mother is more familiar in all sorts of satisfying ways. Maurer and Maurer emphasize that 'from the baby's perspective, his mother is not a special person – nor an object, for that matter: he simply feels comfortable around her because he is encountering a particular set

of familiar sensations and because he is being stimulated appropriately.'[46] This is a happier statement than that of Trevarthen above.

The precondition for real attachment, in this account, is an
understanding that things exist, and the precondition for attachments lasting over time is the ability to recollect things in their
absence. These conditions are only met in normal development
around 8 months of age. And the quality of these attachments, with
their long-term clinical consequences, can range from the secure to
the anxious, the social to the unsocial. We can see from this cursory
review of early development that its investigators, whether they
are of the scientific or clinical bent, use words like 'self', 'person',
's/he', 'boundary', 'fusion', 'awareness', etc., in ways that clash
with each other and which give pause to philosophers. But what
might these philosophical concerns consist of?

DIFFICULTIES WITH PSYCHOANALYTIC DESCRIPTIONS OF INFANT EXPERIENCE

The general problem with descriptions relating adult and childhood experience is that they are vague and insufficiently specific.
Trevarthen insists that the baby has an 'awareness' of other 'persons
as such'. In his work, however, that awareness resides in acts of
perception and signal recognition on the part of the baby, rather
than in acts of symbol interpretation. This is an obvious point so
long as one understands 'persons as such' to mean something like
'human beings as preferred objects of attention'. But some recon-
ciliation is necessary between his propositions that babies 'do not,
at any stage, confuse themselves with objects "outside"'[47] and that
'Towards the end of the first year, the infant develops a clear
awareness of the existence of objects in their own right' and that
they 'become aware of and are interested in the changing directions
of another person's interests'.[48]

Up until that point, by implication, there is no permanent
representation of individual objects such that, when hidden, they
would be searched for. One reason, perhaps, that infants do not
confuse themselves with 'outside' objects is quite simply that they
cannot.[49] Con-fusion involves merging or mixing things such that
their distinctiveness is obscured. There is a strong case to be made
that infants do not 'have a self' of the sort that could be confused

with what is taken to be the not-self. Precisely what could be confused in the case of the infant and the object? Trevarthen seems to be saying that the newborn infant very quickly discerns the distinctness of others (even if it takes the best part of the first year to develop the means for permanent object representation) and is inserted into a complex process of communicational play which, to the attentive observer, requires no such category of 'confusion' to describe what is going on.

Mahler, on the other hand, sees the first six months of the infant's life as a state of 'fusion in which the "I" is not yet differentiated from the "not-I" and in which inside and outside are only gradually coming to be sensed as different'.[50] Here she can sensibly talk of fusion or of confusion, but only if it makes sense to presuppose the existence of 'I' and 'not-I', of 'inside' and 'outside'. A description of the psychic being of the infant as, say, 'an undifferentiated unity', which includes 'Mother', still would not warrant an associated description of 'fusion'. If at that early infantile stage of development there is no sign of anything in the infant's way of acting to suggest the presence of an 'I' as subject – and there is not – then neither can there be a 'not-I', and consequently there can be no such state of fusion as described by Mahler, and endorsed and used by Ellen Spitz. Consequently, there could be no such state, nor any feelings associated with such a state, reavailable for aesthetic experience later on in development.[51]

This reveals a fundamental objection to many object relational, psychoanalytic accounts of the ontogenetic roots of aesthetic absorption. Their languages of description implicitly carry with them dualistic assumptions of the kind that Dewey inveighed against. Their talk of what happens within the psyche or between one psyche and another may seem perfectly reasonable at the level of everyday language, but the assumptions supporting a literal use of such language (as against a merely metaphorical use for reasons of convenience), together with the implications of this use for describing psychological development, are questionable. It may be objected that I am being unnecessarily stringent in my demands for precision in descriptions of the infant's experience, and that Mahler did not really mean 'I' when she wanted a contrast with 'not-I', but was merely reaching for a compelling stylistic phrase. But this objection would have little force either way since imprecision can be as misleading as error. As we shall see in Chapter 4, the empirically investigated (rather than clinically theorized) emergence of I related speech acts is a major achievement of early childhood rather than of infancy and it this sort of evidence with its social–psychological implications that casts doubt on the utility of this type of psychoanalytic theorizing for this particular phenomenon. We may again take Ellen Spitz as the example of this way of thinking for while she regularly calls upon Dewey's aesthetics for quotational support, her underlying concepts of experience, as revealed in her language, are of just the sort to which he opposed his own concepts of experience in general and of aesthetic experience in particular.

The problem begins at the very beginning of her account of absorption and aesthetic experience. Her major question, she writes, has to do 'with what happens in our moments of absorption into aesthetic experience, how it is that we respond as we occasionally do – with intense emotion and pleasure – to music, theatre, painting and literature'.[52] A Deweyan, anti-dualistic position would immediately identify a problem here as residing in the prepositions 'into' and 'to'. (See, for example, the reference in Chapter 2, page 24 to Dewey's criticism of I. A. Richards.) Aesthetic experience is not the sort of thing into which one can be absorbed. In experiences of art objects, other than sentimental experiences, one does not necessarily respond to them with some reavailable or reactivated emotion. For it to be possible to be absorbed *into* aesthetic experience, that experience would have to exist independently of the process of absorption. But the phenomenology of aesthetic experience quickly dismisses this possibility. Absorption is a feature *of* just such an experience. This would, I think, be Dewey's position. Far from Dewey adding authority to an implicitly dualistic position like Ellen Spitz's, the one she advocates would fall into his category of a 'compartmentalized' psychology.

A similar objection can be made to the idea that we respond *with* emotions *to* works of art. The truer, if more cumbersome, description would be this: of the experience which is the joint outcome of the person–art object transaction, particular qualities may be particular emotions. These do not have to pre-exist the encounter of the person and the art object. In an aesthetically open encounter with such an object, qualitatively new emotions may characterize the resulting experience which, in Dewey's terminology, is the art work. 'You are the music while the music lasts,' as T. S. Eliot has it, to which we might add 'new music, new you'. Since art *is* experience, and since the possibilities of art are open-ended, it follows that the possibilities of new emotions and emotional qualities are also open-ended. In other words, art *as* experience, has the power to create new emotions and patterns of feeling in the appropriate circumstances. If, as Susanne Langer[53] believes, art creates forms symbolic of human feeling, it also has the power to co-create, with aesthetically intentionalizing persons, novel experiences with characteristically new qualities of feeling.

A descriptive language that has not formed itself with this understanding of experience in mind will necessarily misconstrue the nature of aesthetic experiences of art and, in the case of our present concern, will misconceive the nature of absorption and its ontogenesis. Thus, when Ellen Spitz identifies as one of the aims of object relations theory the exploration of 'the interactions between the endopsychic self and the external world' in infants, she is assuming that there is such a 'self' that relates *to* 'the external world'.[54] But this description, as I suggest above, is challenged by contemporary evidence. Empirically based theorizing, such as that of Maurer and Maurer, as against clinically based theorizing such as Ellen Spitz's, utilizes concepts like that of the impersonal 'neuronal observer' to speak of an organizing centre of the neonate's experience of movement.[55] This notion bears no relationship to that of an infantile 'endopsychic self' and would not be open to the same criticisms.

Later, in Chapter 5, I shall review some of this evidence and outline one part of a theory of self that relies on an understanding of the consequences for psychic development of symbolic functioning, and that suggests that a different understanding of the nature of the infant mind is required. Unlike psychoanalytic accounts in general, this account builds on an understanding of the fundamental sociality of the human mind, infant or adult, pre-symbolic or post-symbolic. It also distinguishes between the categories of 'person' and 'self' which, it will now be evident, is necessary to clarify our understanding of both psychoanalytic and ethological-type descriptions of the infant mind.

THE FAILURE OF 'REAVAILABILITY' ACCOUNTS OF
AESTHETIC ABSORPTION

Whatever the merit of psychoanalytic intuitions concerning the
nature of the relationship between infantile experience and adult
'oceanic feeling', or between infantile experience and aesthetic
absorption, the psychoanalytic language framing these intuitions is
inherently flawed. Too much is too vaguely conflated, with
argument and analysis yielding to analogy and assertion. Yet the
question of how to think about the continuity of early childhood
experience, especially pre-verbal experience, with later experience
remains.

Ellen Spitz's analogical account of aesthetic absorption as being
'like symbiotic fusion in that encounters with the beautiful may
temporarily obliterate our sense of inner and outer separateness'
melts away as soon as one tries to locate phenomenologically this
'sense of inner and outer separateness' or to imagine what its
'obliteration' might feel like.[56] The heart of her analysis of aesthetic
absorption is, as we have seen, that it is 'the re-availability to us,
during moments of creativity or responsiveness in the arts, of
aspects of our preoedipal life, with its pleasurable sense of merging
and union'.[57] But granting, for the sake of argument, both the
existence and the endurance of such a sense, and granting also the
possibility of its psychological 'reavailability' in moments related to
the arts, this still would not explain aesthetic absorption.

This is because it would not explain the consequential differences
for experience between such a 'reavailable sense' being an object of
attention for me if it occurs as I look at a picture, say, and the same
reavailable sense if it occurs as an unattended-to strand in the fabric
of my experience of looking at the picture. In short, explanations
like this do not say what such reavailable senses of infantile
experiences of 'merging and union' do, other than to carry with
them a pleasant emotional tone. Why should it be such a sense of
symbiotic fusion, rather than any other, that becomes reavailable in
aesthetic situations? To conjure up a 'desire for fusion' (or a
'restoration' of the mother's body as described by Adrian Stokes[58])
which would be satisfied by aesthetic experiences of art does not get
us anywhere. It certainly does not explain absorption as it occurs in
aesthetic experience.

In Chapter 2, we saw that Dewey's ideas about art's powers of restoring 'consciously, and thus on the plane of meaning, the union of sense, need, impulse and action characteristic of the live creature' reject an understanding of this restoration as the simple reinstitution of a previous state.[59] Restoration for Dewey is not reavailability in Ellen Spitz's sense. The restoration concerns forms of relationship, not of states. One can also see that Dewey's references to the origins of aesthetic experience are sometimes phylogenetic, sometimes ontogenetic.[60] When ontogenetic they refer to childhood rather than to infancy, and they centre on 'speech as the mother tongue'. His detailed example from George Eliot's *The Mill on the Floss* is from a time in childhood when objects clearly have their own existence, when perception is capable of delighting in the details of the world and can, with language, give form to imagination.

We also saw in the last chapter that Dewey's understanding of absorption, as a feature of aesthetic experience, involves the surrender or complete engagement of the self 'in what is objectively done'. Were we then to follow the trail of intuitive clues left by Dewey, we would attend to the idea of forms of relating as they develop in the post-infantile, early childhood period of development. We should pay special attention to ways of thinking about the early development of self, since without such an understanding we cannot say much about the development of the capacity to surrender or completely engage the self. This is the path I will follow.

Even if we reject Ellen Spitz's use of Margaret Mahler's theory of development as an adequate description of what happens in aesthetic absorption, there are nonetheless important insights and intuitions to be gained within the psychoanalytic tradition. Some ideas of René Spitz and of Donald Winnicott, for example, are relevant in the context of trying to understand Dewey's intuitions from a developmental perspective as well, perhaps, as trying to interpret certain psychoanalytic positions from a Deweyan point of view. To reject the reavailability account of aesthetic absorption is not to deny the relevance of early childhood experience for later aesthetic experiences. That relevance may be as straightforward as Matisse's insistence on the need to look on the world as though for the first time with the eyes of a child, or it may be as complex as object relations theorists suggest in that the form of aesthetic experience may be linked to forms of the infant's experience. My point is simply that a better account of aesthetic absorption is needed than that currently available from reavailability proponents. Towards that end, I want to conclude this chapter with a review of some psychoanalytic insights and formulations that may contribute to understanding the possible relations between the earliest forms of experience and later aesthetic experiences.

RENÉ SPITZ ON EARLY FORMS OF PERCEPTUAL ORGANIZATION

René Spitz has written about the forms of sensory organization in the first year of life that serve as a basis for the differentiation of 'inner' and 'outer' worlds. He contrasts a form of sensory organization present at birth – he calls it 'coenesthetic' – with a later level of development he terms 'diacritic'. Of these he writes:

> Sensing is extensive, primarily visceral, centred on the autonomic nervous system, and manifests itself in the form of emotions. Accordingly, I prefer to speak of this form of 'perception', which differs so fundamentally from sensory perception, as *reception*. It is an all or none phenomenon operating as a binary system. In contrast to this stands the later development of what I have called *diacritic organization* where perception takes place through the peripheral sense organs and is localized, circumscribed and intensive: it centres on the cortex, its manifestations are cognitive processes, among them the conscious thought processes.[61]

Coenesthesis is a psychological term common in late nineteenth century thought. It refers to an awareness of the body and of its states that arises from sensations stimulated from within the body itself.[62] In using the term 'diacritic' – which in linguistics carries the meaning of distinctiveness – Spitz appears to want to mark off the development of the perception *of* something. By contrasting the two, and by suggesting that they are sequential in the march of development, and potentially coincident once developed, he is highlighting for attention an important aspect of experiential development that is easily neglected. Ideas of self that use notions of 'inner' and 'outer' may possibly have some of their roots in this early phase of development.

My brief discussion of contemporary work on infant development suggests that peripheral sense perception is not nearly so late an achievement as may have been thought when Spitz was writing in 1965. Notwithstanding this, the distinction he makes between these early psychological experiences retains its suggestiveness. Although Spitz's diacritic system evolves from the coenesthetic system, he contends that the earlier system continues to function powerfully throughout life, albeit mutedly in the consciousness of Western man and woman. According to him, the categories of adult behaviour where this more primitive system is evident include the sensory categories of equilibrium, tension (muscular and other), posture, temperature, vibration, skin and body contact, rhythm, tempo, duration, pitch, tone, resonance, clang and others of which adults are hardly aware and which they cannot verbalize. Members of preliterate societies tend to retain and use these sensibilities, or to retain an ability to regress to them when required to by their cultures. Such regression, observes Spitz – in the service of a culturally determined ego-ideal [63] – can be facilitated by stimulus deprivation (such as fasting, solitude, darkness, abstinence) or through drugs, alcohol, rhythm, sound or breathing techniques. He also believes it to be evident in the experience of some mystics, certain psychotics and also in hypnotic trances.

In Western adults, Spitz believes that these categories of perception and communication are usually in a state of atrophy having been replaced by semantic symbols that are diacritically perceived. Nonetheless, there are some groups which retain the ability to use at least some of these sensibilities. These would include composers, musicians, dancers, acrobats, fliers, painters and poets.[64] To use a Deweyan term, these perceptual capacities may be of just the kind which the arts as qualitative symbolizations utilize. In art, Spitz is suggesting that both his forms of perceptual organization are productively at work. More than this is the assumption that, as far as art is concerned, the biological and the cultural formations of experience work in easy harmony.

The arts are meaningful, and a consideration of the developmental origins of artistic and aesthetic competencies must pay attention to the emerging ability of children to make objects meaningful. Within the object relations tradition of psychoanalysis there is one writer whose ideas on the early construction of emotionally meaningful objects have had a special appeal to theorists of art, notably Peter Fuller and Ellen Spitz. He is the English psychoanalyst D. W. Winnicott.

A DEWEYAN REFORMULATION OF WINNICOTT'S IDEA OF 'THE TRANSITIONAL'

In 1951 Winnicott published what was to become perhaps his best known paper, 'Transitional objects and transitional phenomena'.[65] For my purposes, I take this as an account of how very young children can grant meaning to objects – very special objects in this case – and as a theory of the functions and consequences for their developing psychic lives of doing so. Of particular interest to me is Winnicott's use of the idea of 'boundary' as a psychological category.

Winnicott begins this paper by noting that infants, from the earliest days after birth (and, as we now know, prenatally) use their fingers, thumbs and fists to stimulate the regions of their mouths 'in satisfaction of the instincts of that zone', as he puts it, 'and also in quiet union'.[66] After a few months infants like to play with objects and tend to become emotionally involved with one particular object such as a teddy, a scarf or a piece of blanket. Winnicott links these commonly observed phenomena together, and speculates on the significance of this linkage for the infant's developing relationships with the object world.

For this he introduces the idea of 'illusion' meaning 'that which is allowed to the infant, and which in adult life is inherent in art and religion'; he thinks of this as an 'intermediate area between the subjective and that which is objectively perceived'.[67] More specifically, he uses the idea of illusion to identify that emergent feeling of being powerful that infants may have when, wanting something very much, they find it available and present to them. To the observer the infant has found what was already there; but from the infant's point of view, speculates Winnicott, it has conjured into existence exactly what it needed. Herein, Winnicott believes, lies the protean experience of being creative and of its satisfactions. He puts it like this:

> that at some theoretical point early in the development of every human individual an infant in a certain setting provided by the mother is capable of conceiving of the idea of something that would meet the growing need that arises out of instinctual tension. The infant cannot be said to know at first what is to be created. At this point in time the mother presents herself. In the ordinary way she gives her breast and her potential feeding urge. The mother's adaptation to the infant's needs, when good enough, gives the infant

the illusion that there is an external reality that corresponds to the infant's own capacity to create. In other words, here is an overlap between what the mother supplies and what the child might conceive of. To the observer, the child perceives what the mother actually presents, but this is not the whole truth. The infant perceives the breast only in so far as a breast could be created just there and then. There is no interchange between the mother and the infant. Psychologically the infant takes from a breast that is part of the infant, and the mother gives milk to an infant that is part of herself. In psychology, the idea of interchange is based on an illusion in the psychologist.[68]

This last observation, that 'interchange' is an ill chosen term for describing what is happening here, is a cautionary one. In the infant's case, transitional objects, such as a favourite piece of blanket, function as 'comforters' or as defences against anxiety.[69] But it is not the object as such that is transitional, according to Winnicott: 'The object represents the infant's transition from *a state of being merged with the mother* [my emphasis] to a state of being in relation to the mother as something outside and separate.'[70] From this, one can see that Winnicott is describing developmental transitions in experience and their signs, rather than fusions of a presumed 'I' and 'not-I'. His assertion that the idea of interchange between mother and infant is an illusion of the observing psychologist seems to confirm this reading of him.

Although Winnicott does not make this point, one might say that the significance of transitional phenomena for our present discussion is that they present an early instance of the young child granting meaning to an inanimate object in a social context, rather than 'finding' it. 'Meaning' in this case concerns what it is that the particular object does for the infant. Here, perhaps, is an instance of a material becoming a 'proto-medium'. At this point I must re-emphasize that the terms of the problem of absorption during this early stage of development are not those of self–other *differentiation*, as preferred by psychoanalytically oriented writers like Ellen Spitz or Marion Milner.[71] The real problem, which houses that of absorption, is that of self–other *constitution*.

In other words, I want to suggest that self and other emerge from a process of construction *after* this state of infantile undifferentiation; this stage of undifferentiation is not itself the merging of self and other, as presumed by so many psychoanalytically inclined authors. The most succinct formulation I can offer is this: the problem is one of emergence and not one of merging. A similar sort of criticism is offered by Lorenzer and Orban who point to the untenability of arguing for objects that are 'transitional' when those realities supposedly bridged by such objects, namely 'the self' and 'the world', have not yet come into being.[72] Their position, parallel to the one I am proposing, is that self and other do not constitute Winnicott's 'intermediate area of experiencing' but instead differentiate out of it.

The phenomenology of making an object of a novel type, or of formulating a new idea about the world, is difficult to describe and calls out for appropriate metaphors. It may be thought to involve the sense of a 'space between' the maker and the world in which the object or idea 'takes shape', before standing autonomously in the objective world. Once there, it acts to define the boundaries of its maker just as its own boundaries, as made object/idea, are clearly perceptible to other observers. If the present reading of Winnicott is correct, then this is the sort of meaning he wants the idea of 'potential space' to have, especially as it applies to infantile 'transitional objects'. And if it makes sense to speak of a 'location' for cultural experience [73] – and it is not clear that it does – then this is where Winnicott locates play and cultural activity. The experience of the small child 'lost' in play is retained, he felt, in the intense experiencing that belongs to the arts, to religion and to imaginative living, as well as to creative scientific work.

If the separation of the child from its environment is, as John Donne might have it, not 'a breach but an expansion, like gold to airy thinness beat'[74] then Winnicott's account of that continuity, especially as it connects with later experience, is subject to the same general criticisms of psychoanalytic accounts as were made above in relation to Ellen Spitz and Margaret Mahler. How can very early experiences of being 'lost' in activity be retained or reavailable? Is this the best description of the continuity between earlier and later experiences of absorption, or is the similarity due, as I will want to argue, to the exercise of similar functions albeit at different times throughout the lifespan? These are the issues I will investigate in the next chapter from a pragmatic and from a social constructivist perspective.

If Winnicott has identified an interesting and perhaps influential early phenomenon, is his manner of theorizing about these 'transitional phenomena' helpful in advancing our understanding? The English philosopher Antony Flew thinks not, and I am inclined to agree with him.[75] While granting the interest of the fact that very young children do form special attachments to teddies or pieces of blanket, Flew questions the looseness of Winnicott's terminology, especially his definition of a transitional object, while accepting that its importance and meaning for the child lies in its use rather than in what type of object it physically is. The linkage with later cultural experiences, such as are involved in art, via the idea of illusion, is also seen to be problematic. But most controversial is Winnicott's positing of a third 'intermediate' world between 'external shared reality' and 'psychic reality' to which the experiences of transitional phenomena belong. In Flew's respectful if somewhat exasperated encounter with Winnicott, we have an instance of philosophical logic stumbling over psychoanalytic intuition. Given the present focus on aesthetic absorption, what are we to make of Winnicott's work in this area?

Remembering that I am testing the feasibility of applying a Deweyan conception of experience to certain problems of aesthetic experience, it is clear that a formulation in terms of 'inner' and 'outer' reality which interposes a third 'intermediate' realm does not have much appeal. Such a formulation will necessarily favour the idea that some sort of 'merging' occurs, with its correlative separations, whereas my conception favours instead a language of emergence. I have already observed that the language of union and separation has a ready appeal when the attempt is to describe the sequence by which something emerges from the private meanings of its maker, perhaps an artist, into the meanings of the public world. To be seduced by this language of description, however, is to be led like Winnicott to theorize in terms of transitions, whereas the language of emergence will lead to theorization in terms of transformations.

Considered in this way, one would think of the phenomena Winnicott identifies as 'transitional' (and the related ideas of 'potential space' and 'illusion', together with their role in human development) not in terms of a succession of dialectical exchanges between 'inner' and 'outer' reality through the corridor of some 'intermediate' space, but rather as a series of transformations within the unity of a wider experience. In short, the problem becomes that of transformations of subject–object relations, rather than transitions between subject and object. Instead of there being two worlds with a third world of illusion in between, there is the one world of experience. This preserves the heuristic value of Winnicott's intuitions, but within a more satisfactory framework.

CONCLUSION

This analysis of psychoanalytic ways of thinking about the nature and developmental history of aesthetic absorption still leaves us with an important but so far inadequately described phase of aesthetic experience. The earliest developmental history of 'self' remains a problem for psychoanalysis just as it does for other schools of psychology. Having objected to causally linking the concepts of merging, fusion, and transition favoured by these theorists with the idea that these somehow become reavailable during phases of aesthetic absorption in later life, we are still left with the need for a theory of self, however rudimentary, with which to construct a description of absorption. 'I' as a psychological achievement is inextricably semiotic and social, and so, by implication, is the 'not-I' or other. A useful theory of self for our purposes, therefore, must take semiosis and socialization as key contributors to the constitution of self. A number of contemporary schools of thought recognize this need. Within the broad reach of psychoanalysis, for instance, thinkers like Julia Kristeva place these issues at the centre of their work.[76] I mentioned above that the infant is inserted into a complex process of communicational play and that its participation is a vital part of the means whereby self is subsequently constituted. René Spitz also, for example, recognizes the importance of prelinguistic forms of perceptual ability. The body comes into being desiring, and only in time is it transformed within a sign system. Play, as Winnicott recognized, is one especially important social process that shapes this transformation. Kristeva develops these ideas and assimilates them to a semiotic perspective. As Wright puts it, 'Kristeva's child chuckles its way into selfhood, Klein's, a sensitive soul from birth, beats its own breast.'[77] Kristeva accommodates both pre-symbolic bodily desire and socialized symbolic functioning in her conception of emerging selfhood.

In the next chapters I want to offer a description of aesthetic absorption as a process and in doing so to use a theory of self that is heavily reliant on pragmatic philosophical and social constructivist thinking. These are very different from the semiotic and psycho-analytic sources of Kristeva, but not, I believe, unsympathetic to them. In both approaches, childhood and its possibilities are powerful presences.

NOTES

1. Rainer Maria Rilke, *Poems 1906–26*, trans. J. B. Leishman (London: The Hogarth Press, 1968), p. 234; emphasis in original.
2. E. L. Freud, 1975, p. 388.
3. Ibid., p. 389.
4. See Freud's 'The *Moses* of Michelangelo', in *Art and Literature* (1985b, p. 253).
5. For his essays on Jensen's *Gradiva*, Leonardo Da Vinci and Michel-angelo's *Moses*, amongst others, see Freud, 1985b.
6. See Freud's 'Writers and day–dreaming', in *Art and Literature* (1985b, p. 141).
7. Freud, 1985a, pp. 243–340.
8. Ibid., p. 251.
9. Ibid., p. 252.
10. Sachs, 1984, p. 108.
11. Freud, 1985a, p. 254.
12. Ibid., p. 255.
13. Ibid., p. 254.
14. Ibid., p. 255.
15. Ibid., p. 256.
16. This phrase 'requirements of the situation' is a key one in the *Gestalt* theorizing of Max Wertheimer. See Rudolf Arnheim's essay on 'Max Wertheimer and Gestalt psychology', in his *New Essays on the Psychology of Art* (1986), p. 34.
17. See Freud, 1985b, p. 339. Also see Freud, 1985a, p. 271, where he says that 'Psychoanalysis, unfortunately, has scarcely anything to say about beauty either.'
18. See Harré and Lamb, 1986a, p. 169. See also Laplanche and Pontalis, 1980, p. 280.
19. See E. Spitz, 1985. A major influence in the background here is Melanie Klein. Others in this tradition who have written on art are Adrian Stokes, Hanna Segal, Marion Milner and W. R. D. Fairbairn. Anton Ehrenzweig (1967) writes of absorption in its etymological sense of being 'sucked inside' and 'enveloped' by the picture plane. However, I find his speculations and descriptions of this obscure and unhelpful.
20. See Wright, 1984, p. 84.

21. E. Spitz, 1985, p. 141.
22. Ibid., p. 141.
23. Dewey, 1958, p. 15.
24. Ibid., p. 17.
25. Ibid., p. 103.
26. Ethological studies rely upon detailed and protracted observational studies of behaviour. Film and video are frequently used and allow for the study of minute details of individual behaviour and coordinated interactions.
27. Bee, 1989, pp. 48–9.
28. See Trevarthen, 1987a, p. 102.
29. See Maurer and Maurer, 1990. For the last three months of prenatal life, the foetus can, it seems, hear: 'His world is a world of rumblings and groanings punctuated by his mother's utterances. And constantly, through everything, he hears the thumping of his mother's heart' (p. 13). After birth the infant comes to recognize his mother's voice long before his father's (p. 16). And it also seems that babies begin life capable of distinguishing the elements of melody and of speech (p. 145).
30. Trevarthen, 1987a, p. 106. The bases for higher psychological functions begin to be laid sometime between fifteen and twenty-five weeks after gestation when cells of the neocortex move into the cortical plate. Cortical and subcortical cells that later are dedicated to one cortical role have common or proximate origins in the developing brain (pp. 107–8).
31. *The Random House Dictionary of the English Language*, unabridged 2nd edition (New York: Random House, 1987), p. 1926.
32. In Chapter 5, I will introduce a specific notion of 'psychological symbiosis' which Rom Harré derives from the work of Lev Vygotsky and René Spitz.
33. Mahler, 1969, p. 9.
34. Ibid.
35. Ibid., p. 11.
36. Ibid., p. 220.
37. E. Spitz, 1985, p. 142.
38. See Trevarthen, 1987b, p. 363.
39. Ibid., p. 108.
40. Lev Vygotsky (1896–1934), despite a very brief working life, has had a great influence upon contemporary psychology through his insistence on the significance of the nature and function of social relations on the development of psychological process. For an introduction to this see Wertsch, 1985. Also see Bruner, 1986, p. 76.
41. Trevarthen, 1987b, p. 364. Piaget believed that this was developed later through interactions.
42. Maurer and Maurer, 1990, p. 186.
43. Trevarthen, 1987b, p. 365.
44. Daniel Stern's work on infant development, of which Ellen Spitz is aware, can be found in his *The Interpersonal World of the Infant* (1985).

See also Kaye, 1982, for a perspective that is indebted to pragmatic philosophy, especially to Mead, and is critical of the idea that mutual intersubjectivity is a feature of early infancy. Instead he uses the notion of apprenticeship to tackle questions that have to do with becoming a person.

45. Maurer and Maurer, 1990, p. 219.
46. Ibid., p. 220.
47. Trevarthen, 1987b, p. 363.
48. Ibid., p. 367.
49. It should be remembered that the etymology of 'infant' is *infans* which means 'unable to speak'.
50. Mahler, 1969, p. 9.
51. The theoretical possibility of there being some sort of 'self' or 'ego' at the earliest stages of infant development remains controversial within psychoanalysis itself. Here, for example, is Elizabeth Wright's comment on Melanie Klein's reliance on the dualism of life and death instincts from the beginning of life:

    > In this respect Klein remains within the bounds of an id-psychology, but she departs from Freud in asserting that a rudimentary ego is present from the beginning, capable of certain defensive strategies designed to protect a pre-symbolic, pre-linguistic self, whose theoretical status is far from clear, since it seems to have a primitive notion of its own sex.

    For this see Wright, 1984, p. 81. The question raised by my next chapter is whether this idea of a pre-symbolic self is oxymoronic.
52. E. Spitz, 1985, p. 136.
53. Langer, 1953, p. 40.
54. Ibid., p. 138.
55. Maurer and Maurer, 1990, p. 180.
56. E. Spitz, 1985, p. 142.
57. Ibid.
58. See Wright, 1984, p. 85.
59. Dewey, 1958, p. 25.
60. Ibid., p. 18.
61. R. Spitz, 1965, p. 44.
62. *The Random House Dictionary of the English Language*, unabridged 2nd edition (New York: Random House, 1987), p. 398.
63. R. Spitz, 1965, p. 137.
64. Ibid., p. 136.
65. Winnicott, 1974, pp. 1–30.
66. Ibid., p. 1.
67. Ibid., p. 3.
68. Ibid., pp. 13–14.
69. See Davis and Wallbridge, 1983, p. 71. For an application of the ideas of Winnicott, and of others in the object relations tradition of psychoanalysis, to questions of artistic and aesthetic experience see Fuller, 1980, especially Chapter 4 which deals with 'Abstraction and "The Potential Space"'.

70. Winnicott, 1974, p. 17.
71. E. Spitz, 1985, p. 148. See also Milner, 1981.
72. See Lorenzer and Orban, 1978.
73. See Winnicott's 1966 paper, 'The location of cultural experience', in Winnicott, 1974, pp. 112–29.
74. Davis and Wallbridge, 1983, p. 78.
75. Flew, 1978. See also Alfred Flarsheim's reply (1978).
76. See Kristeva, 1980.
77. Wright, 1984, p. 99.

CHAPTER 4

AESTHETIC ABSORPTION AS A CASE OF 'NOT-I'?

in the silence, it won't be I, it's not I, I'm not there yet, I'll go there
now, I'll try and go there now, no use trying, I wait for my turn, my
turn to go there, my turn to talk there, my turn to listen there.

(Samuel Beckett)[1]

INTRODUCTION

References to aesthetic absorption always include mention of the
self, and especially of the 'I'. To adapt Eliot, 'I' am said to *be* the
music while the music lasts, or as Wallace Stevens puts it, I as
reader *become* the book. Obviously, it would not be possible to
expand this description without at the same time developing an
appropriate description of the self. More specifically, the meaning
of 'I' needs clarification since it is the 'I' allegedly that becomes the
book, or the music, or whatever. As the nineteenth century
American painter Thomas Cole put it: 'Our conceptions expand –
we become part of what we behold.'[2]

There are two very important and intimately connected philosophical ideas that can help us to present a more detailed analysis of
the role of 'I' in aesthetic absorption. These are the ideas of
subjectivity and of intentionality. It is a commonplace that how we
feel at any particular moment depends in part upon what we
happen to be thinking or perceiving or imagining at that point in
time, or have been thinking just beforehand. Another way of
putting this is to say that what it feels like to be me at any particular
moment has a lot to do with what happens to be the focus of my
attention at that time. Yet another formulation would be that how

it feels to be me looking or listening or thinking about something depends upon my point of view at that time. In philosophical terms, subjectivity has to do with what it is like to be me doing something, and intentionality has to do with that to which my thinking or perceiving or imagining is directed or is about.[3] The phenomenology of mental states, including states of aesthetic absorption, is jointly composed by subjectivity and intentionality.

This is an important point because describing aesthetic absorption means focusing on the phenomenology of the particular self who becomes absorbed. It means trying to understand how that person's point of view is transformed from a state of being apart from the object of attention to becoming a part of it. What I want to explore is the suggestion that becoming absorbed like this has to do with shifts between types of intentionality together with corresponding changes in subjectivity. The sense of being a centre of my experience depends upon what type of experience that is. Being centred in a field of perceptual experience, for example, is subjectively different from being centred in a field of symbolic thought. What it is like to be me as I intensely gaze at a picture feels subtly different from what it is like to be me as I solve a mathematical problem. If the content and context of my thinking change, my subjectivity will also change.

An example. I am watching my pond. It is raining, and the surface of the pond is a moving pattern of dimpled circles. Self-forgetfully, I gaze at the patterns of circles merging into each other. Then I find myself saying to myself, 'The raindrops are making circles which merge into each other as they hit the water.' Instantly my relationship with the rainswept pond is altered. The rained-upon pond, as the initial focus of my attention, is now verbally mediated and replaced by a thought about it. My gazing has been transformed in that it has been succeeded by a verbal act of signification. This new experience of the pond as verbally signified has distanced me from the previously gazed-upon pond, in that my perceptual experience of it has given way to an experience of it as verbally signified. With that transformation and succession of experiences of the pond as seen, and of the pond as spoken and thought about, has come a shift in the focus of my attention, and more notably a change in the context that directs and houses that focus. The intricate webs of implication and association that form the context of the thought-about pond are different from those of the context of the gazed-upon pond. For now, as I think about the pond, I feel released from its particular presence at this moment. I have, through words, left the field of present actuality and entered the field of imaginative time and possibility where thoughts of Basho's frog[4] are succeeded by schematic memories of photographs from books on water gardens I have read, and all this while I remain physically facing and apparently still looking at the pond.

This is an example of how transformations of types of intentionality have been accompanied by transformations of subjectivity. Take another example from Richard Wollheim's *Painting as an Art*.[5] Wollheim observes that paintings that contain a spectator in the picture face a definite difficulty:

> once the spectator of the picture accepts the invitation to identify with the spectator in the picture, he loses sight of the marked surface. In the represented space, where he now vicariously stands, there is no marked surface. Accordingly the task of the artist must be to recall the spectator to a sense of what he has temporarily lost. The spectator must *be returned from imagination to perception* [my emphasis]: twofoldness must be reactivated. Otherwise the distinctive resources of the medium will lie untapped.

By twofoldness Wollheim means the experience of seeing the marked surface of the painting as well as seeing something in that surface. For this, the spectator of the picture must, in Wollheim's account, adopt and try to maintain a perceptual rather than an imaginative point of view. I believe that the experience of being aesthetically absorbed has something to do with these 'returns' or transitions or shifts and with the type of role the subject of the experience plays in each type of state.

The phenomenology of a mental state is, as Richard Wollheim argues, jointly formed by intentionality and subjectivity.[6] Not all mental phenomena have subjectivity. Only mental states have subjectivity directly. Mental dispositions and mental activities have subjectivity only indirectly, through the mental states that carry them.[7] Subjectivity and thought-content, or intentionality, are intimately linked. Can they then be distinguished? The answer is that such distinctions are very difficult to effect, but Wollheim suggests the following exercise to help isolate that aspect which is subjectivity. He suggests asking ourselves whether we could see exactly what we now think we are seeing (Picasso's *War*, for example), but do so through having a different sort of experience.[8]

He is asking, that is, for 'same intentionality, different subjectivity'. To do this properly,

> it is also imperative that total intentionality, not just a fragment of it,
> is held constant – otherwise we shall drift into imagining a second
> experience that simply includes the original experience or partially
> overlaps with it. If, with these conditions respected, the answer is
> still Yes, then we have isolated subjectivity, for subjectivity is what
> in such circumstances would change.[9]

If imagining 'same intentionality, different subjectivity' is difficult
– I cannot say that I can successfully do it – imagining 'same
subjectivity, different intentionality' is all but impossible. Wollheim takes this to imply that intentionality 'penetrates' subjectivity
more deeply than subjectivity does intentionality.

I have highlighted the subtle relationships between these complex phenomena because of their relevance to the idea that becoming aesthetically absorbed has to do with a change of subjectivity
which is intimately related to a change in the content of thought.
That content and our ability to communicate it is greatly enriched if
we have language. Animals and infants do not have language, but
there is every reason to believe that they are intentional, albeit in a
relatively coarse way. Without language, however, animals and
infants are extremely restricted in their ability to communicate the
subjectivity of their mental states.

The reason for this has again to do with the close link between
intentionality and subjectivity. In practice, we often communicate
how things are for us indirectly by conveying the intentionality of
the mental state. When talking to my doctor on the telephone, for
example, I might say something like, 'I have these terrible pains in
my neck and arms', and leave these verbally articulated thoughts to
convey to her what these pains are like for me. By communicating
my current intentional state I indirectly convey what it is like for
me, my subjectivity. Wollheim suggests that this is analogous to
'the way in which the pigment in a painting of a landscape is the
perspicuous vehicle of innumerable thoughts about the landscape:
which in turn can be connected with the difficulty we have in using
thought to describe the lie of the pigment.'[10]

I can try to convey what my having of a particular mental state is
like more vividly by using metaphors.[11] As against saying 'I have
these terrible pains in my neck and arms' and hoping that this will

adequately convey to my doctor what this is like for me, I might instead say that 'The muscles in my arms feel like washing being twisted dry by ruthless hands, and my neck feels like there are sharp knives stuck in it.' This image may refine her understanding of what it is actually like for me in addition to understanding that these are the sorts of pain I have. Either way, however, I still rely on intentionality to communicate how things are for me. How successful such communication is depends upon the degree to which those communicating share forms of intentionality and subjectivity.

The arts are especially adept in communicating subjectivity because they have the power to induce absorption in such a way that the subjectivity of the represented or depicted other can seem to be capable of being directly apprehended by the reader or viewer. Becoming the other, as we have seen, is a favoured way of describing what happens. Another, more prosaic, way of putting this is to say that the process of aesthetic absorption means that the reader or viewer adopts another point of view. In some contemporary philosophical work, intentionality, subjectivity and point of view are closely linked together, as is the concept of 'I'. I want to look at the relationships between these ideas and use them to fill out a description of how 'I' can become other in an aesthetic experience of art. What I will end up suggesting is that aesthetic absorption involves, at a minimum, the non-deployment of I.

NAGEL ON SUBJECTIVITY AS POINT OF VIEW

In his essay 'What is it like to be a bat?' Thomas Nagel argues that what it is like to *be* an organism has not – at least thus far – shown itself capable of being analyzed in terms of any explanatory system of functional or intentional states.[12] The subjective character of experience eludes full and adequate explanation within such accounts and retains its inscrutability. The reason for this, argues Nagel, has to do with the idea of a point of view. Nagel holds that 'every subjective phenomenon is essentially connected with a single point of view, and it seems inevitable that an objective, physical theory will abandon that point of view.'[13]

Nagel takes as an example the bat whose sonar sense is so unlike our senses, and he examines the idea of what it is like to be a bat.

The best he can do is to imagine what it would be like for him to behave as a bat behaves.[14] But what he wants to know is what it is like for a bat to be a bat. Neither by imaginative additions nor subtractions to his experiential make-up can he do so. Even to form a conception of what it is like to be a bat, let alone to know or experience what it is like to be one, requires taking up the bat's point of view. In short, the experience of what it is like for the experiencing organism is accessible from only one point of view, that of the organism itself.

The purpose of Nagel's argument is to challenge the view that objective physical accounts of the operation of a bat, or of any other high-level animal, could account for the subjectivity of experience, given its linkage with single points of view. The objective factual world of scientific understanding is one that allows approach from many points of view, irrespective of the perceptual systems of those making the approaches.[15] A Martian with no understanding of visual perception could nonetheless understand the rainbow, without understanding the human concept of rainbow or the role of rainbows in the phenomenal world of humans. This is because the rainbow has an objective character that is not exhausted by its visual phenomenology. Whereas its phenomenology is tied to single points of view, its objective character can be approached from many points of view. Objectivity, especially as understood by the natural sciences, is precisely about reducing dependence on particular human points of view and increasing dependence on the evidence of instruments that transcend the private and open up accessibility to multiple public points of view.

But as regards approaches to the understanding of experience as it is for the subject of the experience, any move away from the idea that the subjective character of experience is fully intelligible only from one point of view is a move away from a real aspect of the nature of experience. To understand the objective form of colour, say, in terms of spectral frequencies is not the same as understanding its phenomenal form. Depending upon what it is that one wants to understand, it is appropriate to choose between the variety of relevant points of view in so far as such choice is practically feasible. In the case of understanding the experience of what it is like to be a bat, it is impossible, in Nagel's view, to adopt the single point of view that would enable one to achieve this.

The best option, given our present state of understanding, for approaching questions like 'What is it like to *be* that person/ organism?' or 'What is it like *for* that person/organism?' is for us to use some form of imagination. We must, that is, take up the point of view of the experiential subject by acts of perceptual or sympathetic or symbolic imagination.[16] Without what Nagel calls an 'objective phenomenology' which would allow, at least in part, for a comprehensible description of the subjective character of experience to be given to a being incapable of having such experience, we must continue to rely on imagination.

Nagel has pointed out that subjective experience is always from one point of view.[17] But granting that this is so, need that one point of view always be the same point of view, or more precisely, need it be the same type of point of view? If intercepting the stream of experience at any particular moment will reveal one and only one operative point of view at that moment, could it be that that stream is constituted by a coherent if variable succession of different types of point of view? If so, what might account for that coherence? And might the type of point of view encountered depend upon which intentional mode is in train at the moment of interception? These are questions that have to do with the nature of I.

I have already introduced a general example – the pond example – of how different modes of intentionality can help to weave an experience. I also used an example from Wollheim to suggest the practical operation of perception and imagination when looking at a painting. In the wholeness of any experience it is clear that these modes of intentionality are as closely collaborative as woof and warp. But at any point in time, one or another will be dominant in the stream of consciousness: and at any point in time there will also be only one point of view. The dominant point of view in human experience is generally associated with the I.

I AS A TYPE OF POINT OF VIEW AND THE BODY

A point of view is a position of observation. Its synonyms include standpoint, perspective, stance and angle. Everything seen is seen from a point of view, from a particular point in space–time. But the positions from which any object can be perceptually viewed are potentially infinite; and since an object may generally be viewed only through a succession, rather than through a 'simultaneity', of

viewpoints (barring a situation involving mirrors, say, or Cubist
depictions of the object), it follows that the perceptual experience
of an object is always radically incomplete.[18] And yet our bodies
are, as Merleau-Ponty reminds us, *set to see* more and to experience
as present those sides of the object not currently visible.[19] 'Living',
as Wollheim puts it, 'is an embodied mental process.'[20] There is a
bodily wisdom that antecedes intelligence and incarnates it, and all
understanding of experience must proceed from this fact of
incarnation and its consequences.

One of these consequences identifies tendencies to create 'inner
realities' out of love, hate, shame or anger as erroneous. As
Merleau-Ponty observes, 'They exist *on* this face or *in* those'
gestures, not hidden behind them.'[21] The second consequence of
being incarnated is that experience is always incomplete because it
is inescapably perspectival. There will always be more to what we
see which, were we to see it, would force a reorganization of what
is seen. It is in this sense that objects may be said to arise as the
results of successive perspectives cumulate.

Freud also recognizes the centrality of the body when he writes
that 'The I is first and foremost a bodily I.'[22] But this is to take us
beyond the literal meanings of point of view and into the more
ubiquitous, but metaphorical usages. And in doing so, it takes us
beyond perceptual intentionality and into symbolic and imaginative intentionality. This is where 'point of view' refers to attitudes
of mind rather than to perspectives dependent upon physical and
temporal positions. For Freud, it is the perceptual system that
allows for the development of that most personal of words, the
conscious I.[23] *Das Ich* (the I or ego) has characteristic tendencies to
synthesize and unify, tendencies that are totally absent from *das Es*
(the Id or It). The I, in Freud's view, is ultimately derived from
bodily sensations and especially from the surface sensations of the
body. Freud speaks of it as 'the projection of a surface'.[24] The
orthodox Freudian conception of the I is not of a wholly conscious
control centre; it may be a control centre, but large elements of it
are unconscious. The I's power as a control centre is at best limited
and its success at most partial. Unlike the transcendent, detached
role of the Kantian rational will or of the Cartesian ego, the
Freudian I is inescapably involved in and subject to desires. These
desires may be instinctual, but they may also have to do with the
ideals the I comes to hold for itself. Of central importance is the

insight that the I requires contrast with the not-I in order to exist, a condition which involves notions of boundaries or frontiers. And the body is the core frontier, the nuclear I.

I is quintessentially associated with the most personal of points of view – what, in relation to selves, one could call the abiding point of view – but this association is not unproblematic. For a start, the idea of 'an abiding point of view' in its very formulation tends to reification and to imply singularity. The Freudian I refers to one psychical province or agency, as mapped out by the topographical model of the mind or psyche as a structured organization of *das Es, das Ich* and *das Über-Ich* (It/Id, I/Ego and Upper-I/Superego). Given the unconscious aspects of the Freudian I, and its reference sometimes to a psychic system and sometimes to an agent, it cannot easily be identified with a fixed, lasting, conscious point of view. Orthodox Freudian psychoanalysis illustrates quite well the difficulties with the idea that there is one pre-eminent point of view that is synonymous with I.

Long before Freud, the suspicion that I was a chimera was famously expressed by David Hume. Searching his experience for that to which I refers, Hume concludes that there is no such 'that'. I, he says, refers to nothing. He writes as follows:

> For my part, when I enter most intimately into what I call myself, I always stumble upon some particular conception or other, of heat or cold, light or shade, love or hatred, pain or pleasure. I never can catch myself at any time without a perception, and never can observe anything but the perception. When my perceptions are remov'd for any time, as by sound-sleep; so long am I insensible of *myself*, and may truly be said not to exist. . . . If anyone, upon serious and unprejudic'd reflection, thinks he has a different notion of *himself*, I must confess I can reason no longer with him. All I can allow him is, that he may be in the right as well as I, and that we are essentially different in this particular. He may perhaps, perceive something simple and continu'd, which he calls *himself*, tho' I am certain there is no such principle in me.[25]

If there is no I, no permanent reality to which I refers, then there can be no permanent or abiding point of view associated with it. I clearly is not a thing, and certainly not the sort of thing that can be located, fixed and examined by introspection. And yet our every-day intuition recoils from the apparent implications of this. We know the significance of I for ourselves, we feel ourselves to be more or less unified and continuous over time, and we know the disastrous consequences for selfhood of the failure to develop, or the subsequent loss of, a capacity to use I meaningfully.

A recognition of the reifying powers of language (e.g. the implication that nouns must refer to things), a close attention to the powers of language and symbol systems to create meaningful realities, and a recognition of the ways in which social contexts shape and direct symbolic communication have considerably advanced our analytic grasp of the I. A brief survey of these analyses will serve two purposes here. It will clarify one aspect of the nature of self in order to describe the 'self-forgetfulness' of aesthetic absorption, and it will serve as background to the question of how aesthetic experiences of art objects might lead to changes of self.

I will begin with that consummate introspectionist, and major influence on Dewey, William James.

THE NATURE OF I ACCORDING TO WILLIAM JAMES

In 1904 James published the provocatively titled essay 'Does consciousness exist?'.[26] In it he argues against the idea that consciousness refers to some entity, and for the idea that it is a function. His targets are dualistic conceptions of mind. He opposes the notion of self as some separate and autonomous spiritual entity, and proposes an understanding of it, in Richard Stevens's words, 'as a privileged center of reference within the field of givenness'.[27] This 'field of givenness' is the data of pure experience and according to James's analysis it contains no given distinction between a subject–entity and independent object–entities. At this primitive level are to be found only interrelated patterns of givenness, rather than the I and its acts. Richard Stevens succinctly presents William James's ideas on this early, differentiated form of self-awareness:

> But, among the data which present themselves, we may detect a polarization about a functional center which, though given as a content of experience among other contents of experience, seems to be a 'here' in reference to which the other contents may be defined as 'there'. James contends that this functional polarization of the data of pure experience represents our most primitive form of self-awareness. It should be noted that his awareness occurs in the accusative. The self is presented within the field of givenness as a privileged content to which all other contents are related. The active

dimension of selfhood, the pure subjectivity of conscious activity, does not appear at all as a content of the stream of experience. [28]

In such primitive self-awareness there is what I will call below a non-deployment of I. Just now, however, what is of interest is the characterization of the self as an organizing function rather than as an entity, and the associated idea that I is an indexical. Indexicals are fascinating players in psychological life and can play a key role, I believe, in the psychology of aesthetic experience. But what are they?

Indexicals are words that require a familiarity with the context in which they are being used before that to which they are referring can be known. 'This', 'here', 'now' are indexicals. But 'this', 'here' and 'now' depend upon where I am. And in this sense 'I' too is an indexical. Indexicals, or demonstratives as they are also called, appear to lack a content that can be described, and to imply a particularly immediate association with their referents. To understand the statement 'I am writing this here and now in Dun Laoghaire' requires, if it is to be fully understood, that you know who I am, where Dun Laoghaire is, and the time at which this is being written. To whom I refers depends upon who is using it to locate and refer to him/herself. A great deal of philosophical attention is now being paid to the logic of demonstratives or indexicals such as these. [29] My interest, however, is not in the logic of indexicals, but rather in their psychology and especially in how an understanding of their acquisition and use can further the description of self. [30] In effect, I want to ask how the indexicality of the linguistic I influences the context dependency of the psycho-linguistic I.

For William James, it is the body that is the living nucleus of the community of selves collectively known as the 'self'. And that 'self' is an organized and organizing activity, and not an entity or a fixed substance. The field of consciousness is given with the body as its centre. Indexicals and demonstratives such as 'I', 'here', 'now', 'this' and so on (as well as 'you', 'there', 'then' and 'that'), are connected in the way they are as a consequence of the body being a centre of the organized, experienced world. In this view, the words 'I' and 'me' signify no mysterious transcendental substance. James insists that they are 'names of emphasis' [31] Thought emphasizes the distinction between 'I' and 'you' or 'it' in exactly the same way as it distinguishes 'this' from 'that', 'here' from 'there', 'now' from 'then'. But just as it would be an unilluminating exercise to discuss what a use of 'now' might be without first discussing the context of its use – so as to specify its boundaries (this second, or day, or month, or historical era ?) – so also would it be for any discussion of the meaning of I. Indexicals always insist on bringing their contexts with them. [32]

But if I can know myself only as an object, then clearly there is a problem in my knowing my present knowing I. James calls the I that posits the world, including its self, the pure ego. This is the agent that synthesizes self as part of the objective world (in his terms, the material, social and spiritual selves that together constitute the empirical or objectively known self). [33] The problem here is to account for the unity and continuity of identity of this agent. For this, the pure ego or presently knowing subject or I would need to somehow remain the same over time. Rejecting as superfluous and uneconomical the dualist solution of a separate spiritual substance which somehow supports the stream of experience, and rejecting Hume's dismissal of the need for a principle of unification other than that supplied by the laws of association, and dismissing Kant's transcendental ego as a ' "cheap and nasty" edition of the soul', [34] James presents his own theory of the passing, appropriating pure ego. [35]

Normal everyday use of I carries the meaning of a stable, continuous, active source and sense of personal identity. Rather than think of this I as some thing lasting through time, James conceives of it as referring to an active and dynamic process. It is one's present thought that supplies James's principle of unification. I is the origin of a complex system of coordinates, an active centred position from which and to which references are made. I is the core point of view. And it is from this position that my life is surveyed and judged to be continuous and one. But the key point is that this position is not fixed and given; it is instead incessantly mobile. It is the leading wave of the stream of experience and of its nature can do nothing other than flow forward with its stream. In James's account, the I's location is the present judging thought, and the continuity between this and past or future judging thoughts is to be found in the temporal structure of what he calls the 'specious present'.

Each present moment of consciousness has fringes which overlap with moments just past and with the moments about to replace this present moment. No present thought can ever, in James's view, have itself for its object. But part of the object of any present thought is always the immediately preceding thought as it fades from the horizon of the present. Each present thought appropriates the earlier thought as its own, and in this way each succeeding thought appropriates the previous one, thus ensuring the continuity of consciousness. Property rights are thus transmitted from one thought to the next in a continuous succession. But of the present judging thought nothing can be known until it becomes an object for the succeeding one. 'The present moment of consciousness is thus . . . the darkest in the whole series,' and furthermore, 'Its appropriations are therefore less to *itself* than to the most intimately felt *part of its present Object, the body, and its central adjustments*, which accompany the act of thinking, in the head.'[36] In other words, the I (the pure ego or present thought) assigns and integrates all that is relevant in the preceding thoughts to the me or empirical self. This passing thought *is* the thinker or I. And if one were to ask why each passing thought should inherit the possessions of its predecessors, then James's answer is that the reason, if there is one, must lie in the total meaning of the world.[37]

Central to James's account, then, is this process of appropriation by a succession of pure egos/Is of what is relevant in the past, and their projection of this on to the objective empirical ego, the focal centre of which is the body. And the unique feature of my body is that it is both an objective part of my world and the locus of my perspectives on that world. It is only when I assume the viewpoint of the other and represent my bodily 'here' as his 'there' that my body becomes a more fully objective reality for me. As thought, the pure ego has powers of selective attention, choice and cognition which support its activities of appropriation or rejection.

Richard Stevens has compared James with Husserl on the structure of the self and found many points of agreement.[38] James's treatment of the idea of self continues to be widely influential. Both his terminology and his ideas, for example, are strongly echoed in Jonathan Glover's work on personal identity. Glover, for instance, argues that 'to be a person is to have a single stream of I-thoughts'[39] and that 'A person is someone who has the self-conscious thoughts expressed by using "I".'[40] Dewey had reservations about the dualistic position James adopted, partly for methodological reasons, in his discussion of the self in *The Principles of Psychology*, but

he observed how James came to abandon this in his later work.[41]
Were we to think in terms of 'the course of experience' rather than
of 'the stream of consciousness', Dewey felt that the substance of
James's account would be preserved and the residual subjectivism
eliminated.[42]

The identification of the 'abiding point of view' with the I puts
into question the very idea of such a point of view as 'abiding'.
More precisely, it queries both the singularity and the permanence
of such a point of view. For if the I is best described as an extensive
series open to the changes attending the changes of context at
points all along that series, then the identification of point of view
with those Is implies a successive, changing plurality of points of
view, rather than a single abiding point of view.

And if the I is indeed a word of position and emphasis as William
James would maintain or, in contemporary linguistically slanted
thought, an indexical, then it also follows that I is of its nature
intimately linguistic as a psychological phenomenon. And given its
reliance for proper functioning on context and – language's
primary function being social – especially on sociolinguistic context, it follows that point of view, or at least that point of view
identified with I, is also fundamentally dependent for its functioning on social context.

Under what social conditions does I come into play? An answer
to this may clarify types of point of view which need not be
coincident with I, but which are associated, for example, with
some perceptual intentional states.

SOME CONDITIONS FOR THE DEPLOYMENT OF I

The 'point' in a personal point of view is always a point in the
stream of consciousness. This simple assertion reflects a beguilingly
complex psychological phenomenon. For example, any such point
in the stream is always the present thought which, in Jamesian
terms, is the locus of the pure ego, the point at and from which all
appropriations to the empirical self take place. This is a moving
point, rather like the restless cursor on a computer screen. It moves
and changes with the stream of experience. It especially changes
with shifts of intentionality. Wollheim's point about the stronger
influence of intentionality (thought-content) on subjectivity (what

it is like for the subject) could be taken further to imply that
changes in subjectivity are linked to changes in intentionality,
although not, perhaps, exclusively linked. More simply, changes in
the contents of thought involve changes in points of view, or at
least in what it is like for that subject to have those thoughts in that
way. And if another person wishes to understand what it is like for
this person to have those thoughts, we should advise her to try
and see it from this person's point of view. To the degree that this
can successfully be done – by a Rogerian-style psychotherapist,
say, attempting to understand what a client's world is like – we
might say that this particular relationship of subjectivity to intentionality has been re-created.

Analyses of the stream of consciousness reveal an extraordinarily
rich and responsive web of intentionality. Images, perceptions of
all sorts, half-sentences uttered *sotto voce*, memories, and half-
articulated desires all jostle, configurate, disintegrate and flow.
Sometimes they are shaped under the guidance of a purposeful
subject, sometimes under the power of the current object of
attention, but most usually as a result of an experiential dialectic of
both. Unless one has worked to free oneself from what is taken to
be the illusion of self, as in Theravadin and Zen Buddhist
meditative practices,[43] for example, one is likely to share the
common-sense conviction that the agency of the self is a central
organizing principle of experience.

In the sentence 'I believe that it is I who am experiencing at the
moment and that I have some power to change and shape that
experience in directions which I may choose', the word 'I' is used
four times. But the understanding of the function of I in each case
will differ depending upon whether one's theory of I is referential
or non-referential. The belief that experience as given is structured
around a centre has led to the development of referential theories in
which I is taken to refer to a subject or self. Such theories may differ
greatly as to the nature of the referent of I, whether it is body or
soul for instance, yet agree that it does refer to some entity with its
own properties. Non-referential theories deny that I refers to any
thing with properties. There is no subject to which I refers, only I-
thoughts. In this sense, William James and John Dewey are non-
referentialists, as are such contemporary writers as Anscombe,
Glover and Harré.[44]

But the non-referentialist's claim that I does not refer to a given empirical subject but functions instead to indicate the location of the utterance and its uniqueness, still does not explain how I-thoughts are so unified in personal experience. As Harré puts it, 'it does not follow that because there is no empirically given unifying *entity* that there is no unifying *concept.*'[45] For Harré, the function of I is not to refer to a subject but to label a speech as mine. Later, I will present Harré's argument that I does indeed function to organize and unify experience, not because it refers to a subject, but because people develop a theory that they are selves, or psychologically unitary beings and that, within the holding of this theory, I functions in much the same way as *g* does in the theory of gravity.[46] There is no such thing as *g*. It is an abstraction which finds its meaning and enormous practical utility as part of the theory to which it belongs. Analogously, I finds its meaning and usefulness by virtue of belonging to a particular theory of self which new members of a culture acquire and use to organize their experience.[47]

Where might the possible limits of the point of view associated with I be? If I does not refer to a substantial subject or self which stands outside experience, but is instead an active functioning part *of* experience, then asking what functions I performs will go some significant way towards delimiting the point of view associated with it. Within the non-referentialist account so far presented we can see that the use of I is clearly contingent upon the acquisition of language and the ability to think symbolically. Learning to speak a language and to think symbolically are themselves contingent upon an adequate socially shaped period of development. And within these conditions the acquisition and correct use of the first person personal pronoun, I, is plainly a fundamentally sociopsychological phenomenon.

Once acquired it functions in at least two centrally important ways. First, within the public world of persons it serves to distinguish the I-using self from other selves. In this way the ownership and location of speech acts are indexed by the use of I. This indexical function of I is a quintessentially social act which serves to ground both interpersonal and intrapersonal relationships. 'I think x' means not that there is an I which thinks x, but that the x-thought is mine rather than somebody else's. Therefore any social situation that requires the identification and location of responsibility for an act is one that calls for the deployment of I: 'I am/am not the person who did or spoke or thought that.' It also comes into play intrapersonally when, during a process of reorientation, the person tries to centre and adapt him/herself to changing circumstances ('Where am I? What am I to do?' etc.). But not every act of experience requires the acknowledgement of its possessor in this way. Perceptual and imaginative acts need not necessarily do so.

The second major function of I is as an organizing concept of personal experience. This is the function that participates in the unification of experience, and helps construct the sense of the continuity of self. These two major functions are intimately connected with each other. But it could be argued, using Wollheim's distinction, that the indexical function of I is most likely to characterize mental states whereas the organizing function of I is best understood as a more lasting mental disposition. Presuming this for the moment, and considering just the phenomenon of aesthetic absorption as it occurs as a feature of an aesthetic experience rather than the disposition to seek or to have such experiences, it is the indexical rather than the organizational function of I that may provide the best avenue for describing aesthetic absorption. On the other hand, attention to the organizational function of I as a disposition may pay dividends when one asks about the ways in which self may change as a consequence of experiencing art aesthetically.[48]

I have now filled out the ideas of intentionality and subjectivity, of I and 'point of view' and of how they are associated, and of some of the conditions under which I is deployed. But are there other psychological points of view that do not depend upon the deployment of I?

I acquires its social–psychological power because it belongs to a symbolic system. It comes into play when there are social demands for it to do so (and intrapersonal relationships are taken to be as essentially social in origin and operation as interpersonal ones). There is no real problem in attributing a point of view to a high-level sentient animal like a bat, as Nagel does. But clearly that point of view is not linguistic and therefore not associated with an I. Searching for a succinct way to characterize it one might say that the bat's point of view is an integrated, perceptuo-motor point of view. All bats of the same species may share the same perceptual motor equipment, but its use is always by single bats who embody the living use of that equipment in their particular transactions with their particular world. The highest-level integration of these transactions at any point in time constitutes the bat's point of view. What this is like subjectively is in principle available only to a bat. It is unlikely, however, that it appreciates its point of view as 'mine'. That would require the sort of powers of appropriation and personal possession – symbolically based powers – that, as we saw above, can generate self and I. The bat's point of view is of a different order.

Within the symbolic order of human beings there are also innumerable impersonal points of view open to being occupied by any individual capable of doing so. The developmental psychology of moral judgement, for example, charts a progression from intensely egocentric-type judgements (basically, 'It is wrong because I say so') to judgements grounded in the impersonal perspectives of the community ('One does not do such things'). Or, as I noted above, to learn to think scientifically is to learn a set of methodologies for experiencing the world which allows it to be approached from many points of view quite independently of one's own unique set of viewpoints. This can be done in quite a different way in the arts. Stories may be presented from the perspective of a narrator which a reader may adopt for all or some of the reading of the story. To the extent that one does not deploy one's own perspective but stands in a relationship to the narrative happenings which is the narrator's, then to that extent the reader's I has occupied that other perspective.[49] I will return to this later.

Comparisons could be made between the qualities of absorption that can characterize intense intellectual engagement (such as a mathematician utterly 'sunk' in the solution of an equation), practical–social engagement (like that of an individuality entirely sacrificed to membership of a mob), or creative artistic engagement (as with a pianist possessed by the concerto s/he is playing). But my interest is in just one type of absorption, aesthetic absorption. The ability to perceive is vital for aesthetic experience. However, one can be centred differently when perceiving than when thinking symbolically.

'CENTREDNESS' IN THINKING AND PERCEIVING

Harold Osborne's concept of 'percipience', as we saw in Chapter 1, refers to a preoccupation with a thing, which involves a special kind of awareness. The object is framed for attention and is intentionalized perceptually and not conceptually. My 'location', so to speak, is centred in and about the object rather than on my own moods and emotions. This centring on the object precludes tangential flights of association and imagination. My awareness of time and place, as well as of my body, is diminished and replaced by the object that occupies the field of attention. It is very much a 'here and now' experience. While I am absorbed 'in the object', there continues to be what Osborne calls a 'residual awareness' of myself as spectator, listener or reader, an awareness which is a central logical requirement for its being aesthetic. Without this implicit awareness of myself as observing, however 'residual', the distance necessary for aesthetic experience would not be possible. . This type of mental state lasts for a short time and, while it may be 'about' anything, it is deliberately invited by art objects.

As a phase in the stream of experience, this ends and a different phase begins as soon as I begin actively to question and think about the object and about my passing aesthetic experience of it. As soon as this happens, thoughts governed by phrases like 'I wonder if' or 'I don't think that' and so on, begin to take their place in the stream. In other words, what occurs is a shift of intentionality with a corresponding shift of subjectivity, a shift from Kenneth Clark's impact stage to those of scrutiny and of recollection.

As the content and functions of the experience change so also does the feeling of what that is like for the person. It is as though the person's position has been transformed so that now s/he is returned to again being the centre of the experience, separate from but relating to whatever is being thought of. What I self-consciously thinks is centred on the subject of the sentences thought, however telegraphic and truncated the structure of this inner speech might be. And the subject or owner of such thoughts is the particular I who has them.

Matisse offers an example of this from the point of view of a working artist. In his discussion of portraits and portraiture in 1954, he includes this comment:

I find myself before a person who interests me and, pencil or

charcoal in my hand, I set down his appearance on the paper, more
or less freely. This, in the course of a banal conversation during
which I speak myself or listen *without any spirit of opposition* [my
emphasis], permits me to give free rein to my faculties of observation. At that moment, it wouldn't do to ask a specific question,
even a banal one such as 'What time is it?' because my reverie, my
meditation upon the model, would be broken, and the result of my
effort would be seriously compromised.[50]

In using the phrase 'without any spirit of opposition', Matisse is
referring to the idea that I is inevitably set over against the not-I
once it is deployed. The sort of situation that requires its deployment includes the social one of being asked a simple question. Once
this occurs in a phase of experience such as the one he describes as
reverie or as meditation, it ends and is succeeded by an I-centred
experience.

The subjective centre of an act of perception need not necessarily
be an I. Bats perceive, and have a point of view but no I. But
deliberate voluntary acts of perception by human beings, which are
part of larger acts of adjustment and which contribute to the
thinking necessary to succeed – G. H. Mead's manipulative phase
of the act[51] – may well have an I deployed as subject. If while
climbing a cliff face I become aware that I am in a very dangerous
predicament, then every act of visually judging distance and
kinaesthetically assessing the adequacy of toe-holds may be pre-
meditated and could well feature the I very prominently. 'Oh God!
I wonder if I can reach that crevice? I think it might just about do
the job' might be the sort of inner speech in such a dilemma. But
such a situation is far from routine and demands novel solutions if it
is to be successfully resolved. On the other hand, in dangerous
situations which throw me into immediate action, like running
from a knife-wielding attacker in a blind panic, I am unlikely to be
aware of myself. The difference between these two dangerous
situations is that in one I have time to plan and in the other I do not.
In G. H. Mead's view it is only with such time to plan that I can
think and be self-conscious.[52] Mediated action favours self-
awareness of the kind clustered around I, immediately required
action less so. Perception, thought and imagination work very
closely together in tasks which are demanding, especially when
there is a threat to personal survival.

But in the absence of threat, and in situations where there is no
strong and immediate demand to think about and to account for

what I am seeing or hearing, the phenomenology of certain
perceptual experiences reveals a type of viewpoint which may be
less centred 'in' the perceiver and less 'distant' from that which is
perceived. Much of the staring and gazing of everyday experience
offers examples of this. Merleau-Ponty insists that:

> We must take literally what vision teaches us: namely, that through
> it we come in contact with the sun and the stars, that we are
> everywhere all at once, and that even our power to imagine
> ourselves elsewhere . . . borrows from vision and employs means
> we owe to it.'[53]

I have already observed that the indexical I carries the 'here' and
'now' indexicals with it, rather like parasites. Now I want to
distinguish certain experiences of perceptual centredness from
experiences where I is the active centre. Gazing at my pond, for
example, with its fish enjoying the sun at the surface, my sense of
myself is of being where my pond is, or lying on the grass staring at
a lazily drifting cloud I can seem somehow to be that cloud, and not
necessarily by virtue of some act of empathy or identification in the
sense of Theodor Lipps.[54]

In such acts of perceiving there can sometimes occur the sense of
a coincidence of my perceptual point of view with the current
object of my attention. It is as though I have temporarily been
recentred and am where the object of my perception appears to be.
The field of experience within which the act of perceiving takes
place seems to undergo a recalibration, and phenomenal distances
diminish. The particular object almost entirely and exclusively
occupies my field of awareness – its now is my now; but my here
somehow becomes its there.

In such acts of non-instrumental perceiving, the sense of boundaries of time and space between perceiver and perceived is erased,
though not quite to the point of invisibility since Osborne's
'residual awareness' remains. But although I am anchored in my
body and take my bearings from the physical location of my body,
at the level of perceptual consciousness the felt location of myself
can seem to be that of the cloud I am gazing at, or the blackbird I
am listening to. In these cases, perceptual points of view can seem
to have a twofold mobility: they can move as the body moves but,
phenomenologically, they can also seem to be where their intentionalized object is. Understood like this, one could say that in
certain acts of perception the there and now, as it were, can carry

the perceptual subject with them, just as the subject as indexical I carries the here and now.

Peacefully sitting in a twilit room, or in a starlit garden, seem to be particularly conducive ways of experiencing what I am talking about, where relations of size and distance, of here and there, of I and it, are phenomenologically recalibrated. In 'A Rabbit as King of the Ghosts', Wallace Stevens captures the sense of what these experiences can be like:

> No matter. The grass is full
>
> And full of yourself. The trees around are for you,
> The whole of the wideness of night is for you,
> A self that touches all edges,
>
> You become a self that fills the four corners of the night.
> The red cat hides away in the fur-light
> And there you are humped high, humped up,
>
> You are humped higher and higher, black as stone –
> You sit with your head like a carving in space
> And the little green cat is a bug in the grass.[55]

What I am suggesting is that the type of centredness typical of I can be distinguished phenomenologically from the type of centredness characteristic of certain acts of perception. In the flux of ordinary experience, however, they are normally indistinguishable collaborators, a well functioning team.

In all likelihood there is, as Freud and Merleau-Ponty suggest, a developmental link between them.[56] Bodily perceptual centredness is psychologically prior to the linguistically constituted I that it grounds, and the functions of perceptual centredness differ from those of I as a centre of experience. In other words, the subjectivity of each as a type of intentionality differs. Once again, I do not think that Dewey would quibble with Merleau-Ponty's judgement:

> The speaking 'I' abides in its body. Rather than imprisoning it, language is like a magic machine for transporting the 'I' into the other person's perspective. . . . There can be speech (and in the end personality) only for an 'I' which contains the germ of depersonalization.[57]

It is this conclusion that leads to my formulation of the 'non-deployment of I' hypothesis for aesthetic absorption.

AESTHETIC ABSORPTION AND THE NON-DEPLOYMENT OF I

In Chapter 3, I reviewed the difficulties certain psychoanalytic theories face when trying to account for aesthetic absorption in terms of the reavailability of particular experiences from infancy. That critique motivated the search for a better description of aesthetic absorption. Behind both approaches is Dewey's assertion that:

> the uniquely distinguishing feature of esthetic experience is exactly the fact that no such distinction of self and object exists in it, since it is esthetic in the degree in which organism and environment cooperate to institute an experience in which the two are so fully integrated that each disappears.[58]

The source of any such distinction would be the self, more specifically the I. Aesthetic absorption is described as characterizing the initial pre-reflective phase of the overall experience of the art object, a phase in which self operates minimal control over the nature and direction of the stream of experience during that time. I have maintained that Dewey's intuitions concerning the restorative powers of art should not refer to the idea that states are restored or made reavailable during this phase of the aesthetic experience of art objects, but rather that a harmony of a degree that does not ordinarily exist between forms of relating is what is restored. The general forms of relating are intentional modes such as perceiving, thinking symbolically and imagining.

Symbolic thinking does not require the presence of its referents for sense to be made, although they may of course occur in the stream of thinking. In this chapter, I have argued that the first person personal pronoun (which is itself a linguistic symbol finding full meaning in its use within a particular self theory, as argued by Harré) is the typical 'functional centre' (James and Husserl), or point of view (Nagel) of symbolic thinking. One could, with reservations, say that it is always an I that acts as a functional centre for symbolic thoughts, but that in many (though not by any means in all) acts of perception it is not always around an I as centre that perceptual experience is organized.

The subject and point of view of an act of perception need not be an I, nor need it be susceptible to the same limitations and functions as apply to the use of I. The intentional object of perception must always be present to the perceiving subject. To perceive something visually is to see it here and now; to imagine that same object is to intend it as if it really was present. Perception, symbolic thinking and imagination do not operate independently of each other but are all intimately collaborative in structuring the stream of consciousness and its intentional objects. Husserl reminds us that 'perception is an act which determines, but does not embody meaning'.[59] Significative acts embody meanings that perceptual acts fulfil. Husserl discusses this in the context of considering 'this' as a demonstrative pronoun whose meaning cannot be found in perception itself, but may be expressively fulfilled in perception as, for instance, with 'this pond' or 'this blackbird'.

Given this, can aesthetic absorption be most simply and generally described as a response by self to the demands or requirements of aesthetic situations? Has aesthetic absorption to do with changes of points of view? Perceptual points of view, as in Osborne's 'percipience', facilitate the minimally differentiated self–object relationship described by Dewey as the distinguishing feature of aesthetic experience. But it can be objected that the phenomenon of being 'lost in thought' is a form of absorption which relies upon no shift *between* thinking and perceiving, but which occurs *within* acts of symbolic thinking or imagining. I can, for example, become minimally self-aware in thinking through a conceptual problem in much the same way as I do during the absorption phase of aesthetic experience.

The answer to this objection involves the issue which has occupied most of this chapter. This issue is the psychological nature of I, its functions and the circumstances which invite or demand its deployment. I am at my most self-aware when I can use 'I' fluently. This has to do with I's indexical function as defining a location distinct from that of other persons. In one sense, it is only a properly functioning I that can know that it is not somebody or something else. It is an I which takes up a stance over and against the not-I. In certain phases of perceiving, as I have suggested, there can seem to be a virtual merging or fusing of the subject's perceptual position with the 'that' which is perceived. In intellectual absorption, however, there is not the same merging of self or position with the intellectual content: instead there is a non-deployment of I. In other words, there is not the presence of a new self–thought unity, but simply the absence of I-functioning thoughts. And the reason for this is that there is no need for them, at least not until such time as the situation requires them, whether for reasons of an intrapersonal or interpersonal kind. Only when there is a need to identify the source or ownership of thinking – to answer questions, to appropriate thought to the empirical self, or in some other way to become aware of that thinking as an object – will the deployment of I-thoughts become psychologically necessary.

This points the way to an economical description of aesthetic absorption. I can judge that I have been absorbed only from a state in which I am not now absorbed, but am self-aware. In other words, it must always be a backward look from a point in the stream of experience, which is now symbolically intentional, that allows me to say that I was, for instance, aesthetically absorbed. If I come to understand that such forms of experience can be deliberately brought about – a task for real aesthetic education – I may look to the prospect of being so absorbed again in the future. When that time comes I am likely to be quite aware of what I am doing when I sit down in front of my chosen picture, say, and begin to gaze at it. It will be as I gaze that I slowly 'enter' the picture's 'world' and the phase of aesthetic absorption begins. After a period of time, which as Kenneth Clark testifies is usually short, I become more self-aware and find myself thinking about the picture or about my experience of the picture or whatever. Both the before and after states require the deployment of I with its attendant self-consciousness. The 'percipient' state did not, but it did deploy its own point of view which, being temporarily freed of involvement with the indexical I, acquired a mobility that allowed it to 'occupy' the picture or, in Deweyan terms, to co-constitute the experience which is the picture. This period of occupation is the period of aesthetic absorption. So it is the absence of the conditions demanding the deployment of I that enables the phase of aesthetic absorption to occur. Subjectively, situations that, while making many rigorous demands upon participating selves, do not include amongst them prominent demands for the I to assert its position or responsibilities, are the types of situation that are called absorbing. Aesthetic situations are like this, and aesthetic absorption understood as self-forgetfulness is, amongst other things, a consequence of not having to deploy that particular form of self-centring which is I.

I offer this as the most economical description of aesthetic absorption and suggest that it sits more happily with that other characteristic of aesthetic experience, immediacy. Yet, superficially at least, it seems less at ease with Dewey's comments on memories from childhood than do the psychoanalytic accounts.

WHICH ACCOUNT WOULD DEWEY FAVOUR?

Throughout Dewey's aesthetics, as we have seen, there are scattered references to the importance of childhood and early memories for aesthetic experiences of art. He writes of the 'deep-seated memory of an underlying harmony the sense of which haunts life like the sense of being founded on a rock'.[60] and later of ' "Transferred values" of emotions experienced from a childhood that cannot be consciously recovered'.[61] Dewey also refers experiences which have a 'mystic aspect of acute surrender' back to a person's early relations with the world.[62]

Ellen Spitz writes approvingly of Dewey's assertion that 'the artist cares in a peculiar way for the phase of experience in which union is achieved' and immediately goes on to attribute to Dewey an implicit awareness of the Freudian unconscious and primary process thinking.[63] She seems to take Dewey to be a crypto-Winnicottian and to interpret his talk of union and restoration as meaning that 'aspects of our preoedipal life, with its pleasurable sense of merging and union' are reavailable to us during moments of creativity and responsiveness to the arts.[64] But a truer reading of exactly the same passage reveals support, not for a simple reavailability explanation, but for the type of explanation offered in this chapter.

In the passage quoted by Spitz, Dewey is talking in very broad terms of the significance for living creatures of their being integral with their world. Living is a rhythm of disruption and restoration of such harmonies. What is peculiar about human beings is that they are capable of being conscious of this rhythm. Purpose, emotion and interest emerge with this consciousness. The union to which Dewey is referring is this:

> With the realization [of harmony], material of reflection is incorporated into objects as their meaning. Since the artist cares in a peculiar way for the phase of experience in which union is achieved, he does not shun moments of resistance and tension. He rather cultivates them, not for their own sake but because of their potentialities,

bringing to living consciousness an experience that is unified and total.[65]

A more valid interpretation of Dewey here is that he is underlining the distinctive powers of people in general, but of artists in particular, consciously to pay attention to the dialectic of equilibrium and disequilibrium that humans have with their world. Artists care for the solution that unifies experience as an end in itself, whereas scientists use solutions as means of moving on and solving other problems. But more significant for our description is Dewey's observation that 'the material of reflection' is what gives objects like art objects their meaning by being incorporated into them. This is close to Husserl's statement that acts of perception determine but do not embody meaning. Acts of symbolic thinking do that. It is the union of these that Dewey is referring to in this passage.

That Dewey's own account of absorption depends upon recognizing that certain changes of intentionality are accompanied by changes of subjectivity can be seen in this passage:

> but absorption in a work of art so complete as to exclude analysis cannot be long sustained. There is a rhythm of surrender and reflection. We interrupt our yielding to the object to ask where it is leading and how it is leading there.[66]

In the terms of this chapter, this involves the rhythm of intentional shifts with corresponding transformations of points of view.

Dewey continually reminds us that speech is the mother tongue. Psychoanalysts are right to stress the foundational importance of the early prelinguistic phase of life for our later, symbolically saturated lives. But that phase is mostly beyond conscious recall and reveals itself to us in ways such as René Spitz describes in Chapter 3. This pre-verbal world is predominantly a perceptuo-motor world, one in which the young child comes to experience the world first as it 'feels' before in time coming to construct it 'consciously and in the level of meaning'. The perceptual mode of intentionality developmentally grounds the later developing imaginative and symbolic modes. It is certainly a form of rock on which life is grounded. And no doubt all sorts of early events recur as kinds of memory and phantasy throughout later life. But as sources of description for aesthetic absorption such explanations are unnecessary.

However, if this was all one could say to describe the dynamics of aesthetic absorption, it would be a rather thin description. What I have offered so far is a negative description: it identifies some of the functions of self that are *not* involved in aesthetic absorption. But there remains the question of what does or can go on during aesthetic absorption in the absence of these controlling functions. In their absence, or minimization, other functions of self are allowed freer play as Matisse testifies. My approach to describing the interplay of these other functions will be to continue to focus on the idea of the 'centredness' of self, on the sense, that is, of being a centre within a dynamic field of experience. Specifically, I now want to review the developmental psychology of forms of self-centredness.

In the course of the investigation so far, I have proposed that to be a self is to be centred in a variety of distinct but related ways, depending on the requirements of the particular situation. These may be described, for example, as perceptual, symbolic or imaginary. In this chapter I have paid special attention to the role of 'I'. In the next chapter I will concentrate on the developmental psychology of self as 'centred' in order to introduce the idea of 'recentring'. I will argue that recentring is one of the positive processes of aesthetic absorption when the controlling I is not deployed. This connects with a traditional claim for the benefits of art in terms of its facilitating vicarious experience. I will want to redescribe that claim as an aspect of aesthetic absorption and to ask whether, in the light of the theory of self presented here, self changes during aesthetic absorption.

NOTES

1. Samuel Beckett, 'The unnamable', in *The Beckett Trilogy* (London: Picador, 1979), p. 377.
2. McClatchy, 1990, p. 362.
3. 'Aboutness' and 'pointing to' are the defining features of the concept of intentionality. The concept has its origins with the Scholastics and derives from the Latin verb *intendo*, meaning to point at or aim at or extend towards. Brentano revived the idea when he used it as the definitive distinction between the physical and the mental. He observed that to be conscious is always to be conscious *of* something, and that only mental phenomena exhibit such intentionality. Mental

acts are intrinsically relational. Brentano accepted the Cartesian presumption that when one is aware of a 'representation' (a sound, say) one is simultaneously aware of the act of representing it to oneself (to the act of hearing the sound, for example). Brentano insisted that this was one act, but with two objects. Edmund Husserl took over and developed Brentano's ideas on intentionality, moving away from the psychological concerns of Brentano and towards his own phenomenological philosophy and descriptive psychology. There is also a twofoldness about intentionality in the sense that consciousness is about some object, but also that objects themselves may be about and point to other objects. See Brentano, 1973. Also see Kearney, 1986. According to Richard Kearney, Husserl speaks of perception, imagination and signification as being three main modes of intentionality (pp. 25–7). In Husserl, relevant discussions on this are to be found, for example, in his *Logical Investigations* (1970, vol. 2), *passim* but especially Investigation 6, pp. 707–18. Following Brentano and Husserl, the concept of intentionality continues to play a key role in philosophical psychological thinking, if not in psychological thinking generally. For a recent application in aesthetics, see Lord, 1988.

4. Basho's 'frog' must be the most famous haiku:

> Breaking the silence
> of an ancient pond,
> A frog jumped into water –
> A deep resonance.

For this see Basho, 1981, p. 9.

5. Wollheim, 1987, p. 166.

6. See Wollheim, 1984, pp. 42–3. For the idea that subjectivity is 'what it is like for the subject' to have a particular mental phenomenon, Wollheim is indebted to Thomas Nagel (1979, Chapter 12).

7. Mental *states* are episodic and transient. More than one mental state may occur in a mind at any one time but there is a definite limit to the number that may do so. These might be perceptual states, imaginings, moments of terror, and so on. By contrast, mental *dispositions* (beliefs, desires, emotions, memories, phantasies) are persistent phenomena that occur intermittently. They have histories that are made up of events. Mental *activities* are those that bring about mental events or that bring mental dispositions into play. Examples would be thinking a thought, or perhaps repressing one. For this analysis, see Wollheim, 1984, p. 38.

8. Wollheim's use of 'experience' here is of course the commonly held 'subjective' version, and should not be confused with Dewey's formulation.

9. Wollheim, 1984, p. 39.

10. Ibid., p. 42. For Wollheim's treatment of some objections to this see ibid., p. 41.

11. Wittgenstein's private-language argument is relevant to the question of what subjectivities can or cannot be discussed either with others or

with ourselves (Wittgenstein, 1958). On this see, for example, Kenny (1973).

12. Nagel, 1979, pp. 165–80. J. E. Tiles offers a critique of Nagel from a Deweyan perspective. Were this sustainable, it would present difficulties for my argument. For the reasons why I find that particular critique unconvincing see Benson, 1991–2. For other uses and objections see Jackson (1990), Levin (1990), and Nemirow (1990).
13. Nagel, 1979, p. 167.
14. For an extended description of what it would be like for a self to behave as something utterly alien, in this case a dung-beetle, see Kafka, 1971. Kafka's character, Gregor Samsa, continues to think as himself despite his physical metamorphosis and conveys what it is like for him to have physically become a dung-beetle but not what it is like for a dung-beetle to be a dung-beetle.
15. See Nagel, 1986.
16. Nagel, 1979, p. 176n.
17. In a comment on an earlier draft of this chapter, the Swiss phenomenologist Eduard Marbach agrees with this statement only if what is meant is 'an actually occupied' point of view. He continues:

> However, with mental states of *representing* something in its absence (as occurs in remembering and imagining something), I think that the phenomenological account is able to make plausible that there is *more than one point of view at the same time* that is involved in the state in question. There is a kind of 'parallel processing' at stake, namely of one's still perceiving (if only marginally, dimly, etc.) one's *actually present surroundings* (i.e. as it is given to the *actually occupied point of view*) 'in parallel', or 'simultaneously' with one's representing (more or less clearly, etc.) *the absent, represented situation* (scene, object, etc.) that is given *only as it were, not actually, to the represented point of view* occupied in my past, or occupied in a merely imagined space–time, etc. (Personal communication; emphasis in original)

18. Michael Kubovy speculates that

> the Renaissance artists were exploring the nature of egocentrism and ways of using perspective to *free* oneself from one's special vantage point. To do so is a sign of one's ability to transcend egocentrism. One might argue that the Cubists were engaged in a similar exploration.

See Kubovy, 1988, p. 171; emphasis in original.
19. See the 'Translator's introduction' by Hubert and Patricia Dreyfus to Merleau-Ponty, 1964a, p. xii. See also Merleau-Ponty, 1981. James and Dewey, like Husserl and Merleau-Ponty, oppose the idea – favoured by Descartes and Kant – of a detached subject who grounds his/her relatedness to the world in his/her own conscious acts of relating to that world. Husserl and Dewey both grant the object its due recognition in the dialectical constitution of lived experience with the person. As Merleau-Ponty puts it, 'there is no inner man, man is in the world, and only in the world does he know himself' (1981, p. xi). It is by objectifying meanings in symbolic representations that we come to know and create the meaningful in our lives. Byron, for example,

could write in his *Journal* of 1813, 'To withdraw myself from myself (oh that accursed selfishness!) has ever been my sole, my entire, my sincere motive in scribbling at all.' We must step back from the flux of lived experience the better to know it because, as Merleau-Ponty observes, 'our existence is too tightly held in the world to be able to know itself as such *at the moment of its involvement* [my emphasis], and that it requires the field of ideality in order to become acquainted with and to prevail over its facticity' (1981, p. xv). A similar point is made by William James in his 1890 account of self. It is this 'moment of involvement' that is so important for an understanding of absorption. But we should also note that for Merleau-Ponty, consciousness precedes and forms the ground of language. It is a prelinguistic given. Merleau-Ponty draws on Husserl's distinction between 'intentionality of act' (which has to do with our judgements, and the occasions when we voluntarily take up positions), and 'operative intentionality' (which is what gives us the unity of ourselves and our world, and which is evident in, for example, our desires and evaluations). Operative intentionality furnishes 'the text which our knowledge tries to translate into precise language' (1981, p. xviii). Consequently, we are 'condemned to meaning', as he pithily puts it (ibid., p. xix).

20. Wollheim, 1984, p. 33.
21. Merleau-Ponty, 1964a, p. xiii.
22. Freud, 1984, p. 364. In that original Strachey translation, the text is 'The ego is first and foremost a bodily ego,' but I will follow Bruno Bettleheim's insistence that the correct translation of *das Ich* is not 'ego' as Strachey had it, but the personal pronoun 'I'. For this see Bettleheim, 1985, p. 53.
23. In lamenting what he regards as the mistranslation of *das Ich* as the 'ego', Bruno Bettleheim speculates as to whether Freud was aware of Ortega Y. Gasset's observation that to create a concept was to leave a reality behind. Bettleheim regrets the obscuring of Freud's concern with the personal which the quasi-technical translation of *das Ich* as 'the ego' effected. But at a more general level one can turn Ortega's comment on its head and identify as a problem the realities which concepts themselves sometime produce to be encountered. The concept of the 'I' presents just such a problem. See Bettleheim, 1985, p. 55.
24. Freud, 1984, p. 364. For a recent discussion of this, see Glover, 1989, pp. 120–4.
25. Hume, 1969, Book 1, Part IV, Section VI, p. 300; emphasis in original. Also see Husserl, 1970, vol. 2, Investigation V, pp. 549–50, where he writes:

> I must frankly confess, however, that I am quite unable to find this ego, this primitive, necessary centre of relations. The only thing I can take note of, and therefore perceive, are the empirical ego and its empirical relations to its own experiences, or to such external objects as are receiving special attention at the moment, while much remains, whether 'without ' or 'within', which has no such relation to the ego.

26. McDermott, 1968, pp. 169–83. Originally, this was published in the *Journal of Philosophy, Psychology and Scientific Methods*, 1, 18 (Sept. 1904). In *The Principles of Psychology* James was explicitly dualistic in his approach, but quickly abandoned this position. In a paper entitled 'The vanishing subject in the psychology of James' (1940), Dewey charts this change in James's thought and notes that there are two incompatible strains that become most apparent when James deals with the self or subject. Dewey argues that both psychology and philosophy must be purged of dualistic thinking and should avoid descriptions of the phenomena of mind 'in terms of the organism exclusively instead of as aspects and functions of the interactivity of organism and environment' (Dewey, 1940, p. 599).

27. Stevens, 1974, p. 69.

28. Ibid., pp. 68–9.

29. See, for example, Yourgrau, 1990, for a representative sample of contemporary thinking in this area. For a consideration of some logical aspects of 'I' see Perry, 1979.

30. For a discussion of the developmental psychology of points of view see Cox, 1986. Chapter 5 deals with the development of deictic expressions and discusses their role in the development of the child's ability to converse with other people.

31. James, 1950, vol. 1, p. 341n.

32. On this see Glover, 1989, pp. 66–8.

33. James, 1950, vol. 1, Chapter X.

34. Ibid., p. 365.

35. Ibid., Chapter X. For a summary see Stevens, 1974, Chapter IV.

36. James, 1950, vol. 1, p. 341; emphasis in original.

37. Ibid., p. 401.

38. Stevens, 1974, p. 84. James's distinction between the pure ego and the empirical self has a parallel in Husserl's distinction between the pure phenomenological ego and the human ego: Husserl's description of the pure phenomenological ego as a 'functional centre' is very close to that of James. Both insist that the pure ego must be understood as a function rather than as a content, both see the body as the locus or point of origin for consciousness, and both see the flowing present as the source of the life of consciousness and the necessary condition for objective knowledge. Where they differ is in Husserl's insistence that the pure ego continues as one identical subject over time, whereas for James there is a succession of appropriating pure egos. Husserl emphasizes the constituting activities of the pure ego more than James whose primary concern is with the continuity of self. In Stevens's view, James's is the theory that is truest to the fundamental tenet of phenomenology that all consciousness is object oriented. Husserl's pure ego, on the other hand, is a self-identical, permanent subject that is conscious of itself as such.

39. Glover, 1989, p. 61.

40. Ibid., p. 88.

41. Dewey, 1940. What the later James and Dewey objected to was the idea of mind or of consciousness as a separate entity.
42. Ibid., p. 589n2. Although it might seem to encourage a subjectivistic understanding, I will continue to use the phrase 'stream of consciousness' because it has gained a wide acceptance, but I will understand it in Dewey's corrected sense (and in line with the later James) as an interactive 'stream of experience'. I should also note that an opposition to 'subjectivism', as I have identified it in aesthetics, does not preclude investigating the subjective dimensions of experience as I am doing here.
43. Martin Hollis reminds us of how the Buddhist image of the self as a series of candles lit from the stub of the one before appealed to William James. See Hollis, 1977, p. 71.
44. See Harré, 1983, p. 79.
45. Ibid., p. 79; emphasis in original.
46. Ibid., p. 82.
47. This is close to Dewey's assertion that 'Possession shapes and consolidates the "I" of philosophers. "I own therefore I am" expresses a truer psychology than the Cartesian "I think therefore I am".' See Dewey, 1922, p. 116. Dewey synthesizes William James's idea of 'the present thought' (pure ego) with G. H. Mead's ideas on the importance of social action by translating that thought into social action. James's pure ego acts to acquire elements of passing personal experience to be owned by the empirical self and integrated into it. Mead elaborates the extent to which this construction of self depends on the social world of the developing child. See Hollis, 1977, p. 68.
48. We should remember Wollheim's claim that only mental states have subjectivity, and that mental dispositions do not. If this is so, then mental states that involve the functioning of the indexical I will have subjectivity, but mental dispositions that involve the self-organizing function of I will not.
49. On this see, for example, Rimmon-Kenan, 1985. In Chapter 6, she uses the concept of 'focalization' to discuss the ways in which stories are mediated through perspectives.
50. See Flam, 1978, p. 152.
51. Mead, 1938, pp. 16–23.
52. Millar, 1980, p. 47.
53. See Maurice Merleau-Ponty, 1964b, p. 187. He goes on to say that the 'simultaneity' of things visibly together is a mystery that psychologists handle 'the way a child handles explosives'!
54. See Lipps, 1965. Lipps (1851–1914) was a German philosopher and psychologist who argued for the psychological basis of philosophy. This was especially true of his aesthetics for which he developed his theory of empathy (*Einfühlung*). In his view we experience *Einfühlung* when we project ourselves into the 'life' of aesthetic objects. I will return to this in Chapter 6.
55. See Stevens, 1972, p. 151.
56. On this, also see Allport, 1955, pp. 41–3.

57. Merleau-Ponty, 1974, pp. 19–20.
58. Dewey, 1958, p. 249.
59. Husserl, 1970, vol. 2, p. 684.
60. Dewey, 1958, p. 17.
61. Ibid., p. 240.
62. Ibid., p. 28.
63. E. Spitz, 1985, p. 142.
64. Ibid., p. 142.
65. Dewey, 1958, p. 15.
66. Ibid., p. 144.

CHAPTER 5

·

SELF AS 'CENTREDNESS' AND THE PROCESS OF 'RECENTRING': A DEVELOPMENTAL ACCOUNT

perhaps they have said me already, perhaps they have carried me to the threshold of my story, before the door that opens on my own story, that would surprise me, if it opens, it will be I, it will be the silence, where I am, I don't know, I'll never know, in the silence you don't know, you must go on, I can't go on, I'll go on.

(Samuel Beckett)[1]

REVISITING ARNHEIM'S 'OTHELLO PROBLEM'

I referred in Chapter 1 to Rudolf Arnheim's puzzlement over what happens when 'the dynamics of the art product engulfs [*sic*] the self of the performer, creator, or beholder, that is, when the actor *becomes* Othello', and I took it to be a concern with what I call absorption.[2] Arnheim also felt that such mental states as sympathy and identification were insufficiently explored and he concluded that:

> A psychology of the self does not yet exist that is subtle enough to describe the precise difference between situations in which the self acts as an autonomous perceiver of a dynamic state and those in which the self is *the very center* [my emphasis] of such a state.[3]

I want to describe what I believe to be an aspect of self that is germane to aesthetic absorption. I will do this from a pragmatic and social constructivist position. Although it still cannot offer the precision wished for by Arnheim, it does offer a promising approach to the problem.

The assumptions one makes about the relationship between the types of situation in which 'the self acts as an autonomous perceiver of a dynamic state' and those situations in which 'the self is the very

113

center of such a state' will greatly influence the types of concept with which to build such an account. As I suggested in my reinterpretation of Winnicott, I believe that the choice is between understanding this as a problem of *transition* as against thinking of it as a problem of *transformation*. Under the influence of Dewey's concept of experience, my preference is for a language of transformation. One becomes Othello, in other words, not by crossing some boundary from viewer/actor to character, but by a process of partial transformation into that character within the dynamics of a new situation, a situation that emerges from the one preceding it. What are the details of such transformational processes? Dewey does not offer much help on this question, and Arnheim opts to leave the issue open. But helpful ideas can be gleaned from another pragmatist, Charles Sanders Peirce, as well as from contemporary social constructivist thinking on the self such as that of Rom Harré.

My point of entry into this problem, therefore, will focus on what it means for a self to 'be centred' and on the general developmental contexts of such centrings.[4] I will identify a gap in the language of description, one which must be filled if it is to enclose all that is involved in becoming aesthetically absorbed. Developmental psychologists talk of 'egocentrism' and of 'decentring' (not to be confused with its poststructuralist use as in, for example, 'the decentred subject') in relation to children's ability to adopt the perspectives of others. I want to argue, however, that the dynamics of aesthetic absorption, and also of sympathy and identification, can be usefully described by building on the notion of the self as centre, but that this description requires a new concept in addition to the developmental psychological description of decentring overcoming egocentrism. What also needs to be described are the processes of 'recentring'.

The possibility of recentring within the stream of experience requires a language of transformation such as Arnheim's problem with becoming Othello suggests. Within the pragmatic tradition, C. S. Peirce's notes on selves as signs offer some particularly suggestive ideas for this analysis.

C. S. PEIRCE ON SELF AS SIGN

The idea that experience must be understood as continuous over time is common amongst the pragmatists and is utilized in various ways by James, Dewey, Mead and Peirce. I have already described at various points how the first three of these thought about self and continuity. Peirce's views on the self as sign are less well known. Despite their fragmentary form, they are potentially rich and have influenced the thinking of the others in various indirect ways. Peirce is aware of the value to be gained from attending to the development of self-consciousness, self-knowledge and self-control in children. From such considerations, he argues that self comes to be known by inference rather than, as Descartes would maintain, by direct intuition.[5] Peirce says that children have powers of thinking long before there is the sense of an 'I' that is thinking.

In his view, it is only with the development of language that relations between the child and the world can be asserted, relations which the child can agree to or can deny. Peirce gives this example: a child hears it said that the stove is hot, but the child denies this, touches the stove and is burnt. 'Thus', concludes Peirce, 'he becomes aware of ignorance and it is necessary to suppose a self in which this ignorance can inhere.'[6] The point of the example is that the child in this instance learns not only that the stove is hot, but more significantly that *he* did not know that it was hot. For this to become possible, a mastery of language and an establishment of self is necessary. Peirce's claim is that self is discovered by children indirectly via inference and hypothesis rather than directly by intuition, and especially in situations where the children come to see that they are wrong about something. His further conclusion is that we can only know the self as a sign, and that the self, moreover, *is* a sign which is embedded in a context and formed within a community of interpretation. As Michaels puts it: 'This is to say not only that the self interprets but that the self is an interpretation.'[7] Self and other mutually constitute each other, and it is these acts of mutual constitution that deserve our attention.

Peirce left no systematic account of self nor of self-development, but the notes he did leave are tantalizing for any attempt to describe how one self might in some way 'become' another as, for example, in acts of sympathy or identification, or during phases of aesthetic absorption.[8] His theory of self forms part of his larger project on semiotics, key elements of which are the ubiquity of sign processes, the centrality of dialogue and conversation, the essential formative role of social relations and the cooperative nature of inquiry. Peirce rejects the Cartesian notion of the isolated self with its attendant subjectivism, substituting instead a social view of the self as a communicative agent issuing from communicative relations. This conception of self as constituted by and arising from social relations, themselves understood as sign relations, follows on from his theory of semiosis. His conception of the sign is the foundation for his notions of mind and self.

Unlike Saussure's formulation of the sign as a two-term entity (signifier–signified), Peirce's tripartite formulation (object–sign–interpretant) is much more comprehensive and allows for the inclusion of its own notion of self.[9] Peirce defined a sign as 'something which stands to somebody for something in some respects or capacity'.[10] What the sign stands for is its object, and what it stands to is its interpretant (which may be an interpreter but need not be). For Peirce, a sign has a relationship to its object and it brings its interpretant into a corresponding relation to that object. The object of any sign is always determined within the field or context in which the sign process or semiosis occurs. Signs, furthermore, need not be humanly made and natural signs abound independently of human beings. This is relevant to Peirce's notion of continuity (what, with one of his many neologisms, he called 'synechism') and especially to his understanding of self as always being in relation, as being radically continuous with others.

An example of a sign from the arts as offered by Peirce is the performance of a piece of music. The music as played is the sign, the composer's musical ideas are its objects and the listener's feelings (as determined by listening to the music) are its interpretant, in this case an emotional interpretant. Note how an interpretant is understood as being that which the sign determines.[11] This idea allows Peirce the possibility of describing how something functioning as a sign can effect a change of self. A change of context, as I understand him, could mean that what was an interpretant can now become a sign with its own object and interpretant.[12] If, to build on the same musical example, the listener's feelings on hearing this music led him to cry because it reminded him of his native country from which he was exiled, then in this case his feelings function as sign, his nostalgically remembered homeland would be its object, and his act of crying its interpretant. If his wife saw him crying, she might feel pity for him knowing the sadness of his exile. Here, within this new social context, the previous interpretant becomes a sign to his wife, the exile's sadness its object, and her feelings of pity for him its interpretant. And so this could proceed in endless and complex semiotic transformations as part of continuously evolving social situations. Of particular importance is Peirce's understanding of habits (dispositions to act in certain ways in certain circumstances, which partly constitute self) as interpretants. In other words, selves are formed by the cultivation of habits and these are fundamentally semiotic. The task of a semiotically influenced psychology, he argues, is to investigate how habits emerge from the transactions of organisms and environments.

Self *is* an extremely complex semiotic system of hierarchically organized habits, and not simply a user of signs. However, if the self was nothing more than this, then it would be locked into an idealistic prison. But this is not the consequence of Peirce's semiotic theory of the self because he is acutely aware of the significance of the body and of the meaningfulness of the natural world (remember that his formulation of the sign is much broader than simply applying to humanly-made and human-received signs). His understanding of the body is twofold: it is a medium through which the self expresses itself to the world, but it is also the medium through which the world speaks to the self. This notion of the embodied self is what Peirce calls a perfect sign. A 'perfect sign is perpetually being acted upon by its object, from which it is perpetually receiving the accretions of new signs. . . . In addition, the perfect sign never ceases to undergo change.'[13] A self, therefore, is an immensely complex sign in the process of perpetual development, but it is also and essentially an embodied semiotic process in continual dialogue with itself and with others. The complexity of the self is of such an order that the very course of its own development comes, in time, to be partially controlled from within itself,[14] even if the main direction of influence in the formation of self is, according to Peirce, from the outward to the inward, from the public to the private, from the social to the individual.

Self-control is a very significant idea for him. He writes:

> If we could endow a system of signs with self-control, there is very strong reason to believe that we should thereby have conferred on it a *consciousness* even more like that of a man than is, for example, that of a fish.[15]

Selves evolve from minds that can feel, act and learn.[16] Peirce identifies 'I' with the source of actions, as a centre of control and purpose. 'The human self is', in Colapietro's formulation of Peirce, 'an organically embodied center of purpose and power.'[17] The essence of self-control is inhibition of action rather than the origination of anything. It is the inhibition of physical behaviour, according to Peirce, that creates the possibility of inward action. As a result of being educated and of coming to recognize the difference between what they will and what others will, children learn to discriminate between an inner and an outer world. But the forms of that inner 'subjective' world are dialogic, and the dynamics of those dialogues are intersubjective in origin. In short, the form of a person is the form of a community.[18] It is Peirce's theory of the interpretant, according to Colapietro, that provides a way of including subjects within the theory of signs without denying their extrasemiotic nature (e,g. that they are embodied) or the social circumstances in which they are likely to act.

The paradigm of communication for Peirce is the conversation, which he considers to be an exemplary kind of sign-functioning. In conversation, self can be the source from whom discourse flows as well as the object to whom it moves; the conversation can be about self, and it can be a way in which the discourses of others find expression through the self (one of structuralism's key ideas). The body also should be thought of as a medium through which the self finds expression, rather than thinking of a self as being in a body. Again, rather than speak of thoughts being 'in us', Peirce says that 'we ought to say that we are in thought,'[19] an idea we have already seen developed in William James's conception of the 'I' as being part of the present thought. To sum up the essence of Peirce's position, we can say that the being of self is a being in communication, an embodied social semiotic being.

How might this conception of self illuminate the dynamics of aesthetic absorption? Earlier on in Chapter 2 when discussing the idea of a qualitative sign, I mentioned Peirce's classification of signs into three basic types – icons (which involve some resemblance between sign and object), indices (in which there is a dynamic relationship with that signified) and symbols (where the relationship is via some convention). One commentator on Peirce, Max Fisch, suggests that in situations where the indexical aspect of the sign is very attenuated and the iconical aspect very prominent, as with a piece of music, 'we are likely to be absorbed into the qualitative structure of the sign itself.'[20] On the other hand, where the indexical aspect is attenuated and the symbolic prominent – he offers a poem as an example – we are most likely to be drawn into a process of interpretation. Leaving to one side any reservations one might have about Peirce's classification of signs in a post-Goodman era, Fisch's example suggests how different art forms, understood as being differently constituted types of sign, may engage the self in different ways. The promise of the Peircean perspective is that it suggests how that engagement of self and art object, to take just our present interest, might occur, albeit in the most general terms.

What might it mean to say that I was absorbed into the qualitative structure of the music itself, or, after Eliot, that I am the music while the music lasts? Peirce attaches great significance to the nature of our experience, to the fact of sympathy and to the ways in which self can become one with others without at the same time losing its own individuality.[21] The essence of semiosis is the establishment of relations between things that would otherwise remain unrelated. The initially unrelated things that concern us are individual selves, other selves, real or fictional, and the dynamic fields of communicational meaning within which they are made and sustained. Unlike physical things, whose boundaries force degrees of separateness and discreteness upon them, semiotic things with their permeable boundaries and continuities are capable of quite a different order of mobility, interpenetrability and participation in each other. This is the key to the general Peircean description of how one self can become another, as in, for example, acts of sympathy.

Peirce believes that an essential possibility of selfhood is that the self can become one with some other. He speaks of the self as a centre of purpose and power, and of the phenomenology of self as 'a sort of innermost centre within the circle', and of this sense of centredness as being ineffable.[22] But this ineffable dimension is only one aspect of self, most of the other aspects of which are communicable. What the self is in its uniqueness can only be realized in its relations with others, and these others do not necessarily have to exist. They may be imagined. Self is of its nature extended in time. Because of this it is always incomplete and essentially unrealizable. As the existentialists put it, self is a project. Personality, as a coordination of ideas, is a living power realizing itself to some degree in the present, but a power which is also˙

oriented in a flexible way to the future.[23] So strongly does Peirce hold to this view that he maintains that set apart from others and set apart from its future the individual self has a status that is merely negative. As Colapietro puts it: 'A sign cut off from its future interpretants is a sign denied the possibility of . . . being a sign.'[24] A developing self is a self in dialogue with itself and this is part of a wider enveloping dialogue with others. Because of this, it is possible to distinguish different parts of self as different roles in the unfolding conversation of sign with sign. Signs, moreover, do not have to be in the same 'place' at the same time.

The view opposed by Peirce is the subjectivist one such as that of William James in *The Principles of Psychology* where self is understood as irreducibly insulated (James, as we know, later changed his position on this and caused the self, as Dewey remarked, to 'disappear'). On this account we can never know in any real sense the thoughts and feelings of anyone other than ourselves. The idea of becoming one with another is rendered inconceivable by this assumption of insular separateness. All we can do is decode the signs through which the other mind chooses to express its thoughts and feelings, but these remain hidden 'in' the other's mind.

Peirce, on the other hand, insists that the starting point is the public world with its language. What needs to be explained is not how individual private worlds come to be negotiated in some public sense, but rather how from a start in a public world people come to acquire private worlds. This is also the starting point for social constructivists such as Harré, following Wittgenstein, Vygotsky and Mead.[25] According to Peirce, acquiring a private world during the course of development involves coming to know the difference between an 'inner' world of imaginings and an 'outer' one of actuality, and of being able to withdraw from the 'outer' into the 'inner' one. But he objects to the description of mind that considers it to be 'within' a person in a way analogous to one physical thing being located within another. This type of description allows mind, and by extension self as a species of mind, to be located only in one place, namely the body that houses it. But this is not a good description of mind and self. Peirce puts it like this:

> There is a miserable material[istic] and barbarian notion according to which a man cannot be in two places at once; as though he were a *thing*! A word may be in several places at once, [e.g.,] *six, six,*

because its essence is spiritual; and I believe that a man is no whit inferior to the word in this respect. . . . But that he truly has this outreaching identity – such as a word has – is the true and exact expression of the fact of sympathy, fellow feeling – together with all unselfish interests – and all that makes us feel that he has an absolute worth.[26]

If words have the mobility they have because they are signs, then so also have selves to the extent that they too are signs. Mind and self, because they are signs, can transcend their instantiation in the body. This must not be understood as a dualistic formulation in any Cartesian sense. Mind and body for Peirce are two aspects of a unity. The upshot of these semiotic powers of minds and selves is that, far from being insulated from each other, different minds and selves are potentially interpenetrable and this is the existential ground for sympathy and for selves to feel one with another.

This helps us to understand how 'I' can shift in certain circumstances from a position at the centre of 'my' current field of experience to a position centred somewhere in a field of experience which is another person's but which temporarily becomes mine also, with whatever consequences this may have for my relationships with myself and with the other person. For Peirce, self-development or self-realization depends upon the self surrendering to ever more inclusive ideals. The antithesis of this, and the recipe for stagnation, is self-absorption.[27] In this context, aesthetic experiences of art, of which absorption is such a crucial element, can be occasions for self-transcendence and therefore for self-change.

I have proposed a description of aesthetic absorption which hinges on the idea that the situations in which this type of absorption occurs do not, for the period of absorption, demand that the 'I' of the person reading or looking be self-consciously deployed. This, as I said, is to slant the description negatively in the sense that it describes what tends *not* to happen during aesthetic absorption. The positive statement of what does happen, towards which this description is moving, has to do with my occupying a newly centred position within a novel field of experience which some object or event (a book or a picture, for example) and I jointly create. The change to a new centre is what may also be called a change in point of view. It is this process that I want to call 'recentring'.

Points of view are inherently relational: they are points of view on or about something. They are constituted and sustained by interaction with the world, as Dewey's theory of experience would have it. Within this theory of experience, points of view, understood as signs in the Peircean sense, are labile and mobile. They change, and in certain circumstances are invited to allow themselves to be changed. One such circumstance is experience of art. Artists and, from my present interest, visual artists and writers, intentionally incorporate points of view in their work as organizing focuses for the life of those works. Consequently, a spectator interacting with a picture or a reader interacting with a text might be minimally described as a centring being interacting with a centring artefact/event, which has been intentionally constructed by another centring being, the artist or writer. Being centred in this sense might be understood in Peircean terms as an interpretant of these signs.

Granting the heuristic value of the description, I now want to ask about what is involved in the formation of some of these centring processes and about some of the functions they serve in social–psychological life. My approach is once again developmental in order to highlight the many types of ways of being centred in experience. The developmental history of some of these ways of being centred illustrates this, and it also suggests what might be involved when the experience of being centred changes, when, that is, recentring occurs. Peirce's theory of self allows me to do a number of things in this respect. In addition to underlining the continuing relevance of pragmatic thought, Peirce's idea of self as sign suggests in general terms how it is possible for one self to interpenetrate another and share or become part of some aspect of the other's experience. It also allows me to show how close Peirce's enterprise is to that of contemporary social constructivists like Rom Harré and cultural psychologists like Jerome Bruner and Richard Schweder. A review of some of this contemporary work on the development of being centred and integrated will flesh out my description of aesthetic absorption as a process of recentring.

ROM HARRÉ ON SELF AS AN ACQUIRED THEORY

Dewey approves James's formulation that:

> The world experienced . . . comes at all times with our body as its

centre, centre of vision, centre of action, centre of interest. The body is the storm centre, the origin of co-ordinates, the constant place of stress in all that experience-train. . . . The word 'I', then, is primarily a noun of position, just like 'this' and 'here'.[28]

It is the association of 'I' with the likes of 'this' and 'here' that is especially suggestive here, and that links pragmatic thinking on self with that of contemporary social constructivists.

Peirce's ideas on self find a contemporary development in the work of Rom Harré who, with his colleagues, has explored some of the questions posed by the idea of self as sign.[29] Harré describes his theory of the 'appropriation' of selfhood from personhood as a drawing out of the details of G. H. Mead's original insight into the social origins of self, and Mead was influenced by Peirce.[30] The distinction between 'person' and 'self', which Harré owes to Strawson, is of central significance. 'Person' refers to social individuals located in social structures whereas 'self' refers to psychological individuals. In this view one is not a person because one is a self, but one is a self because one is and has been a person. We could say that personhood is a gift by adults which is bestowed on newborn and young children. The young are treated as though they are persons and grow into full personhood as a result. Within individual development, personhood precedes selfhood and determines it.

Harré argues that self is an organizing theory whose form and content is social in origin. This is a much more radical view than, say, the social learning theory of Albert Bandura or the notions of self as self-concept which are associated with writers like Carl Rogers.[31] While theories such as these may be illuminating in their accounts of the social acquisition of certain types of belief, they nonetheless presuppose the 'belief that I am'. It is the form and content of this central belief that, Harré argues, is essentially social.[32] By 'sense of self' Harré means 'the generally "centred" structure of experience'.[33]

In the last chapter, I introduced the idea of an indexical and highlighted its social–psychological importance. 'I' is an indexical and indicates one's individual position in any group of people, but it does not refer to a directly experienced 'subject' or 'centre'. Yet I-thoughts are unified in normal personal experience. We feel that they are part of a coherent entity, our 'self'. Nonetheless, this readily verifiable sense of being does not imply that there is an empirically given, unifying entity to which I refers, something 'contained' by my body. What there is, according to Harré, is a unifying concept. Harré uses this idea to surmount the referential or non-referential dilemma that confronts theories of self.

In this view there is no autonomous self functioning to organize experience. There is only a theory of 'myself as subject of my experience', a theory which organizes beliefs, memories, plans and so on, in much the same way that the theory of gravitation helps organize our experience of moving bodies.[34] We could say that self *is* a higher thought process. It is a high-level theory whose primary function is the constitution and organization of experience. Like other theories it is acquired in the course of development, and is appropriated from a community which has itself acquired, held and perhaps subtly modified the theory over time. It follows from this that if one community differs from another in the theory of self which forms it and which it holds, then members of each community will differ in significant respects from each other in their senses of self and in the nature and organization of their experience. Harré argues that this is just what anthropology and history show.

Central to the acquisition of self, and of I as a 'centred individual', is the acquisition of a concept of I as a person occupying my own position in the array of other persons. The transition from personhood to selfhood is the transition from I, functioning primarily as an indexical, to the theoretical idea of I as a unifying centre of my experience. Personal being is thus a consequence of social being.

To become capable of developing and possessing this concept of self is to gain the ability to constitute and organize experience in a 'self-centred', unified way. A requirement for the development of self is the development of the semiotic function in general, and of verbal language in particular. Self is intrinsically symbolic, as Peirce argued. Without a capacity for symbolization self could not be. Language is inherently constitutive and words, as Bruner reminds us, give an 'apparent ontological status' to the concepts they embody.[35] Self, like other theories, is in large part verbal and this is a reason for its being so easily reified and granted an apparent ontological status as some kind of entity.

Harré emphasizes the psychological significance for self-development of deixis or the acquisition of the ability to use pronouns.[36] Mind is, in his view, grammatically modelled: 'An organized belief system and a corpus of linguistic and practical skills are at least necessary conditions for "mindedness".'[37] Quite what is involved in the development up to the point where it is possible to acquire this system and these skills is worth exploring. Such a developmental sketch – one not offered but enabled by Harré's thinking – is especially worthwhile if we wish to understand how the points of view peculiar to perceiving, thinking symbolically or imagining can cohabit as essential functions of a developed self.

My suggestion is that self is an outcome of cumulated achievements which are eventually integrated in the theory that is, as Harré argues, the self. It is the structure of the theory that can account for the coherence over time of self, as well as the stability of the system of social relations within which it functions. But that theory is itself acquired only over time. A schematic description of the centring aspect of that development will help to clarify what is involved in the idea of self as integrated centres of experience, and therefore with the idea of there being different processes of recentring.

SELF–DEVELOPMENT AND THE INTEGRATION OF CENTRES OF EXPERIENCE

Harré, like James, Dewey and Mead, understands 'sense of self' to mean 'the generally centred structure of experience'. But how does this sense of self develop? In general terms, it has to do with development from impersonal modes of psychological functioning to personal modes. One very important aspect of this is the extent to which a developing self can acquire powers of action or agency. This, however, is not an area that I will deal with. My focus is exclusively on the idea of self as 'centred' and as 'centring' or, to use the earlier formulation, on the development of personal points of view.

Persons as agents intuitively feel that they are the origin of their voluntary actions. In other words, individual experience is of oneself as a point of action. More often than not, point of view and point of action are experienced as being coincident. In Harré's account the developmental transition from early impersonal modes of being, characteristic of the baby, to the personal being of self is a two-step process. In the first place the concepts of point of view and point of action must be acquired. In the second step, to use his formulation,

> the capacity to contemplate oneself reflexively as the unifying principle of these 'origins' implies the separation of the use of indexicals from the deployment of a theoretical concept of the self. . . . Self-consciousness in this view is not a new kind of consciousness but rather a new way of partitioning that of which one is aware by reference to a theory, one's theory of oneself.[38]

These in turn are necessary conditions for that third essential element in human individuality which is the ability to construct and tell one's own story to oneself and to others. The narrator is a part of the unfolding narrative that is self. Point of view, point of action and autobiography are therefore the key elements in this understanding of self as active centredness. A schematic outline of some of the milestones in the development of centredness will help to amplify this description of self.

There is a prototypical centredness in the newborn child's experience. The idea of a centre implies position in space and it implies direction. To have a sense of oneself as a 'centre' of experience implies having a sense of direction. Newborn babies have no developed notion of directionality in the inconstant world that flows around them. The only constancy, as Maurer and. Maurer remind us, lies with the newborns' sensations of their own movements.[39] This 'awareness' of their own movement as a constant in the babies' experience is a primal biological root of later points of view. But since they have no control over movement, there can as yet be no points of action, no sense of being the origin of their own action or the centre of their own experience. At this early stage of psychological development it is not a question of *who* processes and controls information but of *what* does. The achievement of the type of personal being that 'who' assumes still lies down the developmental road.

The body lies at the core of one's sense of being centred, with the brain and the rest of the nervous system as the central control system of the body. From a neuropsychological perspective, consciousness is neuronally grounded in the interconnections within the cerebral cortex and in those connections between the midbrain and the cortex. In so far as these exist and function in a normal baby then that baby can be said to be conscious. But the baby is not self-conscious because there is no self of which to be conscious. In this account of self, self-consciousness must await the development of the theory which constitutes oneself, and which then allows one to categorize that of which one is aware by reference to that theory. There is no 'baby' that is conscious nor any equivalent agent. However, an integration of sensorimotor information does occur. It is to this that Maurer and Maurer refer when they speculate with the idea of an impersonal 'neuronal observer' as a part of the functioning of the newborn's brain.

For the neuronal observer (not 'the baby') the world does not exist. What do exist are the neurochemical movements of the bodily world of which it is a part, rather than objects in the 'outside' world that give rise to many of those movements of neurochemical energy. This has profound consequences for understanding the relations between the newborn and the world. The experience of movement provides an example. Maurer and Maurer believe that 'if we could put ourselves inside the newborn's head, the world would look like clips of movies taken from the cutting-room floor and played back sometimes in slow motion, at other times speeded up.'[40] It would not be as we experience movement.

How does the transition from this non-personal world of neuronal observer and neurochemical energy to a world of light and objects in which the newborn has a definite location and position take place? What is involved in coming to understand neurochemical events as the world? This is a longer story than scientists and philosophers can yet tell. But some aspects of it will help to underscore the points made earlier about how symbolic points of view (such as 'I') with their associated semantic spaces are grounded in and develop from a bodily centredness with its associated perceptual spaces. We know, for example, that by virtue of having extensively touched itself and its uterine environs the foetus's skin becomes virtually mapped by its brain, and that this map functions to measure distance. Coupled with neuronal signals forming sensations and with other regular cycles of the body, biological clocks for measuring time also develop. So the foetus/neuronal observer develops a rudimentary awareness of the relationship of movement to distance and time. The newborn baby's body is thus set to be a standard for measuring distance and time.[41] The point which it is helpful to make here is that ideas of distance and time are central to such semantic spaces as will be required by developing abilities to, say, remember and that these ideas are intellectually developed borrowings from perceptual spaces and time.[42]

But self is part of mind, and it is with the emergence of mind that the neuronal observer begins to be appropriated by and annexed to the simultaneously emerging process of self. Sometime around 8 months the babies' neuronal networks have developed sufficiently to allow two actions to be linked together in a purposeful combination. They can now pull cloths towards themselves to reach the toy on top of them, for example. This ability to combine different actions with different objects involves the splitting apart of object and action. Up to this time it is a case of one action–one object as part of a single unity.

For the babies, objects now begin to exist for the first time, and because their memories have improved they come to know that objects have their own permanence over time. It is now, according to this account, that the neuronal observer 'comes to realize', in ways that we do not yet understand, that neuronal activity represents events and objects in a world other than the neuronal world of the observer. This is taken to be a landmark in the psychological development of mind.[43] The babies have now become competent in a variety of important ways. They can experience space and time, and hence movement, as adults do; psychological 'boundaries' become established such that a sense of the difference between what is part of baby and what is other than baby becomes part of experience; they can now recollect as well as recognize things; and, for the first time, they become capable of learning from other people. Here, with their rudimentary but growing understanding of cause and effect, and with their growing ability to anticipate the actions of others, is the origin of the sense of psychological agency, of feeling themselves to be the origin of actions.

With all of these developmental achievements comes a crucial change in respect of the centredness that is point of view. This has to do with the sense the baby has of being positioned in space.[44] Maurer and Maurer put it suggestively: 'No longer is his body the center of the universe. No longer does a chair revolve about him as he crawls: now he crawls around the chair.'[45] Along with the capacity to recollect and the understanding that objects have their own permanence, comes the ability to function symbolically. And with the development of the capacity for symbolization, and especially the learning of a natural language, comes the basis of what comes to be understood as self. Without a capacity for symbolization there could be no developed sense of self.

Infants learn to speak the language of their culture as a consequence of being spoken to within what Wittgenstein called the language games of that culture.[46] The speech acts of those who speak to the child, acts of addressing, ordering, requesting and so on, are the carriers of language for the infant. And these are complex acts. 'Bye-bye' can be recognized by 8 month old infants and coordinated with the action of waving a hand. In this case the word is an embedded part of the context of an action. There is some evidence to suggest that, at around 18 months, words begin to be taken as objects of attention in their own right, objects which can represent other objects and actions.[47] Their 'detachability' from entire actions begins to be grasped, albeit in a rudimentary way, by the baby. Up to now, for instance, 'bye-bye' means 'waving-your-arms-as-somebody-leaves'. Now 'bye-bye' means 'leaving'. Now too, remembered or imagined objects are no longer necessarily the same as the actual objects that are remembered or imagined. With this comes the possibility of combining words and of forming sentences with the infinite possibilities for creating meaning that this entails. This also means a radical step forward in the formation of self.

These developing abilities of categorization, recollection and symbolization are key requirements for developing the theory that is self. If the world does not exist for the newborn, the newborn certainly exists for the world. From the beginning, and especially in contemporary cultures, newborn babies are treated as persons. For instance, they are named and by as early as 1 month show signs of recognizing that name.[48] Being named means being formally located in the array of other people that are one's family or community. With this will come the possibility of being experientially centred in a way which is qualitatively different from that entailed by perceptual and motoric centredness, but which comes to coexist with them as part of the higher-level integration that is self. To put this another way, we could say that the development of self involves, amongst other things, the integration of successively emerging ways of being centred within corresponding fields of experience, neuronal, perceptual-motoric, intellectual and social.

There now begins the development of that symbolic theoretical structure which emerges from, and comes to partially contain, bodily centredness. Semantically constructed 'spaces' come into coexistence with the already constructed perceptual spaces, and interpenetrate them. And with these come the possibility of different types of 'point' from which to form views and perspectives of the world as perceived, and of the world as understood. High-level integration of function now takes a quantum leap in the complexity of the tasks facing it. Signification annexes and subordinates perception, but never totally as the coexistence of different types of point of view and modes of intentionality remind us. There is no longer any necessity for all understanding to be centred on self as a body occupying a particular point in space–time, as the 'Greenwich of the universe', to borrow Maurer and Maurer's image.[49] It now depends upon the particular demands of particular situations as to what type of point of view and what kind of 'location' are required or available.

We could say that as selves we are spoken into existence. This would in fact be an almost literal description of what is involved in the development of self. It is wider than saying that language is the stuff of self. It recognizes that language is for most practical purposes embedded in the acts of persons and selves, as Dewey believed. We still know relatively little about the dynamics of language games in the early formation of persons and of selves, about the interplay of available symbol systems and preferred social practices in the formation of children. But certain 'hard cases', such as how children who are both deaf and mute can still manage to acquire the cognitive organization of self, point to the power of these social practices, these language games and their speech acts, denuded as they are for these children of the richness of verbal language, to form persons and selves.[50] That is why the phrase 'being spoken into existence' is preferable to some less dynamic formulation such as 'the self is linguistically constituted'.

Against the background of this general review of early psychological development, I can now describe the development of the particular forms of centredness that lie at the heart of becoming a person and becoming a self. If self is a theory of which 'I' is the central construct, its development depends entirely upon a person being reared as a part of a speaking or symbolizing community. What are the most important developmental milestones in the symbolic constitution of self as I, at least as far as 'being centred' is concerned? Answering this question will help me to suggest what must, psychologically speaking, be involved in recentring and occupying points of view other than our own. What is it, in other words, for I to become as another within a given field of experience? If a developmental account can show that I is a relatively late developing aspect of self, founded upon and incorporating earlier senses of self, then this will help towards a description of how self can still involve centredness even when the use of I is not required by the situation, or is minimally deployed, as in aesthetic absorption.

THE EMERGENCE OF I AS A DOMINANT CENTRE OF EXPERIENCE

I have already dealt with the meaning of I and its association with a dominant point of view, with James's ideas on its status as a passing appropriating ego and 'noun of position', and with the conditions under which it may be deployed. All this was done in order to reach the conclusion that aesthetic absorption involved, at a minimum, the non-deployment of I. Now I want to amplify that account with a description of the social developmental origins of I in order to underscore its relational nature and its functions within contexts that have their own dynamics. If I as a sense of self depends upon context, then a change of context can perhaps effect a change in sense of self.

Arising from an idea of René Spitz, Rom Harré reformulates the notion of 'psychological symbiosis' and uses it to describe the learning of selfhood.[51] The idea is this:

> Psychological symbiosis is a permanent interactive relation between two persons, in the course of which one supplements the psychological attributes of the other as they are displayed in social performances, so that the other appears as a complete and competent social and psychological being.[52]

Although this idea has general application across human relationships (teacher–student and parent–child relations being obvious examples), it is especially descriptive of the types of relationship of which babies are a part. Mothers, for example, do not simply talk about their infants' wishes, feelings, intentions and so on: they supply them for the children, and relate to the children as though it were the children who possessed them.

The dynamics of this type of relating on the part of mothers and of others in the children's world, the 'as though' nature of psychological symbiosis in which the children are treated as though they were persons with a clear social position and a developed psychological being, is what creates for children the experience of being just such persons. By supplementing the psychology of their children in these ways, mothers contribute to and shape the construction of their children's psychology. This idea is quite different from Mahler's idea of symbiosis which we met in Chapter 3 and which Ellen Spitz uses to develop her account of aesthetic absorption. Whereas Mahler uses the term to refer to a form of emotional dependence characteristic of the child–mother relationship, Harré's use is to be understood as a much more social and cognitive process. Harré puts it like this:

> The crucial person–engendering language games involving the indexical and referential features of the uses of pronouns, and all sorts of other devices by which concept pairs like 'self and other', 'agent and patient', complementary points of view, continuity and discontinuity of experience, etc. are shared with an infant, take place in conditions of psychological symbiosis. One who is always presented as a person, by taking over the conventions through which this social act is achieved, becomes organised as a self.[53]

It is through such language games and the appropriation of the conventions of such games that the child comes to be centred as a person. It is by appropriating from this public and collective concept of person, so the argument runs, that centredness as a self develops. Self is here understood to be a theory which serves to organize experience 'as the mental life of a self-conscious agent'.[54] Harré speculates that in other cultures the theories available for appropriation may be quite different from Western culture, resulting in different organizations of experience and different phenomenologies of self-centredness.[55] In relation to the psychological significance of indexicals like pronouns, Harré's assertion is this:

> That the transcendental ego, the 'inner self', is not an empirically presented entity, but a shadow cast on the mind by the grammatical forms used in the practices of self-reporting, avowing, etc., deriving from indexical properties of pronouns and their equivalents. Again degree of individual 'centredness' of the members of a culture in matters of the assignment of responsibility, degree of hypochondria, etc. are independent indicators of this or that linguistic convention.[56]

With English speakers, for example, it is the acquisition of personal pronouns such as 'I', 'me', 'you', 'they', and so on that, in addition to bodily and role related forms of centredness, contributes most significantly to the psychological sense of being a centre of one's own experience. If self is understood as being an acquired theory, then first person pronouns are key constructs of that theory, and attention to the way in which they are acquired will help our understanding of the development of self.

There are a number of points to note about the development of deictic forms, and especially about the development of personal deictic or indexical forms such as 'I' or 'me'. Personal deictic forms refer to position in space–time and this is graphically reflected in American Sign Language, for example. Using the body as the centre of a 'sign space', different spatial areas locate different pronouns. 'You' is front-centre; a third person is signed to the right, another to the left and others to the space between. Once, in the course of any single conversation, a person is assigned a space it continues to be reserved for that person throughout the conversation.[57]

This is an especially visible example of what is meant in the use of personal deictic forms. They index the source and locate the position of communications and actions, of points of view and points of action. There is a sequence in which the use of first person personal pronouns is typically acquired. Children's initial self-labelling is likely to be 'baby' and by 21–24 months most can use their own names. Only by about 2½ years of age do children normally begin to use personal pronouns. By 3 years of age most children refer to pictures of themselves using their own names and the appropriate personal pronouns. Furthermore, if we include the possessive pronoun, the sequence of development is typically 'mine', followed by 'me', and finally by 'I'. If 'I' refers to the knowing subject as a potentially private phenomenon, 'me' to the known subject as a potentially public phenomenon, and 'mine' to acts of ownership, then the sequence of pronominal development suggests a progression from public social being to more private personal being, from being 'other' in the first instance to becoming a reflexive self capable of 'I–me' modes of relating. This also adds support to Dewey's comment, noted in the last chapter, that 'I own therefore I am' expresses a truer psychology than Descartes's *Cogito, ergo sum*.

The acquisition of 'I' is never by formal instruction, and the child is always addressed as 'you' or by its name. By the age of 3, most normal children can, however, understand the distinction between 'I' and 'you', 'my' and 'your', and can use them appropriately. The acquisition of 'I' involves more than merely acquiring the word: it is the ability to use 'I' appropriately that takes time to acquire. And in their ability to use these pronouns, children's competence in the use of first person pronouns ('I', 'me', 'my') appears earlier and is used more frequently than their ability in the use of second person pronouns ('you', 'your').[58]

Some writers confuse children's emerging abilities to take themselves as reference points, within the ever-shifting roles of the ongoing conversation of which their lives are a part, with the idea that the children are egocentric or imprisoned by their own points of view. Cox argues against such an equation, as does Tanz who insists that the child

> cannot have grasped this egocentric formula without having understood at some level that other speakers organise the system with themselves as centre. Thus any child who has mastered the shifter properties of 'I' and 'you' or 'me' and 'you' in ordinary conversation has achieved some degree of decentring.[59]

A further significant part of early language development is the growing extent to which the child's words and sentences become detached from the situations to which they refer. As de Villiers and de Villiers put it, 'it is as if the child now carries the context of language around with him.'[60] In time, language itself becomes available as an object of reflection for children and they develop a meta-linguistic awareness. Whereas most 4 or 5 year olds will confuse the word with the thing it names, it is not until around 8 years of age that most children can liberate a word from its referent.[61]

Whatever the difficulties of detaching nouns from their referents, it is a far more difficult task to do the same for context-dependent words like pronouns. Nonetheless, from a relatively early age children become highly proficient in the use of personal pronouns. The use of these acquired ways of organizing experience, action and interaction provides the child with a new mode of being centred, that of being self-centred, of having experience organized around 'I'. In addition to the already developing bodily modes of being centred which are the variety of perceptual and motoric points of view situated in physical space–time, and the social forms of centredness which have to do with learning one's own role in relation to those of others, new psychological modes of being centred emerge. These are symbolic points of view which have to do with I as a construct within the emerging theoretical edifice which is self, and which can be used self-reflexively to situate the child in the semantic spaces of social and personal being.

One of the functions of I in William James's account is to assign and integrate all that is relevant in the preceding thoughts to the me or empirical ego. This functional centre of each present thought, the I, thus has some powers of self-creation in so far as it can augment or diminish the me by acts of claiming as its own and by acts of disowning. Once this organizing construct of I is acquired, with its powers of selectively appropriating and unifying experience, the perceptual and motoric points of view and action are also subordinated to its ownership. Acts of seeing, hearing, touching and so on come to be understood and appropriated as *my* acts. Distinctions can now be made between voluntary and involuntary acts, those that I intended and those that I did not. And even when acts are understood to be involuntary, like sneezing, they may still be appropriated to the self by understanding that their source and point of origin is me even though I did not intend to sneeze.

The development of I marks the emergence of that 'privileged center of reference within the field of givenness' which for James is the self. This self is not an entity, but a symbolic structure or theory which develops within and because of social relations, and which serves to unify experience by enabling it to be organized around a more or less integrated set of centres. Part of this acquired symbolic structure or theory involves the acquisition of personal pronouns. They form a core part of the developed theory that is self in our culture. As theoretical constructs, 'I', 'you' and their like help to constitute symbolic points of view. They also unify these with the other types of point of view; and they unify points of view with points of action. Bodily, social and psychological modes of being centred in experience are, in short, complexly interrelated.

Once these constructs become working parts of a developing personal psychology, self rapidly develops. Because these are the sorts of constructs which, if properly deployed, can take one's own concept of self as an object for reflective attention, and thus give rise to what is called 'self-consciousness', it is then possible for beliefs, evaluations and all sorts of attitudes to be developed about one's self. It is at this stage that the development of self as an essentially historical and cultural construct becomes paramount. This is the idea of self whose structure and sources Charles Taylor has explored. It is the idea of self as constituted by knowing where I stand in relation to some ideal of the good. As Taylor puts it:

> To know who I am is a species of knowing where I stand. My identity is defined by the commitments and identifications which provide the frame or horizon within which I can try to determine from case to case what is good, or valuable, or what ought to be done, or what I endorse or oppose. In other words, it is the horizon within which I am capable of taking a stand.[62]

This further field of self-development is not of immediate relevance to the present stage of analyzing aesthetic absorption except in so far as it might suggest that our interests, and hence our likely liability to become absorbed, will have to do with the particular frameworks of value within which we come to live and according to which we come to be shaped as moral selves. My main concern, however, has been to outline schematically the development of those elements of self that have to do with its characteristic centredness, and only tangentially have I needed to relate these to those other aspects of self that have to do with agency and autobiography.

As it happens, the achievement of the first three years of life is the capacity for that third aspect of personal psychological individuality which is the continuous construction of one's own story or autobiography or narrative self. Psychology and philosophy are coming to recognize this. Jerome Bruner's advocacy of a cultural psychology, for example, happily anchors itself in issues of language, narrativity, autobiography and self.[63] Bruner argues that there is an 'innate' or 'primitive disposition' to organize experience narratively, but that the child's culture soon supplies new powers of narration through the traditions of telling and interpreting in which the child participates.[64]

Autobiographical narrative has an 'I' as its organizing centre, and the telling of one's own story is always from a particular point of view. Change the point of view and the telling changes, and with it what is told, namely the story that is one's self. Now what I took to be true of myself is no longer true. My story has changed because I have changed. And when I change, so also do my points of action or powers of acting. What changes points of view? James might answer that a change in present thought changes the I housed by that thought. But for more extended periods of time, significant events in our lives shift the context of our understanding and with that change of context comes a change in point of view. This is part of what it means to say 'I have changed'.

I is always contextualized; it is always part of a fabric of thoughts, feelings, wishes, intentions, actions and so on. The experience that is I is pervasively conditioned by the nature of the present thoughts of which it is a part. Intentionality and subjectivity are, as we have seen, intimately connected. Such intentional contexts condition how I feel or think at any point in time. More specifically, the contexts that are the home of I can shape and greatly influence the point of view which is I. It follows that if the contexts in which any personal I is experienced are altered, and perhaps especially if they are altered for a prolonged period of time, so that the pattern of appropriations to self that the I executes is also altered, then this might be a condition for more lasting self-change.

In his theorizing about self, Daniel Dennett has also placed the relationship of self and narrativity at centre stage. Selves, he argues, are the product of narrative. Like Bruner, he sees this urge to tell stories as biologically given in humans in a way analogous to web-spinning in spiders.[65] 'Like spider webs', says Dennett, 'our tales are spun *by* us; our human consciousness, and our narrative selfhood, is their product, not their source.'[66] He goes on to say that such streams of narrative issue as if from a single source, and that this encourages their audience to posit what he calls a 'centre of narrative gravity'.[67]

I mention this work to emphasize the ubiquity of the construct of a 'centre' in discussions of self, whether it be at the simpler level of basic structures of self or at more complex levels of narrativity and self-creation. Against these background ideas of self, and the notion of point of view as dynamic centre, I now want to elaborate the concept of recentring. I want to suggest the idea that aesthetic experiences of art objects might alter the contexts of I, perhaps by inviting I and other points of view to occupy temporarily points which are new for them and which may consequently change their view, so to speak, with what consequences this may have for one's sense of agency and autobiography as well as for one's subsequent sense of being centred.

This idea of recentring is not current in psychology or philosophy. The problem it applies to, however, has received a lot of attention. In essence, this is the question of the possibility of one person having the experiences of another, or more specifically, of one person occupying or sharing the same perspective as another. Developmental psychology has something to say about the ways in which young children develop the ability to consider the world as open to being viewed from many perspectives, only some of which may be habitual for them, and about how children come to be capable of adopting perspectives other than their own. A brief and critical review of this work will help reveal the descriptive gap which the concept of recentring may be able to fill. This in turn will help me to describe some of the ways in which aesthetic absorption can be understood as involving processes of recentring.

EGOCENTRISM, DECENTRING AND RECENTRING AS
PSYCHOLOGICAL IDEAS

Piaget considered the young child to be fundamentally egocentric. For the newborn infant, in his view, there are no objects and there is no space that contains objects.[68] There is just a series of different spaces all of which are centred on the body. From a classical Freudian perspective the mouth is the part of the body which, as a centre of experience, is especially significant at this age. But the body can also centre itself in visual, auditory, kinaesthetic and tactile spaces. Piaget would call these 'egocentric spaces'. They are not coordinated with each other, nor is the infant's body included as an element in these spaces.[69] A more precise designation, given my previous reservations about assuming an 'I' at that early age, would have been something like 'corpocentric spaces'. After about 18 months, in Piaget's view, the normal child has developed a notion of general space which integrates the varieties of space (visual, tactile, etc.) and which now includes the body as an object amongst other objects in space. In this respect, Piaget speaks of 'a total decentration in relation to the original egocentric space'.[70]

This 'notion' of general space to which Piaget refers develops during the period when knowing is predominantly a matter of the coordination of sensory and motoric ways of interacting with the world. As such, one could describe this decentred notion of general space as a felt, pre-verbal sense of space. It includes a pre-verbal sense of 'being in space'. This reminds us of those feelings of which René Spitz speaks, feelings which tend to atrophy as objects of attention and use in Western sensibilities, except amongst those whose thinking is, as Dewey says, of the qualitative kind characteristic of artists.

I have no quarrel with Piaget's thinking on this aspect of development. The details of the progression to which he refers are now being spelt out by more refined studies. To offer just one example, we now know that it is during the fourth month of life that babies can, without help from the eyes, locate sounds in the dark with the same precision as adults.[71] But it is not until children learn to creep and crawl that they develop the ability to understand the spatial layout of their environment and to refer directions to points of origin other than themselves. No longer, for instance, does the world turn left as they turn left.[72] This, as I suggest above, is a key development in certain prerequisite capacities for selfhood, such as the capacity to be an organizing centre of experience but also the capacity to refer the positions of objects to some point of origin other than one's own position in space. But this is only one of the abilities needed for sharing and occupying perspectives other than one's own points of view.

To be an infant, as cultural psychologists continually emphasize, is to be part of a social system. Babies engage in 'dialogues' with their mothers. From an early age they show evidence of an ability to share visual experience in much the same way that adults can be cued to participate in sharing another's viewpoint or, more precisely, to share a common object of attention. Babies can follow the direction of another person's gaze, and they can follow the line of a pointing gesture to its selected object. In this way they can share another person's object of attention. Furthermore, babies can share their own object of attention with another person by themselves gazing or pointing at that object. They can also deprive another person of a particular visual experience by acts of hiding. And they can act to attract the attention of another person and to refer that attention to objects of interest by vocalizing and showing.[73]

Thus, the development of a notion of general space in which one's own body is situated, the development of the ability to refer other objects in that space to points of origin (for the purposes of fixing location) other than one's own body, the ability to understand and use such basic gestures of indication as gaze and pointing, and the coordination of acts of attention are prerequisites for sharing perspectives and for occupying points of view (albeit perceptual ones in the case of very young children) other than one's own. As early as the end of the first year of life, the normal infant shows considerable mastery of these requirements. Scaife and Bruner's judgement is this: 'In so far as mutual orientation implies a degree of knowledge in some form about another's perspective then the child in its first year may be considered as less than completely egocentric.'[74]

This brief review shows that two concepts are repeatedly used in developmental psychological discussions of perspective sharing: they are egocentrism and decentring. In essence, 'egocentrism' means that all objects are indexed exclusively in relation to one's self or body or position or role, whereas 'decentring' is used to refer to an act by which a reliance on one's own current point of view is relinquished and some point of reference other than one's self or body or position or role is chosen. What one does not encounter in this developmental psychological literature is the concept of recentring, by which I mean the process whereby points of view other than one's own are subsequently occupied.

To say that it is by an act of 'decentration' that an act of 'recentration' takes place would not be enough. It is easy enough to envisage what happens when the point to be occupied is a point in physical space and the view is a perceptible one. The difficulties would arise when the point to be occupied is part of a symbolically constituted or imaginative space. Once the child begins to represent the world symbolically and to construct a 'semantic space' (a symbolic space occupied, amongst many other things, by the idea or theory which is 'him- or herself'), the problem of describing emerging and novel types of perspective, and of how they may be shared or occupied, enters a new order of difficulty.

How these emergent semantic spaces might relate to the previously developed notion of general space is an unanswered question, and beyond my scope here. Intuitively, however, we can have a real sense of being in a realm of meaning which, when examined, is abstract and symbolic. We can speak meaningfully of entering into the world of a painting or of a book, or of being trapped inside a way of thinking. On the assumption that there are parallels between the sense of being located in a general physical space and of subsequently being located in semantic space, we could try and draw out some of the analogical correspondences between physical and symbolic spaces, particularly those symbolic spaces which are our ideas of ourselves, of other people and of other things.

The subjectivity of both types of space, for example, includes a sense of being 'located' within them, and of being a significant point of reference for other objects occupying the same spaces. In the case of general physical space, that sense can reside in the infant as a perceiving, feeling, moving body. But in the case of the newly emergent semantic spaces that follow on from the mastery of symbolization, in what would such a sense of location inhere? One ready answer is that it is the child's self that serves as a central point of reference and, in a related way, the child's role as a child within his/her social world. If we understand self to be as already outlined, then this sense of being located in a semantic space has to do with the *abstractum* or theory we are taking self to be. At the heart of this theory which is self is the idea of 'myself as subject of my experience'. If to be a self is to be, in part, a functional centre of experience, what then is the nature of this active centre?

Two elements of the answer to this question have already been introduced. The first is the process whereby infants are positioned in their social milieu as named persons, a process which is foundational for the progress of subsequent self-development. This is a social, role related process. The second is the process whereby the acquisition of the ability to use correctly indexicals like pronouns serves to elaborate children's ability to locate themselves in both physical and semantic spaces, to become capable of self-reflection with the consequences this has for the construction of personal narratives, and to inaugurate a whole new set of possibilities for sharing and occupying perspectives that do not depend upon the constraints of real space–time. Now, in addition to being centred in real space–time as a perceiving, feeling body, the child becomes centred in the symbolic space–time which is the stuff of a developed psychological life.

But those newly developed selves – which include children as they are for themselves – somehow acquire the powers of, temporarily, not being centred upon themselves, but of merging with and of being centred in another. Alternatively, it could also be, in line with Peirce's thinking about the fundamentally semiotic nature of self, that what children acquire is the power to exercise an already existing capacity. Of course this merging is not true in a physical sense, but it can be true in a psychological sense. Even though they are for much of the time functionally centred in their bodies and functionally act and view the world as 'I', children also become capable of decentring and of understanding the feeling of the world as it is for a 'you' or a 'she' or an 'it'.

For much of the time, such acts of decentring and recentring are acts of thought. They are, that is, analogies and deductions, often based upon similar personal experience of what must be subjectively the case for another person or thing, given that certain things have happened or are happening to them. Notions of empathy or *Einfühlung*, which are understood as involving a sense of our own feelings but *in* the object, would seem to involve some act of recentring as I am using the term here.[75] But empathy and sympathy are two states or dispositions that are frequently confused in the psychological literature and in the next chapter I will return to the idea of sympathy as it features in aesthetic theory. For the present, I want to stress the inadequacy of the idea of decentring as an account of the ability to occupy another point of view.

The ability to decentre is a necessary but not a sufficient condition for the achievement of the fullest form of occupancy of other perspectives. Decentring, somewhat like the non-deployment of I, is a negative description of what may be happening. But what does happen when self, whether it is understood as physical location or as role or as a centring I, is not the dynamic or functional or controlling centre of a flow of experience? My suggestion, as will now be clear, is for the additional process of recentring to answer this question.

One particular form of recentring, for example, involves what Richard Wollheim calls 'central imagining' by which he means imagining an event from 'inside' a particular protagonist who need not be oneself.[76] This is another formulation of the idea of 'identification', and I will examine it in the next chapter where I will use the idea of recentring to describe how the arts as experiences can be especially directed to enable radical recentrings of viewpoints, within fields of experience re-created by readers or spectators. I especially want to explore the proposition that the phase of aesthetic absorption can involve the relinquishing of personal senses of being centred, and can enable intense, if shortlived, recentrings in ways that have been intended and incorporated by artists in their work.

The foundation for the mobility with which selves can occupy, or perhaps come to appropriate as their own, the perspectives of others is the very sociality that enables the emergence of selves as centres of psychological life in the first place. Succinctly, one might say that subjectivity is rooted in intersubjectivity or, to amend Sartre's existentialist dictum, that coexistence precedes essence. The more similar the forces that constitute selves, the easier those selves tend to find communication since, as we find, so much can be taken for granted. Pre-eminent amongst cultural achievements, the arts build upon and elaborate these possibilities.

If self is a sign or interpretation as Peirce suggests, or if it is in Harré's terms a theory or in Dennett's an *abstractum*, then my description of its development shows the social bases of its fabrication. Like other signs, it continually points to what is not itself and finds its meaning in its relations with what is other than itself. These relations sustain and develop self. In a uniquely distinctive way, art as experience can 'expand' the sense of self, and one of the ways in which it has been traditionally understood to do this is by somehow enabling its recipients to have or to benefit from the represented or depicted experiences of others, real or fictional. This is the question to which I now want to turn, and in considering specific examples of the ways in which particular art forms incorporate points of view, I will put the concept of recentring to work as part of a description of how selves as centres can transact with centring objects, and of how they may in the process be changed.

NOTES

1. Samuel Beckett, 'The unnamable', in *The Beckett Trilogy* (London: Picador, 1979), pp. 381–2.
2. Arnheim, 1966, p. 318.
3. Ibid., p. 318.
4. My view on the need for a developmental approach to understanding these aspects of aesthetic experience is similar to that of Harré when he discusses the relations of language and social reality. Harré writes: 'A developmental approach thus opposes the prevailing structuralist and transformationalist practice of making the synchronic study of states methodologically prior to that of development. In fact it is argued,

purely synchronic analyses are likely to be explanatorily inadequate.'
For this see Mühlhäusler and Harré, 1990, p. 13.
5. For a discussion of Peirce on this see Michaels, 1980.
6. Quoted by Michaels, ibid., p. 193.
7. Ibid., p. 199.
8. I am largely indebted for what follows to Colapietro, 1989.
9. See Eco, 1977, pp. 14–16, and *passim*.
10. Ibid., p. 15.
11. See Colapietro, 1989, p. 14.
12. Ibid., p. 57.
13. Ibid., p. 58.
14. Ibid., p. 110.
15. Ibid.; emphasis in original.
16. Ibid., pp. 88 and 112.
17. Ibid., p. 92; emphasis in original
18. Ibid., pp. 112–18 and 43.
19. Ibid., p. 120.
20. Ibid., p. 16.
21. Ibid., p. 104.
22. Ibid., p. 74.
23. Ibid., pp. 76–7.
24. Ibid., p. 77.
25. See Harré, 1983, p. 8.
26. Colapietro, 1989, p. 103; emphasis in original.
27. Ibid., pp. 96–7.
28. James, 1912, pp. 169–70.
29. For an instance of Harré's explicit use of Peirce see Harré, 1991, Chapter 11, entitled 'Corporeal semantics'.
30. Harré, 1983, p. 256. Mead, of course, was strongly influenced by Peirce and especially by Dewey. Harré's theoretical account of the development and nature of self is widely indebted to such writers as Strawson, Wittgenstein, Mead and Vygotsky and to such disciplines as anthropology, social psychology, cognitive psychology and the philosophy of science. The transactional nature of his theory of individual psychology or 'personal being' harmonizes with pragmatic philosophical ideas of experience. For a Marxian-type review of some of these issues see Burkitt, 1991.
31. See, for example, Bandura, 1985 and Rogers, 1951.
32. Harré, 1983, pp. 77–8.
33. Ibid., p. 78.
34. For an application of this idea see Dennett, 1988, pp. 1016, 1028 and 1029. Like the physicist's theoretical notion of a 'centre of gravity', Dennett pursues the idea that 'a self is also an abstract object, a theorist's fiction' (p. 1016). He concludes by echoing David Hume's inability to see or find a self:

> The fact that these abstract selves seem so robust and real is not surprising. They are much more complicated theoretical entities than a centre of gravity. And remember that even a centre of gravity has a

fairly robust presence once we start playing around with it. But no one has ever seen or ever will see a centre of gravity. (p. 1029)

35. Bruner, 1986, p. 64.
36. The Greek word *deixis* means 'pointing'. Within Harré's theory, deixis

> refers to the process or act by which reference is made to spatial, temporal, social or personal aspects of a situation. The use of the pronoun *she* to refer to a third person, or the selection of the pronoun *vous* in French polite discourse to signify formality of address or distance of social relationship with a second person are both deictic acts. Widely different dimensions of deixis are encoded in the languages of the world. However, on closer inspection these differences can be reduced to a number of basic deictic dimensions. For instance, there is distance from a reference point of *self as speaker*, the degree of power or control over another, while acceptance or rejection of responsibility of the speech act itself is yet another important dimension of deixis.

See Mühlhäusler and Harré, 1990, pp. 9–10; emphasis in original. For a discussion of the development of the use of deictic expressions in children see Cox, 1986, Chapter 5.

37. Harré, 1983, p. 92.
38. Ibid., p. 104.
39. Maurer and Maurer, 1990, p. 168.
40. Ibid., p. 182.
41. Ibid., pp. 184–5.
42. I say 'spaces' because the phenomenology of visual space, for instance, differs from that of auditory or of kinaesthetic space.
43. Maurer and Maurer, 1990, pp. 200–1.
44. For the purposes of his inquiry into the purely perceptual nature of centredness in pictorial and sculptural composition, for example, Rudolf Arnheim offers this glossary definition of 'self':

> A viewer's awareness of his location in space and the direction of his activity. Although outside the reach of the work of art, the position of the self determines the spatial aspect of three-dimensional works and is accommodated to by two-dimensional ones. The self acts as a center of forces in the field that comprises the viewer and the work of art.

For this, see Arnheim, 1982, p. 218.

45. Ibid., p. 202.
46. See Wittgenstein, 1958. There, Wittgenstein speaks of language games as 'Those games by means of which children learn their native language,' and also as 'consisting of language and the actions into which it is woven' (p. 5e). Wittgenstein has this to say on indexicals: '"I" is not the name of a person, nor "here" of a place, and "this" is not a name. But they are connected with names. Names are explained by means of them. It is also true that it is characteristic of Physics not to use these words' (p. 123e).
47. Maurer and Maurer, 1990, pp. 202–3.
48. Ibid., p. 189.
49. Ibid., p. 167.

50. For an informative introduction to the nature of sign language and deafness see Sachs, 1989.
51. The idea of 'psychological symbiosis' was developed by René Spitz in his *The First Year of Life* (1965) to which I referred in Chapter 3.
52. Harré, 1983, p. 105. Vygotsky's 'zone of proximal development' and Bruner's 'scaffolding' are similar sorts of idea.
53. Harré, 1983, p. 106.
54. Ibid., p. 108.
55. Mühlhäusler and Harré, 1990, p. 18.
56. See Mühlhäusler and Harré, 1990, p. 5. To my knowledge, this is the most comprehensive and detailed interdisciplinary investigation of the social and psychological significance of pronoun development.
57. Crystal, 1989, p. 22.
58. Cox, 1986, p. 74. On this Cox writes:

> What seems to be happening, then, is that a child first *understands* the pronouns used by others which refer to herself ('you', 'yourself', etc.); later she understands the pronouns used by others to refer to themselves ('I', 'me', etc). When the child comes to *use* pronouns herself, it is those which refer to herself ('I', 'me', 'my') which she uses first, and then later those which refer to others ('you', 'your', etc.); in the meantime, she uses proper names to refer to other people. (p. 74)

Cox explains this in terms of the ease of mastering terms that have a limited set of referents compared with those that have more. When the child is spoken to as 'you' she is the only referent whereas 'I' and 'me' refer to many speakers. When she comes to speak herself she is the only referent for 'I' and 'me' whereas she uses 'you' in relation to many others. For an interesting comment on the difficulties autistic children have with pronouns see Frith, 1989. There, Uta Frith writes: 'Thus pronoun use improves when reciprocal social interactions improve. This relationship suggests that autistic children's difficulties in pronoun use are not specific but have the same root as their other difficulties in social interaction. This root could well be a poor conceptualization of their own and others' mental states' (p. 136).
59. Tanz, 1980, p. 162.
60. De Villiers and de Villiers, 1979, p. 86.
61. Ibid., pp. 90–1.
62. See Charles Taylor, 1989, p. 27.
63. See Bruner, 1990.
64. Ibid., p. 80.
65. See Dennett, 1989.
66. Ibid., p. 169; emphasis in original.
67. See note 34 above for Dennett's use of the analogy of self and centre of gravity. For an extended treatment of these ideas see Dennett, 1991, especially Chapter 13.
68. See, for example, Piaget, 1974, Chapter 1.
69. Ibid., p. 15.
70. Ibid., p. 16.
71. Maurer and Maurer, 1990, p. 140.

72. Ibid., p. 232.
73. For a summary of this evidence see Cox, 1986, Chapter 1.
74. Scaife and Bruner, 1975, p. 266.
75. This is a central concept in the aesthetic writings of Theodor Lipps (1851–1914) and of Vernon Lee (1856–1935). See Lipps, 1965 and Lee, 1913. An influential application of Lipps's ideas has been Worringer, 1953.
76. For an extended discussion of this and other related ideas see Wollheim, 1984. For a further use of the idea as it plays a role in certain types of painting see Wollheim, 1987, Chapter 3.

CHAPTER 6

———— · ————

ART AND NOT BEING ONE'S SELF: AESTHETIC ABSORPTION AS RECENTRING

A picture lives by companionship, expanding and quickening in the eyes of the sensitive observer. It dies by the same token. It is therefore a risky and unfeeling act to send it out into the world.

(Mark Rothko, 1947)[1]

INTRODUCTION

'Who', asks Alexander Solzhenitsyn, 'would be able to bring home to a bigoted and obstinate human being the distant grief and joy of other people, the understanding of relationships and misconceptions that he himself has never experienced.'[2] Art and artists, is his emphatic answer. Why? Because art, he maintains, is the only thing that can take the place of experience we have not lived. He writes:

> Art and literature can perform the miracle of overcoming man's characteristic weakness of learning only by his own experience, so that the experience of others passes him by. Art extends each man's short time on earth by carrying from man to man the whole complexity of other men's life-long experience, with all its burdens, colour and flavour. Art re-creates in the flesh all experience lived by other men, so that each man can make this his own.[3]

Solzhenitsyn's optimistic assessment of the moral powers of art rests on the assertion that one person's experience can somehow be appropriated by another 'as his own' and 'in the flesh', and that this happens through the agency of art. But how might this happen?

Self is constructed and sustained by interactions with what is other than itself, and the processes of self, as I have outlined them, arise from the conversation of social relationships. It follows that any significant reconstruction of those relationships would entail some corresponding reconstruction of self. Solzhenitsyn's view is that art as vicarious experience is a potent instrument for self-change. I want to ask whether a self *recentred* in a work of art is a changed self, whether for that moment alone or lastingly. Is this process illuminated by describing it in terms of recentring? Does it differ, for example, as between visual art and literature?

The phenomenology of recentring and of aesthetic absorption will differ across different artistic media and forms. Narrative fiction works differently from pictures, as I will show. But important differences, both large and subtle, will also be evident in music, dance, film, poetry, architecture and other art forms. For reasons of scale, however, I can only alert the reader to these possibilities for further exploration. My own examples of how recentring can be facilitated come from pictorial art and literature.

The experience foregrounded in this chapter has to do with a depicted or represented perspective becoming the perspective of a viewer or reader. I want to describe it in terms of the self being recentred. This is an old problem for aesthetics. Among the variety of processes that have been used to describe the transactions of selves and art objects are those of contemplation (Kant), aesthetic empathy (Lipps and Lee), psychic distance (Bullough), aesthetic sympathy (Lind[4]), interpretation and understanding (Goodman), as well as the more psychoanalytic ideas of projection, introjection and identification. Given my focus on aesthetic absorption (understood as a phase of experience in which the reader's/viewer's 'I' is not deployed to function as it normally does, but instead is either not deployed at all, or if it is, is deployed in a recentred form as the 'I' of another), projection, identification and sympathy are processes to which I will pay particular attention.

In the rich untidiness of lived experience, the possibilities for variability in the substance of aesthetic experience are endless. But if there is a possibility for self-change as a consequence of aesthetic experiences of art, then this change is wrought, I suspect, to a considerable degree in and through the transactions of the brief, intense, 'self-forgetful' moments of being absorbed 'in the world' of an other. These transactions have to do with an intrinsic flexibility and mobility of self. The understanding of the self as sign, coupled with the idea that the self as linguistically composed is founded on the perceptual powers of the body, as Merleau-Ponty convincingly reminds us,[5] opens up ways of replacing analyses that cast the problem in terms of an autonomous subject trying to reach over to an autonomous object. A language of emergence and transformation needs, as I have argued, to replace a language of merging and transition.

READING AND THE EXPERIENCE OF INTERIORITY

> All night I sat reading a book,
> Sat reading as if in a book
> of sombre pages.[6]

Is the reader 'in' the book, or has the reader, as in Wallace Stevens's earlier quoted poem, 'become' the book? Or perhaps the book is 'in' the reader having started by being 'out there'? How is this aspect of the experience of reading to be described? John Berger asks us to remember what it was like as a child to be told a story.

> Were not the excitement and assurance of that experience precisely the result of the mystery of such a fusion? You were listening. You were in the story. You were in the words of the story-teller. You were no longer your single self; you were, thanks to the story, *everyone it concerned.*
>
> The essence of that childhood experience remains in the power and appeal of any story which has authority. A story is not simply an exercise in empathy. Nor is it merely a meeting place for the protagonists, the listener and the teller. A story being told is a unique process which fuses these three categories into one. And ultimately what fuses them, within the process, are the discontinuities, the silent connections, agreed upon in common.[7]

Granting that story-telling and listening work to the degree that there is an unspoken consensus on the terms of the transaction, what is this experience of ceasing to be your single self and becoming whom the story concerns?

Georges Poulet describes the experience well as it occurs during reading. He speaks of it in terms of 'interiority'.[8] The interesting questions posed by aesthetic absorption have to do with the dynamics of breaking down initially given divisions. This is the starting point for Poulet's description of the experience of 'interiority' during reading. 'In short', he writes, 'the extraordinary fact in the case of a book is the falling away of the barriers between you and it. You are inside it; it is inside you; there is no longer either inside or outside.'[9] Like Wallace Stevens's reader, you become the book. So what is happening while this division of self and other is falling away? In the case of reading, Poulet speaks of being aware of the book as 'a consciousness' that invites him to think what it thinks and to feel what it feels. The book as object disappears, and becomes a series of words and images and ideas that now exist in 'my innermost self'.[10]

This notion of an innermost self is a problematic one, but not perhaps as problematic as might seem at first since, as Poulet puts it, it is the significations that make themselves at home in his mind. The constructive activity of the object is acknowledged. The book as meaning becomes dependent upon the reader's consciousness. But now '"I" become the prey of language.'[11] The distance between the reader and the read diminishes, allowing Poulet to speak of 'subjectified objects'. He identifies the greatest advantage of literature as being that 'I am persuaded by it that I am free from my usual sense of incompatibility between my consciousness and its objects.'[12]

How is this union of self as reader with what is read to be described? What does it mean to say that in the process of reading I can think the thoughts of another person, whether fictional or actual? In offering answers to questions like these, Poulet seems to be giving examples of what is involved when selves (understood as personal centres) encounter objects that have themselves been organized around centres of their own kind. His focus is on the 'I' and on what happens when the book as physical object 'disappears', and the intimate relationship of mental objects with the reader's consciousness begins. As a reader, the thoughts I have as I read are the thoughts of another. But it is I who am now their subject. It is not so much that I am thinking them as the thoughts of the other; instead, as I think them they are mine. Remembering William James's conception of 'I' as part of the present thought, one might also add that I am theirs. 'My consciousness behaves', says Poulet, 'as though it were the consciousness of another.'[13]

In this sense, thoughts and ideas are mobile and in a similar way to that in which I believe Peirce would have understood the mobility of self as sign. Thoughts are 'mine' in this sense for as long as 'I' think them, for as long that is as I am their subject and they are my present thoughts. My initial description of aesthetic absorption, however, hinges on the idea that absorption of this type is favoured by the non-deployment of I. How can this be reconciled with Poulet's account of being absorbed while reading, an account involving my thinking and feeling as another thinks and feels? Poulet's answer is that the reader's I is in a sense displaced by that of the other. It is another's I that is deployed during the act of reading. The thoughts of the reading self have as their subject what we might call for shorthand purposes the 'read self'. With the thought comes a subject other than that of the reader. Poulet says that 'as soon as something is presented as thought, there has to be a thinking subject with whom, at least for the time being, I identify, forgetting myself, alienated from myself.'[14] To put this in terms of the descriptive language I have used so far, the act of reading involves a shift from one centre around which present experience is organized (i.e. the reader's I) to another centre around which the now present experience is organized (i.e. the read I). This shift during the act of reading, and by extension during the act of looking at a picture or listening to music, is an example of what I want the idea of recentring to mean. In more abstract terms, my subjectivity alters with the alteration of intentionality; with the change in my thinking as I read there comes a change in what it is like for me as I read.

Such recentring in the act of reading does not, according to Poulet, interrupt my activity as a subject. What happens is that 'I am on loan to another, and this other thinks, feels, suffers and acts within me.'[15] Wollheim's idea of central imagining, which I will discuss below, is another way of describing this. There is a sense in which this other I is the I of the book's author, but this is not a sense favoured by Poulet. For him, the other I can only exist in the work itself. What matters is to live, for the time of reading, inside the work that is 'inside' me. A work of literature 'is a mind conscious of itself and constituting itself in me as the subject of its own objects'.[16]

This way of putting it seems capable of reinterpretation in terms of Peirce's idea of the self as a sign continuous with other signs. If we take the I of the text as a sign and its object as a narrator or character, say, then the interpretant of that sign could be the nature of the reader's identification with that protagonist. In this process, the reader's I is brought into the same relationship with the protagonist's I as the I of the text bears to that character. For as long, perhaps, as this relationship obtains between these elements of the semiotic process what happens to the protagonist can have parallel subjective consequences for the reader.

This does not, of course, involve a loss of consciousness on the part of the reader. What Poulet means is that the 'reading I' shares the use of its consciousness with the subject lying at the heart of the work, but with the latter being the most active during that act of reading. Precisely who or what this presiding subject of the work might be is left obscure and unformulated by Poulet. In the end he speaks of it as being a mental activity which is engaged in objective forms but which, at another level, transcends them, 'a subjectivity without objectivity'.[17]

The experience described needs a psychological elaboration. Its complexity is such, however, that one is more likely to find philosophers trying to disentangle the conceptual undergrowth so that a better path might become available for psychologists interested in exploring the questions raised by the experience. Dewey does have something to say about it, and so too does Richard Wollheim. In fact, what each has to say is unexpectedly similar to the other and for this reason they are worth comparing at this point. This comparison concerns the processes by which selves and books or pictures, for example, relate during aesthetic experiences.

Should these relations be understood as meetings, thus implying continuing separation, or should they be conceived as fusions, with the implications this would have? Assumptions of dualism would underpin the former description whereas a philosophy of continuity, such as Dewey's, would favour the latter. Some central psychological concepts relevant to this question are those of projection and expressive perception. What follows has more immediate relevance, I think, to looking at pictures than to acts of reading, although these are of course complexly related.

PROJECTION, EXPRESSIVE PERCEPTION AND SEEING

In line with pragmatism as a philosophy of continuity (James's 'stream', for example, and Peirce's 'synechism') Dewey's aesthetics emerge from his ideas on the continuity or stream of experience. His philosophy of experience tries to take due account of levels of interaction (biological, psychological, social and cultural) and, in the case of the arts, of the interrelations of artists, objects and their publics. Since the first edition of *Art as Experience* in 1934, trends in the theory of criticism have moved from a focus on the artist (in part a Romantic legacy), through a focus on the text or 'object' (the new criticism, formalism and structuralism), to a variety of concentrations on the reader/spectator (phenomenology, reader-response criticism, psychoanalysis, and some versions of the poststructuralist position).

Dewey's theory of experience as interaction strains to unite the artist, the art product and the aesthetic public whose active re-creation is the work of art as experience. Wollheim's recent attempts to 'repsychologize' the theory of art are similar in intention.[18] Paintings are Wollheim's great love and he insists that they be understood within a theory of action. He opposes any attempt to assimilate pictorial meaning to linguistic meaning, a project he identifies with hermeneutics, semiotics and structuralism. He offers instead a psychological account in which pictorial meaning is located in the mental state (understood in a general sense as 'intention') of artists, the way in which this causes them to paint, and the experience that an informed and sensitive spectator can be expected to have on looking at the picture.[19] This mirrors Dewey's position when he insists that a work of art is complete only when it works in the experience of people other than the work's creator. This could of course include the creators, but only if they now occupy the role of spectator in relation to their own work. As for Wollheim, the 'triadic relation' of artist, object and receiver lies at the heart of Dewey's theory of artistic meaning.[20]

Dewey would also have had problems with the idea, most lucidly argued by Nelson Goodman,[21] that each of the arts is radically conventional and that each, albeit distinctively, requires decoding on the part of the spectator or 'reader' of the artistic language in question. Dewey felt that:

> there are other meanings that present themselves directly as posses-sions of objects which are experienced. Here, there is no need for a code or convention of interpretation; the meaning is as inherent in immediate experience as is that of a flower garden.[22]

He goes on to say that whereas art may not have meaning similar to that of flags used as semaphore, it does have meaning of the sort possessed by flags decorating the deck of a ship for a dance. If the languages of science state meanings that lead to experience then, in Dewey's view, those of art 'express' or 'constitute' or 'immediately realize' meaning and intent. 'The expressiveness, the esthetic meaning, is the picture itself.'[23] The relationship of spectator and painting, in this view, requires more than the sort of understanding involved in the deciphering of codes. Such understanding may indeed be an important part of it, but a more direct, intimate and participatory type of perceiving may also be involved. Let me first present what Wollheim has to say on this, and then let Dewey comment.

Wollheim argues that the visual artist works with a clear reliance upon a spectator who possesses and is able to use three perceptual capacities he calls 'seeing-in', 'expressive perception' and 'visual delight'. These parallel the powers of the painter to represent external objects, to express mental phenomena, and to induce a special kind of pleasure.[24] 'Expressive perception' is, Wollheim argues, a genuine type of seeing that in turn grounds a distinctive kind of pictorial meaning. Here again, Wollheim's analysis echoes Dewey. Expressive perception, according to Wollheim, is the capacity we have for seeing a painting as expressing, say, melancholy or serenity or many more subtle varieties of feeling that are inexpressible in words. He also asserts that what is expressed is invariably a psychological phenomenon.[25]

Expressive perception, while finding its best elaboration and refinement in art, is rooted in an already existing part of our psychology. What Wollheim has in mind is the process of projection, for which he is indebted to psychoanalysis. He reworks this concept of projection, however, in order to widen its scope. He compares expressive perception to two familiar kinds of experience. One is the type of experience in which our whole world seems to be coloured by a dominant feeling. We feel sad and depressed, for example, and everything we encounter also seems lacklustre and in agreement with our feelings, and is so because of how we are at that time. 'All looks yellow to the jaundiced eye,' as Alexander Pope succinctly put it. Wordsworth's unhappy 'night-wandering man' who, in 'The Nightingale', 'filled all things with himself / And made all gentle sounds tell back the tale / Of his own sorrow,' would be another example.

The second type of experience is where it is the world that seems to possess a feeling which then creeps over us. We feel good but find ourselves in a depressing milieu which, as we say, 'gets in on us' or 'gets us down'. In the first type of experience, the feeling flows from us to the world; in the second type, it flows from the world to us. Romantic poets seem especially adept in complex projection. Take Tennyson's 'Song', for example:

> My very heart faints and my whole soul grieves
> At the moist rich smell of the rotting leaves,
> And the breath
> Of the fading edges of the box beneath,
> And the year's last rose.[26]

Transience seems part of things in late autumn and causes the poet's heart to faint and his soul to grieve. These examples also remind us of the way in which a pervasive quality, according to Dewey, unites a situation and governs the relevance of its parts.[27]

Wollheim believes that expressive perception is prefigured in experiences of this second kind. It is not enough, however, that the feeling, once engendered by what is seen, is then 'associated' with the perception. Circuits rather than additions describe the relationship of feeling and perception here. 'The emotion must effect how we perceive what we perceive. Expressed emotion and perception fuse.'[28] But to understand how expressive perception works we need to know how it originates, and this is where the idea of projection comes in.

To explain how expressive perception involves certain forms of projection, Wollheim needs to be able to say how, in an experience, some aspect of what is seen invites or is responsible for that projection. In other words, he must say how the projection is a joint process of self and object, rather than merely a function of intrapsychic demands, which is how it is commonly understood in psychoanalysis.[29] To do this, Wollheim differentiates a simple from a complex form of projection.[30] In the simple form, people alleviate the anxiety caused by a feeling of sadness, for example, by projecting their sadness on to some other figure in their environment. They now believe it is this other figure who is sad and not themselves.

In cases of simple projection people end up with beliefs about the figure on to which they have projected their feelings; with complex projection, however, the consequence is what Wollheim calls 'a way of experiencing' the world. In this case, a person 'begins to experience the external world as of a piece with his sadness'.[31] Positive as well as negative emotions and feelings may thus be projected. But the essential difference between both forms of projection is that with simple projection what the projecting person now comes to believe of the other is the same as that which he/she started feeling and then projected; but with complex projection, the property the person now experiences the world as having is not the same as the feeling he/she started with. We could say that whereas simple projection tends, as it were, to repeat a feeling or emotion, albeit differently located, complex projection is more open to new forms of experiencing the world. The world as it were suggests how it is to be seen and experienced by virtue of those of its qualities that are available to be perceived.

Wollheim uses the phrase 'projective properties' to describe the properties the world is experienced as having as a result of complex projection and he argues that expressive perception is perception of projective properties. Taking Tennyson's 'Song' once again as an example, the 'heavy' stalks of the 'mouldering' flowers, and the fact that the hollyhock 'heavily hangs', are projective properties. The poem's protagonist may not have started with a fainting heart and a grieving soul, but the sight of all these heavily hanging flowers just prove too much for him and through the process of complex projection he ends up in this fashionably melancholic state.

In a Deweyan idiom, I might say that projective properties are properties of the world as experienced, which are the outcome of the joint construction of self and other and for which the image of 'fusion' is appropriate. But if this describes what happens in Wollheim's complex projection, how are we to understand the contribution of the object in the creation of novel projective properties and in the avoidance of the repetitiveness of simple projection? Emerging novelties of experiencing need to be explained if expressive perception is to be included in a description of how aesthetic experiences of art change selves. So how is the projected–upon world responsible for the projection? What do projective properties owe to the constructive powers of the world upon which projections are cast?

Wollheim tells us that there is no simple answer, and that trial and error and all sorts of influences forge the relevant correspondences.[32] He falls back on a psychoanalytic account of projection, influenced by Melanie Klein, in which 'expulsive phantasy dyes the world, and it is this dye that gives the world its new projective properties.'[33] Unfortunately for those who find Kleinian formulations obscure, this fallback by Wollheim to his psychoanalytic influences does not seem to advance our understanding of the role played by the object or world in possessing these projective properties.

Notwithstanding that Dewey might object to some of Wollheim's apparently dualistic phrasings, such as speaking of something perceived giving rise to 'an emotion in us',[34] the thread of Wollheim's thinking on these matters is notably parallel to Dewey's presentation of 'esthetic perception'. Dewey also insists on fusion rather than association in his discussion of 'esthetic perception' and of how a perceived object can possess a value of expressiveness. As with Wollheim's requirement that spectators be both sensitive and informed, that they possess a relevant 'cognitive stock' for looking at paintings, Dewey also sees the development of suitable responses as being necessary if 'esthetic perception' is to occur. The emotions that occur in acts of 'esthetic perception' need to be directed along paths that have in part been laid out by previous experience. But a balance needs to be struck if these patterns of response are not to override a perception of what is being expressed.

Another condition of 'esthetic perception', according to Dewey, concerns the 'meanings and values extracted from prior experiences and funded in such a way that they fuse with the qualities directly presented in the work of art.'[35] His objection to the idea that these meanings are 'associated' with the qualities of the work is that this maintains a kind of separation, as against the idea that there is a fusion of meanings and qualities into a single whole that is the emergent experience. The former aesthetic theory, in his view, is founded upon a psychology that insists on the persisting separation of the relevant perceptible qualities of the object and the meanings brought to it by the perceiving subject. This associationist psychology leads to two contrasting but false conceptions of aesthetic expressiveness, the one object-centred and the other subject-centred.

One conception attributes expressiveness directly to the perceptible qualities of the object; the other attributes it to the meanings and experiences brought to it by the person. Taking the popular example of straight and curved lines as exhibiting expressive differences that are intrinsic to themselves and that are immediately apparent to the eye, Dewey once again reminds us that lines are the boundaries of things and that eyes never function in isolation from other powers like hands.[36] Lines habitually carry with them the properties of objects. Lines, and other abstracted and thematized aspects of the world, owe their expressiveness, in Dewey's view, to their having 'become subconsciously charged with all the values that result from what they have done in our experience in our every contact with the world about us'.[37] This is Dewey's refutation of the object-centred theory of aesthetic expressiveness that follows on from an associationist psychology.

The second type, where expressiveness is considered to be a function of the perceiving subject, is exemplified by some of those theories that hinge on the idea of empathy. Dewey's objection to these theories, notably Vernon Lee's theory of empathy (and by extension to theories that would rely on Wollheim's simple projection) is their insistence that what happens in empathy happens 'solely in ourselves'.[38] Fusion, in his view, rather than association, addition or superimposition, is the necessary condition for aesthetic expressiveness: a fusion of what we bring and of what is brought to us in a process of cumulative continuity. 'Art would not amplify experience if it withdrew the self into the self nor would the experience that results from such retirement be expressive.'[39] The world a self experiences becomes a part of that self in so far as its meaning and value are retained. This is close to Wollheim's understanding of complex projection and expressive perception. Dewey does not doubt that aesthetic encounters change selves. But if Dewey objects to concepts of empathy as explanations of aesthetic expressiveness, he objects on similar grounds to certain concepts of projection.

Once again it is the implicit separation of self and object that bothers him. Dewey's starting point is the experience itself and he finds no separations in it. Separations and divisions are, in his view, post-reflective imports back into experience rather than given parts of experience. On these grounds, he objects to Santayana's definition of beauty as 'objectified pleasure' preferring instead some such formulation as 'pleasure in the object' where 'in' means that 'the object and pleasure are one and undivided in the experience.'[40] Of course, not every field of inquiry requires this union of self and other. Scientific method is purposively designed to diminish the confusion of self and other, to embody Nagel's 'view from

nowhere', and to avoid the sort of situation where what is claimed
to have been found is indeed a projection of what one desired to
find.[41] Instances of prejudice and preconception are also instances
of similar projection. Good thinking requires a detachment of self
and other. But to deploy this strategy of detachment in relation to
art or, more accurately, in seeking to experience art aesthetically, is
simultaneously to prohibit the possibility of aesthetic absorption
which, as I have argued, is at the heart of aesthetic experience.

Dewey would lift his objection to the notion of projection if it
recognized that experience is caused by the ways in which selves
and objects interact. He puts it like this: 'Projection in fact is a case
of transferred values, "transfer" being accomplished through the
organic participation of a being that has been made what it is and
caused to act as it does through organic modifications due to prior
experiences.'[42] This formulation of projection exemplifies a
number of Dewey's key ideas: the insistence on starting from pre-
reflective experience; the primacy of interaction – with the associated idea of participation – from which he mounts all his attacks on
subjectivism; and the idea that experience must be understood as
forming and unfolding over time in a cumulative, continuous and
constantly changing way. The parallels with the idea of complex
projection are compelling.

It is the demand for control of experience that differentiates the
union of self with an object from the detachment of self and an
object. Experience is produced by the interaction of self and other.
In aesthetic experiences, self is absorbed in the experience produced
by the interaction of self and art object. When there is a need to
control the development of experience, as in planning how to
extricate oneself from an unpleasant situation for example, then self
does tend to remain detached and to be, as it were, the possessor of
the experience rather than to be possessed by it.[43] But one must
inhibit this tendency to detachment and to self-controlled thought
if one is to become unified with the material of an art object in an
aesthetically absorbing experience.

Another way of describing what is involved in aesthetic absorption, as I described it earlier, is to say that aesthetic absorption can
only occur when selves relinquish or attenuate control over the
shaping of the experience. If control is not placed in abeyance, at
least for the duration necessary for absorption to occur, then the
type of intimate participation of self with the art object, which is

necessary for the production of aesthetic experience, cannot occur. Following on from the earlier argument, this type of control by self‾ is the kind where 'I', as the active subject/centre of experience, is not deployed.

As both Dewey and Wollheim insist, the qualities directly presented in the work of art, even if not consciously acknowledged by the perceiver, actively contribute to the 'fusion' of self and other that results. And even if we lack the confidence to endorse Wollheim's Kleinian account of the developmental origins of projection, both he and Dewey think of it as a process of participation and fusion rather than of association and imposition.[44] But more than that, this complex form of projection includes an openness to the emergence of novel experience rather than a reduction to existing patterns of experience. This is the understanding of projection that underlies aesthetic or expressive perception. What is perceived shapes the subjectivity of how it is perceived, and allows for novel expansions of perceiving.

Expressive perception, with its underpinning in complex projection, is an idea that helps to describe how both self and object contribute to the intricate experiences that develop from their transactions. But how can art objects, and in particular literary narratives and pictures, be structured so as to facilitate experiences in which the reader or spectator is recentred in a deliberately intended way? One obvious structural aspect of both literary narratives and of pictures would be the ways in which they themselves are centred. In what ways might this form part of the dynamic of recentring during aesthetic absorption?

CENTRES IN STORIES

What does it mean to share, or to participate, in another's perspective or point of view? There are a variety of ways in which I might be able to share the points of view of other people (actual or fictional) or, more specifically, to sense what it is like for them to organize their experience around the particular points of view or centres that they do. Physically, for example, sharing a perspective means having more or less the same view as another person because you are perceiving a scene from the same physical position and at the same time. This is the simplest sense in which one can share another's perspective – the perspective of 'witnesses' – and involves the body as a location or centre or origin of coordinates in space–time.

Taken psychologically, sharing another's point of view means apprehending some event or condition in a similar way to that in which it feels for, or means to, the other person; this involves adopting a similar set of interpretive strategies and a drawing of similar conclusions in relation to oneself. This meaning of 'sharing˙ a perspective' relates to the idea of subjectivity I used in the last chapter, and refers to a form of sharing that is subjectively similar for the sharer as for the shared.

Sharing a perspective can also be understood in terms of social centredness, especially as this relates to the organization and constitution of experience around social roles. So I can understand, with feeling, what it is like to be the sort of person who occupies the same sorts of role as I do. As a son/father/master/slave/wife/husband and so on, I can share the role-related points of view of sons, fathers, masters, etc. 'As a mother, I know what it must be like for her,' is a commonly heard claim when someone else's child suffers a misfortune. The 'must' in the statement tells us about the commonalities between similar types of role-centred experience. Finally, I can share a point of view morally or politically or ideologically, in so far as I share with someone else similar beliefs and values about what is desirable or undesirable.

These, of course, are not mutually exclusive and as they are more or less integrated in normal self-centred experience, so they are likely to be integrated in the participation of one self in the experiences of others. My sharings are not necessarily restricted to direct personal experiences of my own, nor to the experiences of 'real' people. If I have the ability, I can imagine, and be helped to imagine, what it is like to be a different type of organizing centre within fields of experience which are different from those of which I have direct personal knowledge or acquaintance. By having my context of experience changed, and my intentionality or thought-content determined for me (as described by Poulet), if only for relatively short durations during a process of reading or viewing, 'I' can be changed. A change of intentionality can result in a change of subjectivity. So what is it about the structure of literary narratives or of pictures that might facilitate changes in the selves of readers or viewers? In particular, how might they facilitate the sorts of recentrings of self that, I am arguing, characterize aesthetic absorption?

An obvious choice for the organizing centre of a literary text would be its narrator. Norman Friedman speaks of Henry James's obsession with the problem of finding a 'centre' or 'focus' for his stories, and of how James solved this problem by framing the action inside the consciousness of a character within the plot.[45] This avoids the need, predominant in nineteenth century literature, for an omniscient narrator situated outside the story. But this is only one solution to the problem of how to filter – or to centre – the action in a text.

Whatever point of view is chosen as the organizing centre or focus of the text, it will open up or diminish the range of information available to the reader, and it will determine how close or how distant the reader can personally become to the represented life of the text. This can easily be shown within the taxonomy of narrative points of view proposed by Norman Friedman. This taxonomy uses criteria such as degree of omniscience available to the narrator, and hence to the reader, and the degree to which the narrator is personally present in the narrative. Of any narrative one can ask whether the narrator has an unlimited, 'bird's-eye' point of view, and whether he or she regularly intrudes his or her views and opinions into the text. If so, then this is an instance of what Friedman calls 'editorial omniscience'. If the author speaks impersonally in the third person and does not intrude – a preferred method of Aldous Huxley where a superior tone dominates the consciousness of his characters – then this is an instance of 'neutral omniscience'.

If the text is to have the quality of suspense, then the solution to the problem of centring the text and of limiting knowledge of the outcome, is to have a narrator who speaks in the first person as a witness to the events. This is what Friedman terms ' "I" as witness'. Conrad's *Lord Jim* would be an example. If, as with Pip in *Great Expectations*, the problem is to trace some autobiographical development, then ' "I" as protagonist' may be the solution. But if the intention is to release the narrative from a single, personal point of view, then the solution may be 'multiple selective omniscience' where there is no narrator, and the story is filtered through the minds of many characters in the manner of a mosaic. Virginia Woolf's *To the Lighthouse* would be an example of this solution.

If, on the other hand, the reader is to have access to the mind of only one character as a fixed centre in the narrative, as with Stephen Dedalus in Joyce's *A Portrait of the Artist as a Young Man*, then 'selective omniscience' is Friedman's term for this solution. He argues that this allows the reader to 'catch a mind in a moment of discovery'.[46] When author, narrator and mental states are eliminated – as in Hemingway's *Hills Like White Elephants* – then we have the 'dramatic mode'. The reader is now limited to what the characters are represented as doing and saying, rather than thinking and feeling. The reader listens only to the characters, as in a play where 'his angle of view is that of the fixed front (third row center), and the distance must always be near (since the presentation is wholly scenic).'[47] Finally, if the aim is to convey a segment of life without apparent selection, and apparently without a selector, then the solution may be to adopt, as it were, the 'eye of the camera'.

This summarizes some of the technical ways in which the problem of centring a text may be solved, each of which has different consequences for the reader. Since Friedman offered his analysis of point of view in fiction, a further useful distinction has been made between narration and 'focalization' by Shlomith-Rimmon-Kenan.[48] A story may be mediated through some perspective or point of view that is verbalized by the narrator but that may not necessarily be his or hers. Borrowing from Gerard Genette,[49] Rimmon-Kenan calls this mediation 'focalization' to distinguish it from narration. Narrators may be, but need not be, focalizers. Narrators may speak of what they see, but they may also speak of what someone else sees. Discussions simply in terms of point of view, like Norman Friedman's, are prone to confusion here. Friedman, for example, speaks of the selective omniscience of Stephen Dedalus in *A Portrait*, where almost everything is seen through Stephen's eyes.[50] But Stephen Dedalus is both focalizer and narrator. In the beginning of the novel – 'Once upon a time and a very good time it was' – the language is not Stephen's nor is he the narrator. Examples like this lead Rimmon-Kenan to conclude that 'In so-called "third-person centre of consciousness" (. . . Joyce's *Portrait*), the centre of consciousness . . . is the focalizer, while the user of the third person is the narrator.'[51]

We can see from this survey of the technicalities of representing 'centres of consciousness' or points of view in narrative fictions, that there are many ways of refracting and anchoring fictional realities in texts. All this talk of 'centres' may not, of course, find favour with structuralists or poststructuralists. But my contention throughout has been that to be a self is to be, in part, variously but integrally centred, and sustained by one's relations and transactions with the world. This cannot be reconciled with a view of self as radically decentred, as a 'space' merely for the play of language. Early in its development self acquires powers, albeit curtailed powers, of self-making and unification, of stability and coherence.

The nature of the narrator or focalizer makes a difference to the experience of becoming other; to the process, that is, of recentring. But if, within literary narratives, the choice of type of centre makes a difference for the experiences of being recentred, so too do the qualitatively different sorts of choice that can be made within pictorial art.

CENTRES IN PICTURES

Are points of view in pictures analogous to their role in narrative fictions? Kendall Walton thinks not.[52] Walton asks whether there is anything comparable to narrators in depictive representations such as pictures, sculpture and the visual arts generally. At first sight, there does not seem to be a mediating personality when one looks at a picture. As Walton says, we 'see for ourselves' what is going on in the picture world. But perhaps it is the artist, or what Walton terms the 'apparent artist', who fulfils some of the functions of the narrator. Somewhat like people, many works of art visibly convey to the spectator the history of their making. Some, like a Jackson Pollock, give a sense of how they were physically constructed; others, like a George Grosz, convey the intention that guided the way they look; some suggest the personality of their maker, like a Bosch or a Munch. The impression conveyed by such works may not actually be true, and it is to cover this contingency that Walton speaks of the 'apparent artist'.

Much that has to do with the style of a work can be explained, according to Walton, in terms of the apparent artist: 'A work in a compulsive, or carefree, style is (very roughly) one which seems to have been produced in a compulsive, or carefree, manner.'[53] Here there is a parallel with narrators. Just as narrators are not often described in a novel, so the apparent artist is not depicted. But both are revealed by what they say or make. But how far does this analogy go? Do apparent artists mediate depicted fictional worlds for their spectators like focalizers do in narrative fictions? Walton argues, convincingly I believe, that they do not mediate in the same way since it is quite feasible for a spectator to investigate a pictorial fictional world without having to take into account its apparent creator. In a narrative fiction, however, this is not possible.

This is not to say that apparent artists do not indicate the perspective they have on the world depicted. Moral, political and other perspectives of apparent artists may well be evident in the picture. But, argues Walton, whereas the narrator belongs to the fictional world, the apparent artist does not. The consequence of this is that the narrator views the fictional world 'from the inside', and the apparent artist views it 'from the outside'.[54] The spectator of a picture has what is depicted immediately available to him or her, and he or she can decide on their implications for other fictional truths without having to take into account what they imply for the apparent artist. But the reader of narrative fiction cannot discount the mediating narrator in the same way.

Take Walton's example of a Brueghel painting in which Icarus is portrayed from the perspective of a person with normal vision who is looking from above. Who is it that sees Icarus from above in broad daylight? In narrative fiction, it would probably be a narrator–focalizer or a character–focalizer. But with pictures Walton argues that the only plausible candidate is the actual spectator (including, we should add, the artist in the role of spectator). He concludes that in depictions there is no counterpart to a mediating narrator:

> One does not have the sense of going through another person, of 'seeing the fictional world through someone else's eyes', as the reader of a narrative representation does. A depiction does present the fictional world from a particular perspective or point of view, but it is not the perspective or point of view of any specific (fictional) person (other than the spectator himself).[55]

Experiences of reading texts are different from experiences of looking at pictures. The ways in which pictures and narrative texts are organized with respect to being centred or focused or to incorporating points of view differ, amongst other things, in the ways in which they invite the engagement of their spectators and readers. The process of recentring that is part of the dynamic of aesthetic absorption will differ significantly as between reading and looking. This difference has to do with differences in the qualities of the media and with related differences of phenomenology. With Georges Poulet's analysis of the reading process, we gained some idea of what it might be to be recentred during certain acts of reading. There, we met the claim that the reader's 'I' is somehow fused with or taken over by the subject of the thoughts currently being read. Consequently, to be aesthetically absorbed in a book of narrative fiction is, in part, to be in the same state of thinking and feeling as that other 'centre of consciousness' in so far as that other centre becomes, for the duration, my centre. But this would depend upon the presence of some form of mediating focalizer. Since, however, that direct mediation by a focalizer is not a pictorial option, at least not in the manner of narative fiction, how are we to describe, in terms of being recentred, what it is to be aesthetically absorbed in works of visual art? And will the nature of recentring in experiences of visual art be distinctively different from experiences of literature?

I can best answer these questions by reviewing some of the ways in which perspectives mediate spectators' access to pictorial worlds. I have argued that to be a self is to be centred in a variety of integrated ways, as a perceiver and mover, as a thinker, speaker and imaginer. To be a subject of my thoughts is subjectively different from being a subject of my perceptions. Perceiving is tied to the here and now in a way that thinking is not. As Merleau-Ponty says, 'Perception does not give me truths like geometry but presences.'[56] Perception is indexed to my bodily position in a field of perceptible objects. All aesthetic experiences of art, including reading liter-ature, are experiences rooted in the present. However significant and moving it might be, remembering a painting seen is not the same as seeing the painting, even though memory is of course crucial to any meaningful act of perception. Looking at pictures is first and foremost a visual perceptual experience. So the first types of centring, and of possible recentring, I will consider are percep-tual centrings in real or depicted space.

The creation of pictorial space depends to a large degree on the artist's choice of perspectival system. As Arnheim points out, two radically different views enclose the range of all possible views for any picture with pictorial depth.[57] At one extreme is the view determined by the optical projection only. This would be completely flat with all objects lying in the same plane and with size controlled by distance. It would correspond to the description a flea-sized surveyor would make as it crawled across the surface of the picture. In this case the centre of the picture would more or less coincide with the centre of the framed surface. At the other extreme, the spectator would see the depicted world as having the same spatial properties as the lived-in physical world. It would be like looking at a scene through a window, and the centre of this scene would be halfway between the window plane and the visible horizon.

In actual experience neither extreme is realizable because of the effects of psychological constancy adjustments that compensate for changes of size and shape as the physical relationship of the perceiver and the perceived changes. In looking at both the 'real' spatial world and the pictorial spatial world, the degree of depth visible will lie somewhere between these extremes. Despite the supreme achievements of Renaissance perspective painting, the eye can effortlessly distinguish between spaces that, as Arnheim puts it, are 'walkable' and those that are not.

With reflection, one can note the contradiction in a space that is perceived as having depth but that is simultaneously known not to be physically real. But within the experience of looking – what Arnheim calls the phenomenological experience – there is no such contradiction. There are, however, qualitative differences between physical, 'walkable' spaces and pictorial spaces, and spectators can voluntarily shift from projection-based pictorial views to 'real' walkable ones. The context in which pictures are conventionally seen, in a frame hung flat against a flat wall, further emphasizes the contrast between the two-dimensional and three-dimensional spatial worlds. We need not concern ourselves here with the psychological and compositional technicalities of depth perception in pictures or in the lived world, other than to note that over the history of art many techniques for pictorial spatial projection have been devised that can have a variety of consequences for the engagement of the spectator.

A picture might have a number of centres other than the 'balancing center of the picture as a whole'.[58] Pictorial traditions differ in their expectations of what, to adapt a phrase from literary theory, the 'implied spectator' for the pictures should be. In the European tradition, pictorial perspective generally tends to have in mind a spectator who will stand more or less at horizontal eye-level. Parallel (one-point) perspective is the most commonly used perspectival system in Western art. With this system, all the receding lines appear to come to a point on the horizon that is the same as eye-level. Botticelli's *The Calumny of Apelles* is a classic example of this system.[59] By using a number of vanishing points, as in Paolo Veronese's *Marriage at Cana*, a powerful panoramic view can be achieved that seems to include the spectator. Systems of angular (two-point) perspective utilize right-angular planes, each of which has its own vanishing point at eye-level. Although not commonly used, a notable example would be Toulouse-Lautrec's *M. Boileau at the Café*.

The diagonal compositions of Japanese prints are a major influence here and the cutting off of the corners of the depicted scene, for example, has the effect of personally and immediately involving the spectator in the scene. Architects employ oblique (three-point) perspective to achieve the sense of an aerial view of the scene. Cézanne, on the other hand, uses perspective not to draw the viewer into the picture but to refer him on her back to the surface picture plane. And Cubism radically develops pictorial experiential possibilities by utilizing multiple viewpoints. These examples are given in order to illustrate how artists have devised many ways of creating pictorial spaces, of shaping the experience a spectator of those works will have, and of effecting the viewer's access to these pictorial worlds. And, of course, deformations of perspectival systems, as in German Expressionism, can yield all sorts of expressive possibilities for artists.

The point of view from which the spectator enters the fictional pictorial world is the spectator's own, unmediated by any equivalent of a literary narrator or character. But that entry is not uninfluenced. What viewers see, and the extent to which they are invited to become engaged with what is seen, has a lot to do with the viewpoints of others which may sometimes be a visible part of the depiction and sometimes not. During aesthetic experiences of pictures, and notably when aesthetically absorbed, the range of 'places' where the self as viewer can 'be' is as large as the possibilities of art itself. Furthermore, while aesthetically looking at a picture there may be a series of differently centred experiences – perceptual, imaginary, critical – each of which constitutes the subject differently and is differently organized.

The type of recentring I illustrated with Poulet's analysis of the reading process – where 'I' becomes the subject of another's thoughts with whatever subjective consequences this may have – does not seem appropriate for the visual arts. As I look at a picture I see a depicted scene, and, depending on the picture, I may see that it, or part of it, is what another person, depicted or perhaps undepicted, also sees. But I do not necessarily think the thoughts of that other person as I would if that other were a literary narrator or character whose thoughts I happened to be reading. This is not in any way to suggest that such experiences do not involve think-ing.[60] Everything I have said so far about the arts as demanding qualitative thinking should make that clear. But the visual arts are, before all else, *visual* arts. Any type of recentring that may occur during experiences of them must be inextricably linked to visi-bility. Richard Wollheim continually emphasizes this and, with his analysis of central imagining in relation to certain pictures, offers an example of recentring in the experience of pictures.

RECENTRING: CENTRAL IMAGINATION AND SYMPATHY

Wollheim makes much of the interplay between pictorial surface and what one may be able to see as standing in front of that surface, or perhaps behind it. This phenomenological feature of seeing is what he calls 'twofoldness'.[61] In looking at any pictorial surface, I can deliberately attend just to its surface qualities or, if the surface is appropriately differentiated, I can attend to that which I see 'in' the picture. The recent history of art has many artists, such as minimalists, making pictures of a sort that will restrict spectators to the two-dimensional surface so that their attention will be focused on what are often highly refined, pictorial qualities. An aim here is often explicitly to prohibit this natural perceptual tendency to 'see in', and to disappoint the culturally induced tendency of spectators to expect pictures to have depth.

As a result, the spectators' experience of these non-representational pictures can be as varied as the ingenuity of their makers. Within Op Art, for instance, I can stand before a large Bridget Riley with its unstable vibrating qualities, and can quite literally feel myself being physically destabilized and 'thrown off centre'. Concentrated viewing of the coloured concentric squares of a late Josef Albers, on the other hand, can be an almost mantric meditative experience. One is tempted to think that these are exclusively optical experiences, but should remember that in this case the eye, as Dewey always reminds us, is an outpost of the self. The type of phenomenological 'relocation' or recentring that can occur as one becomes absorbed in looking at these types of non-representational picture has most to do with the perceptual centredness of self.

Wollheim's idea of central imagining, on the other hand, comes into play in the context of representational or figurative pictures. I have already considered those points of view that, depending on the perspectival system chosen by an artist, perceptually engage spectators, shape their potential occupation of the pictorial space and, to some extent, condition their experience. But there can be other points of entry to pictorial worlds and to their meaning. These have to do not just with compositional points of entry but with points of entry facilitated by what the artist represents and also with what the spectator is capable of seeing 'in' the picture and of expressively perceiving. Specifically, the spectator might identify with some protagonist in the pictorial world, and in that way unlock some of the picture's significance. This is the sort of situation Wollheim has in mind when he speaks of the play of central imagination in the spectator's experience of certain types of picture. But what is it to imagine centrally or to identify with a protagonist?

I referred earlier to Arnheim's observation that sympathy and identification are insufficiently explored. That continues to be true, but some analytic progress has been made since then.[62] Solzhenitsyn, in his belief that art involves a sharing in experiences that are not initially one's own, implicitly involves the idea that such sharing will be to some degree sympathetic. The processes of sympathy and of identification are closely related in that each can be understood as an aspect of imagining. Let me take the idea of sympathy first and consider its meaning.

In his influential *The Psychology of Interpersonal Relations*, the philosophically inclined psychologist Fritz Heider schematically distinguishes four types of reaction of one person to the lot of another person.[63] 'P' refers to the person who is reacting and 'o' to the person to whom s/he is reacting. If o has a positive experience that is also positive for p, then this is what Heider calls 'sympathetic enjoyment'. If o has a negative experience that is also negative for p, then this is 'sympathy' or 'compassion'. Both of these reactions involve what he calls a 'sympathetic "identification"', in which there is a congruence of feeling between p and o, in which the feelings may be congruently positive or congruently negative.[64]

For Heider, sympathy implies p favouring o in some way or other. For the remaining two types of reaction there is a discordance or imbalance. If o has a positive experience that is negative for . p, this is what Heider calls 'envy'. But if o has a negative experience that is positive for p, then this is what he calls 'malicious joy' or, as the Germans would call it, *Schadenfreude*. Heider qualifies this fourfold classification of reactions to the lot of the other at some length. For my purposes, it is sufficient to stress that in the forms of sympathy, whether positive or negative, the requirement is for a congruence rather than for an identity of feeling. Although in sympathy with o, p's feelings need not be as intense nor qualitatively identical with those of o. Much depends, however, upon how p judges o, whether s/he likes him/her or not, and on how p feels about him/herself and his/her lot when compared with that of o. A requirement here is that p be able to infer something about o and be able to construct or to possess what Wollheim calls a 'repertoire' for o.

Wollheim's understanding of sympathy is different from Heider's in so far as he conflates Heider's useful distinction between sympathy and *Schadenfreude*; on the other hand, Wollheim puts his analysis to a use highly relevant for my concern with the processes of recentring. In his analysis of 'iconic imagination' – a subset of iconic mental states that also includes dreams, phantasy and a type of memory – Wollheim develops a description of iconic mental states using the analogy of the theatre with its roles of dramatist, actor and audience.[65] As part of this theatrical description of iconic mental states, he asks how the mental states of the audience are to be related to those of the characters in the drama. His answer is that the mental states of the audience may relate to those of the characters in one of three ways.

The audience may retain a position of detachment. It may note and understand the mental states of the characters, but feel nothing in response and not get involved.[66] Or it may be sympathetic or empathic. With sympathy, the mental states of the audience are determined by the mental states that are represented for the benefit of the audience, and also by how favourably or unfavourably that audience regards the characters.[67] With empathy, as Wollheim formulates it, one character is selected at the outset by the audience which then 'duplicates' the mental states of that character, and responds to the other characters and to the unfolding narrative as from the perspective of the one chosen protagonist.

The mental states of the chosen character and of the audience are 'in unison', and the audience responds as it thinks that character would. On this account, empathy is quite different from favour. Favouring, according to Wollheim, starts as an intellectual act that may or may not become a matter of feeling. Wollheim illustrates these distinctions by taking the feelings of a character and then predicting how detached, sympathetic and empathic audiences would react.[68] Were the character to feel terror then the detached audience, while noting and understanding the character's state of mind, would itself feel nothing; the sympathetically favourable audience would feel solicitude; the sympathetically unfavourable audience would feel triumph;[69] but the empathic audience, like the protagonist, would feel terror. Were the character to be represented as feeling sad, then the feelings of the audience would be feelings of detachment, pity, pleasure and sadness respectively.

The distinction of most interest to my account of aesthetic absorption and recentring is that between iconic mental states that possess points of view internal to what they represent and those that do not. This is the difference between what Wollheim calls 'centred' and 'acentred' iconic mental states.[70] In memory, an example would be what Wollheim calls experiential memory; in imagination, an example would be what he calls 'visualizing' or 'centrally imagining'. Although it is often the case that I am the protagonist of my own imaginings, it need not necessarily be so. I can imagine a scene from inside some or other protagonist.

I can, for example, imagine that I am Napoleon on St Helena whiling away my defeated days. I can feel the disappointment, experience the longing, see the island, be bored by the routine, and dream of the past as though I were Napoleon. In this, I would be imagining being on St Helena from Napoleon's point of view. This is an example of central imagining. I could also conjure up the scene of Napoleon on the island, but from the point of view of no protagonist in that historical situation. I could visualize it in a detached, uninvolved way and imagine that he was bored, disappointed, longing and so on. This would be to acentrally imagine the scene. However, it would not have the same consequences for me that centrally imagining the scene might have.

To centrally imagine being Napoleon I must know something about him, what he was like and how he behaved. I must, in Wollheim's term, possess or be capable of forming a 'repertoire' for him. Using the theatrical description elaborated by Wollheim, it can be said that I am the dramatist in so far as I can create the *mise-en-scène* and script for the action, and also that I am an actor within it. But more than that, the act of centrally imagining has consequences for those imagining, what Wollheim calls cogency. In brief, it tends to leave them in a condition similar to how they would be had what they imagined actually happened.

To centrally imagine myself, for instance, as a protagonist within an erotic scenario would tend to leave me erotically aroused. Outside that centrally imagined enactment, however, and returned to my own routine point of view, I may, depending upon my attitude to such matters, find my state of arousal to be a source of amusement or of shame and guilt. Within the theatrical description, this effect can be described in terms of the effect on the audience of the drama. It is thus the cogency of central imagining that can lead to self-change. Wollheim sums up the three essential features of centrally imagining as point of view, plenitude and cogency.

Some clarifications of central imagining will avoid misunderstanding. To centrally imagine myself as Napoleon is not to imagine myself as identical with him. Identity is symmetrical but, as Wollheim points out, 'imagining myself being Napoleon' is not synonymous with 'imagining Napoleon being me'. I should note here that sympathy is also asymmetrical in that if p sympathizes with o there is no necessary reciprocation of sympathy of o for p. Just as the focus of sympathy is the person with whom one sympathizes, so the core of central imagining is the choice of the protagonist. Once chosen, the imagined mental states of the protagonist 'act, in virtue of their intentionality, as windows open on to the world, through which characters other than the protagonist can climb into the story', and also, let me add, into the picture.[71]

This brings us back to the question of recentring while looking at pictures, and of gaining access to pictorial worlds via a depicted or undepicted protagonist. We can follow Wollheim's application of the idea of central imagining to his analysis of certain pictures that contain a spectator.[72] In embodying a spectator in a picture, the artist first determines the identity of the spectator and then assigns him/her a repertoire of dispositions that will shape his/her being. The function of the spectator in the picture is to enable spectators of the picture to gain a distinctive access to its content.[73] First, the viewers see what there is to be seen in the picture; then they centrally imagine – from the 'inside' – what the depicted spectator is seeing in the depicted world and how s/he thinks and feels about it; this has an effect on the viewers (the 'cogency' of central imagining) which then alters how they view the picture.

By central imagination, in other words, the viewers identify with the spectator in the picture and so open up another route into its content.[74] 'In a licensed way', writes Wollheim, 'he [the spectator] supplements his perception of the picture with the proceeds of imagination and does so so as to advance understanding.'[75] Central imagination is a necessary part of the actual constitution of pictures like this. The consequence of this identification for the viewer, according to Wollheim, is that:

> Though imagining from the inside someone's inward responses doesn't require me actually to have these responses myself, the upshot of the imaginative project, or the condition in which it leaves me, is that it is for me as if I had responded in those ways. Imagination . . . delivers the fruits of experience.'[76]

Transformation of intentionality, in such cases, involves transformations of subjectivity for the spectator or reader. For Wollheim, the concepts of empathy, identification and central imagining are similar.

To ensure that the repertoire of the protagonist with whom the viewer (or reader) can identify is rich enough for the spectator to benefit from it, it must be constructed and inscribed by the artist in the work in such a way as to enable the viewer (reader) to retrieve it. This brings us back to Wollheim's, and Dewey's, formulation of pictorial meaning as depending on the mental state of the artist, the way this causes him or her to mark the surface, and the mental state this marked surface induces in a suitably sensitive and informed spectator. It also recalls Wollheim's theory of expression which is taken to rest on expressive perception 'in which emotion, aroused by what we see, comes to colour our perception of what we see.'[77]

CONCLUSION

This discussion arose from the question of how art might enable us, as Solzhenitsyn believes, to experience 'in the flesh' the thoughts and feelings of others. It has, not surprisingly, turned out to be a most complex process and one that has taken us through a variety of intellectual terrains. The excursion has helped me to sketch an outline and to fill in certain details of what it means to understand aesthetic absorption in different art forms as distinctive processes of becoming recentred in novel fields of experience. It has, in short, been an extended reading of Seamus Heaney's apparently simple description of listening to poetry with which I began, and one which I take to have more general application – the experience of 'daydreaming in sympathy'. I offer it tentatively and in the certain knowledge that better descriptions can be offered, but I am also convinced that this long neglected phenomenon deserves the attention it has received here, and more.

NOTES

1. See *Mark Rothko 1903–1970* (London: The Tate Gallery, 1987), p. 83.
2. Solzhenitsyn, 1972, p. 14.
3. Ibid.
4. See, for example, Lind, 1988, Chapter 4.
5. See Merleau-Ponty, 1964b, where he writes: 'The perceived world is the always presupposed foundation of all rationality, all value and all existence. This thesis does not destroy either rationality or the absolute. It only brings them down to earth' (p. 13), and 'it is perceptual experience which gives us the passage from one moment to the next and thus realizes the unity of time. In this sense all consciousness is perceptual, even the consciousness of ourselves' (p. 13).
6. Wallace Stevens, 'The Reader', in W. Stevens, 1972, p. 101.
7. Berger and Mohr, 1989, p. 286; emphasis in original.
8. Poulet, 1980. This was reprinted in a shortened form from *The Structuralist Controversy: The Language of Criticism and the Sciences of Man*, ed. Richard A. Macksey and Eugenio Donato (Baltimore: The Johns Hopkins University Press, 1972), pp. 56–72. Also see Iser, 1974. Iser assumes that all perception, including reading, is constituted by a subject–object division (p. 293), and finds Poulet's description problematical. Iser judges his 'substantialist conception of the consciousness that constitutes itself in the literary work' unsatisfactory. He suggests a different line of development for certain of the points

made by Poulet. If reading involves dissolving the division between the reader as subject and the book as object, then it also involves instituting new divisions within the reader, according to Iser. 'I' as reading subject gives way to the 'me' of the text that supplants it. Iser then talks of linked levels of reading that involve 'the alien "me"' and 'the real, virtual "me"'. This real, but virtual, 'me' forms a variable background depending on the text being read. He goes on to quote approvingly an objection made by D. W. Harding to the idea of 'identification' with what is read, and to observe that 'our faculty for deciphering' is what is formulated along the lines set by the text rather than by the reader. But this talk by Iser of 'reading literature [as giving] us the chance to formulate the unformulated' (p. 294) seems to miss the point of Poulet's attempted description, and to fail to develop it intelligibly. The problem of describing what is involved for the reading subject (or, in the case of pictures, the viewing subject) in sharing or participating in the artistically presented thoughts and feelings of another remains. Specifically, how are we to think about self and text/picture during the phase of aesthetic absorption? On this see Harding, 1962. What Harding actually queries is not the idea of identification, but that of wish-fulfillment, which is quite a different matter. Harding is objecting to the reductionism implicit in the idea of wish-fulfilment and intends to support the openness of literature to new meaning with his alternative idea of 'wish-formulation or the definition of desires' (p. 144).

9. Poulet, 1980, p. 42.
10. Ibid.
11. Ibid., p. 43.
12. Ibid.
13. Ibid., p. 44. This is reminiscent of the comments in 1930 of a disgruntled Georges Duhamel in the face of the rise of cinema: 'I can no longer think what I want to think. My thoughts have been replaced by moving images.' This is quoted by Walter Benjamin in *Illuminations* (1979, p. 240).
14. Poulet, 1980, p. 45.
15. Ibid.
16. Ibid., p. 47. Poulet's analysis has a relevance beyond literature. Speaking of an intuition he had when seeing the Tintoretto collection in the Scuola di San Rocco in Venice, Poulet writes:

> When looking at all these masterpieces, brought together and revealing so manifestly their unity of inspiration, I had suddenly the impression of having reached the common essence present in all the works of a great master, an essence which I was not able to perceive, except when emptying my mind of all the particular images created by the artist. I became aware of a subjective power at work in all these pictures, and yet never so clearly understood by my mind as when I had forgotten all their particular figurations. (p. 48)

17. Ibid., p. 49.
18. Wollheim, 1987.

19. Ibid., p. 44.
20. Dewey, 1958, p. 106.
21. See especially his *Languages of Art* (1976).
22. Dewey, 1958, p. 83.
23. Ibid., p. 86. And let us remember that the picture is experience, in Dewey's view.
24. For a discussion of 'seeing in' see Wollheim, 1987, pp. 45–79, and for a consideration of 'visual delight' see pp. 98–100 of the same work.
25. Ibid., p. 80.
26. See Wilson, 1991, p. 100.
27. It is also similar to the way in which Rudolf Arnheim thinks of 'expression' as being 'found' in one's perception of the world. In his 'New version' of *Art and Visual Perception* (1974) Arnheim writes that 'Visual expression resides in any articulately shaped object or event' (p. 451). He observes that in the modern Western world, we are accustomed to differentiating the animate from the inanimate and the mental from the physical. 'But', he goes on to say, 'in terms of expressive qualities, the character of a given person may resemble that of a particular tree more closely than that of another person' (p. 453). He argues that in great works of art, 'The deepest significance is transmitted to the eye with powerful directness by the perceptual characteristics of the compositional pattern' (p. 458).
28. Wollheim, 1987, p. 82.
29. For an analysis of the meanings of 'projection' see Laplanche and Pontalis, 1980, pp. 349–56.
30. Wollheim, 1987, p. 82.
31. Ibid.
32. Ibid., p. 83.
33. Ibid., p. 84.
34. Ibid., p. 82.
35. Dewey, 1958, p. 98.
36. Ibid., pp. 100–1. Wollheim makes the same point, with the stress on the hand being guided and directed by the eye. See Wollheim, 1987, p. 89. Arnheim likewise insists that 'Our senses are not self-contained recording devices operating for their own sake. They have been developed by the organism as an aid in reacting to the environment' (1974, p. 455). Arnheim concludes 'that even the simplest line expresses visible meaning and is therefore symbolic' (p. 461).
37. Dewey, 1958, p. 101. For a discussion of 'thematization' see Wollheim, 1987, pp. 19–20.
38. Dewey, 1958, p. 102. Arnheim's position is similar, even though Lipps, in his view, made an advance within the associationist way of thinking by pointing out that the perception of expression involves the activity of forces. With his theory of empathy, Lipps wanted to explain how inanimate objects could be expressive. When looking at a column, for example, I know from past experience the pressures involved in columns and I also know, argues Lipps, how I should feel if I was in their place. What is happening is that I am projecting my

kinaesthetic feeling on to the columns. But the activation of these memories draws in others that Lipps describes in the following passage quoted by Arnheim:

> When I project my strivings and forces into nature I do so also as to the way my strivings and forces make me feel, that is, I project my pride, my courage, my stubbornness, my lightness, my playful assuredness, my tranquil complacence. Only thus my empathy with regard to nature becomes truly aesthetic empathy. (1974, p. 448)

The difficulty with this position as Arnheim points out, as do Dewey and Wollheim, is that it relies for its efficacy on learned association and denies any intrinsic relationship between the appearance perceived and the expression conveyed. For Arnheim, it is in the 'perceptual qualities of the stimulus pattern' that expression resides (p. 449).

39. Dewey, 1958, p. 103. Again, Arnheim also holds that 'For art the distinctions between the outer and the inner world and the conscious and the unconscious mind are artificial. . . . There is no way of presenting the one without the other' (1974, p. 461).

40. Dewey, 1958, p. 248.

41. For a discussion of Nagel's thinking on the 'centreless' conception of the world see his *The View from Nowhere* (1986).

42. Dewey, 1958, p. 249.

43. Ibid., p. 250.

44. Similarly, in speaking of Michelangelo's *Creation of Man*, Arnheim says that:

> The forces that characterize the meaning of the story come alive in the observer and produce *the kind of stirring participation* [my emphasis] that distinguishes artistic experience from the detached acceptance of information. (1974, p. 460)

45. Friedman, 1955, pp. 1160–84.

46. Ibid., p. 1180.

47. Ibid., p. 1176.

48. Rimmon-Kenan, 1983, Chapter 6.

49. Genette, 1980.

50. On this Wayne Booth suggests that 'any sustained inside view, of whatever depth, temporarily turns the character whose mind is shown into a narrator.' See Booth, 1961, p. 164. Also quoted in Rimmon-Kenan, 1983, p. 72.

51. Rimmon-Kenan, 1983, p. 73. The focalizer is a character within the represented world. S/he is an agent whose perception guides the presentation of what s/he perceives. Sometimes s/he is the narrator, other times not. This theoretical distinction now enables one to speak of the narrator–focalizer as distinct from a character–focalizer. We can see that the distinction between focalizer and narrator parallels that between the experiencing self and the narrating self. Two criteria can be used to identify the type of focalization at work in a narrative text. The first of these is the position of the focalizer relative to the text. If the focalizer is represented as being external to the story, then its vehicle may be a narrator–focalizer or a first person narrating self. If

the focalizer is inside the represented events, then usually this will be a character–focalizer. The second criterion is the degree to which the same voice persists throughout the narrative. Sometimes a single fixed voice speaks throughout, sometimes two or more voices alternate. Whichever of these solutions an author opts for will again influence the reader's experience, since the 'centres of consciousness' represented will vary in what they know, and in how what they know matters to them. These distinctions enable Rimmon-Kenan to propose her own analysis of external and internal focalizers in terms of the perceptual, psychological and ideological aspects of focalization.

52. Walton, 1976.
53. Ibid., p. 51.
54. Ibid., p. 57. 'Inside' and 'outside' here do not parallel the earlier distinctions between narrators who are 'internal' and 'external'.
55. Ibid., p. 60.
56. Merleau-Ponty, 1964b, p. 14.
57. Arnheim, 1982, p. 182.
58. Ibid., p. 186. See the whole of Chapter VIII for a discussion of these issues. Arnheim summarizes the varied meanings of 'centre' as it relates to visual artistic composition in this way: -

> Geometrically, the center is defined purely by location as the point equidistant from all homologous points of a regular figure. Physically, the center is the fulcrum around which an object balances. Perceptually, the *balancing center* is the point at which all the vectors constituting a visual pattern are in equilibrium. In a broader sense and irrespective of location, any visual object constitutes a *dynamic center* because it is the seat of forces issuing from it and converging toward it. (p. 215; emphasis in original)

59. For this and the following examples see Malins, 1980, pp. 46–65.
60. See Arnheim (1969) and Goodman (1976) for examples of arguments, from the *Gestalt* and semiotic traditions, for the cognitive nature of seeing pictures.
61. Wollheim, 1987, p. 46.
62. For a recent example of social–psychological thinking on sympathy see Wispé, 1991.
63. Heider, 1958, especially Chapter 11.
64. Ibid., p. 27.
65. Wollheim, 1984, Chapter III.
66. Heider fails to identify and discuss emotional indifference or uninvolvement in his schematic division of possible reactions.
67. This is similar to Thomas Nagel's idea of 'sympathetically imagining' where we put ourselves in a conscious state that resembles the mental states or events of others, or of ourselves. This is distinguished from 'perceptual imagining' where we put ourselves into a conscious state resembling the state we would be in if we perceived the particular object or scene. Solipsism arises, in Nagel's view, by misinterpreting sympathetic imagination as though it worked like perceptual imagination. When this is done, it seems impossible to imagine any experience

that is not one's own. By implication, it is sympathetic imagination that allows us to imagine experiences that are not originally our own. Nagel notes but does not elaborate on 'symbolic imagination'. See Nagel, 1979, pp. 175–6n11.
68. Wollheim, 1984, pp. 68–9.
69. This category of the 'sympathetically unfavourable' is equivalent to Heider's *Schadenfreude* or malicious joy . Heider's taxonomy is, I think, the clearer one.
70. Wollheim, 1984, p. 72.
71. Ibid., pp. 76–7.
72. Wollheim, 1987, Chapter III.
73. Ibid., p. 129.
74. For a discussion of psychoanalytic meanings of identification see Laplanche and Pontalis, 1980. As they make clear, identification in its everyday meaning overlaps other psychological concepts like imitation, empathy, sympathy, mental contagion, projection. In general they describe it as a:

> Psychological process whereby the subject assimilates an aspect, property or attribute of the other and is transformed, wholly or partially, after the model the other provides. It is by means of a series of identifications that the personality is constituted and specified. (p. 205)

75. Ibid., p. 129.
76. Ibid.
77. Ibid., p. 138. Wollheim's own application of the idea of central imagining here is a subtle argument for the existence of what he calls unrepresented internal spectators in the landscapes of Caspar David Friedrich, in the single-figure paintings of Edouard Manet, and in the group portraits of Frans Hals. Were we to look for depictions of the appearance of being absorbed, we would be hard-pressed to do better than those portraits by Manet that Wollheim describes as possessing a 'mood of preoccupation', 'of self-absorption', of 'momentary absence' and 'abstraction' before the figures 're-enter the moment'.

POSTSCRIPT

Two things we may learn from little children from three to six years old; that it is a characteristic, an instinct of our human nature to pass out of self. . . . And not to suffer any one form to pass into me and become a usurping self.

(Samuel Taylor Coleridge)[1]

The goal of life, for Dewey, is self-realization and this is to be achieved socially, through what he calls 'associated living'. The necessity of social being for personal fulfilment is not a denial of individuality; becoming an individual is a sophisticated achievement of social being. Self-absorption is the enemy of self-realization, aesthetic absorption is its ally. Self-absorption is a closed circuit whereas aesthetic absorption always requires something other than itself. A self aesthetically engaged is opened to possibilities of experience that are actively sealed off by the dynamics of self-absorption.

Aesthetic absorption as a type of experience is exceptional in this respect since it is the psychological nexus of the public and the private, of the body and symbolic meaning, of perception and sign, intuition and interpretation. It is a transaction of deep constructive intimacy. What is constructed or reconstructed in these intimate moments when self becomes other than itself? Feelings for others and understanding of them may be altered; new registers of feeling and fresh angles of understanding may contribute to an 'expansion' of self and self-meaning; new vocabularies of experience may be acquired and old ones extended; and there may be a special pleasure qualifying the time during which this happens. These contrast sharply with the stagnancy of self-absorption.

If aesthetic experiences, and especially the axial experience of aesthetic absorption, can lead to changes of self, should we then assume that all such change is always for the better? I raise this question now because throughout this investigation I have been aware of certain problems lurking in the background. It is not self-evidently good to hand oneself over to something other – like a novel or a film or a painting – for intimate and subtle formation and reformation. Perhaps the dynamics of aesthetic absorption, or at least of ceding control of self to something other than oneself, are capable of being brought under the manipulative control of social forces whose primary interest is not respect for individual self-realization. There are institutions and ideologies whose own realization and perpetuation require members who are centred not in themselves, but are instead psychologically centred where these forces want them to be. Religious and political fundamentalists, for instance, are likely to instil great caution, and perhaps active denial, into their adherents when it comes to art and aesthetic experience, whereas liberal democracies may value these cultural possibilities precisely because self-realization is a core value of democracies like this.[2]

Art as experience, in other words, is as liable as any other form of experience to be recruited for ends other than for itself. It could become a technique to reach within the warm, deep recesses of individual selves, especially during aesthetic absorption. By the manipulation of these powers in experience, institutional and ideological forces of all types can infiltrate the selves of their adherents, and shape them accordingly. Such selves would be, to use a fashionable word, colonized.

But what selves are not colonized, especially when it is argued as I have done that the fabric and foundations of self are social? If our very ability to choose and this ability's subjectivity is shaped, at least in part, by what is other than ourselves, then who can say who is free and who is a serf? Were this true, then all we could say is that the option is not between being colonized or not being colonized, but between types of colonization. And even then, because choosing itself is always concretely situated, such choices are partial and historically conditioned.

Walter Benjamin's contrast between contemplation and distraction – 'A man who concentrates before a work of art is absorbed by it. . . . the distracted mass absorbs the work of art' – is suggestive here. He was contrasting painting and film, and observing that the crisis of painting in an age of mechanical reproduction has to do with its inability to be present as 'an object for simultaneous collective experience'.[3] Architecture, film, video, music, theatre, photography and literature are much more amenable to such simultaneous collective experience, especially in this mass marketed age engendered by the technologies of reproduction. But what might the difference be between contemplative absorption *in* the work as against the distracted absorption *of* the work?

In one commonplace view, according to Benjamin, it is the work that makes demands of the spectator and 'the mass' that makes demands on the work. Here contemplation has distraction as its opposite. But this contrast, it seems to me, becomes paradoxical when we ask in which the individual self has more control. It would appear that to be distracted is to be controlled: to contemplate is to choose freely. The one is an abdication of freedom, the other a continuing exercise of it. The consequence of yielding oneself to the other in distraction is to become 'absent-minded' and to allow the object of distraction to occupy a vacated space. This is a form of absorption but it is not aesthetic absorption. Benjamin again:

> Reception in a state of distraction, which is increasing noticeably in all fields of art and is symptomatic of profound changes in apperception, finds in the film its true means of exercise. . . . The public is an examiner, but an absent-minded one.[4]

Contemplation, on the other hand, is a form not of absent-mindedness but of being present-minded elsewhere, as enabled by a novel or picture or film or passage of music. Both distraction and contemplation end after a time, but with different consequences. Distraction, or escapism as we would call it today, returns people largely empty-handed to the situation they left, other than with the knowledge that they can probably be similarly distracted again. This can of course be a refreshing experience, but the enrichment is the refreshment and not much else.

Aesthetic absorption, on the other hand, makes different demands of its participants since it demands different forms of engagement. It does not ask the object to mask feelings of boredom or unease; it does not arise from having nothing to do or from wanting to avoid something one would rather not do; it is not a swallowing of some experience as a panacea for an underlying feeling of alienation; it is not a passive activity; and it does not invite occupation by some 'usurping' form. The engagement of self in aesthetic absorption is active, chosen, informed, attentive, demanding, and – depending on the quality of the art – enlarging. It is itself the outcome of achievement as well as contributing to further achievement. It is rooted in interest and not in evasion.

There is another reason why aesthetic absorption might prove more resistant to simple-minded manipulation than would, for want of a better term, distracted absorption. Aesthetic absorption is but a phase, albeit a vital one, within aesthetic experience, a phase that is rhythmically paired with reflection. Dewey's phrase was 'a rhythm of surrender and reflection'. Reflection requires what Dewey calls 'funded experience' and what Wollheim calls 'cognitive stock' if the spectator or reader or listener is to be 'suitably sensitive and informed'. And that requires some form of disciplined education, as Dewey clearly understood even if many of his disciples did not. Again, I have not been able to deal with the fascinating questions posed for aesthetic education by my description of aesthetic absorption. All I can say at this point is that it seems reasonable to suppose that those who receive an education in which personal openness is fostered in tandem with critical reflection, will be less susceptible to crude colonization through art forms. But to follow this would take us into the troubled waters of 'humane literacy' as an educational aim and its efficacy, and that is another day's work.

There is another related portfolio of questions that has shadowed me throughout this book. These are questions about the relationship between perception and knowing, between Dewey's 'primary experience' and reflection, between bodily wisdom and interpretive understanding. Aesthetic experiences are very complex in terms both of their organization and of their constitutive materials. These 'materials' are relationships of all sorts and at many levels. Aesthetic experiences spread out over time and, as we saw in Chapters 1 and 2, different phases can be distinguished in them. Kenneth Clark could speak of looking at pictures as a recurrent pattern of impact, scrutiny, recollection and renewal. At its briefest, we could say that aesthetic experience is characteristically immediate, absorbing, ineffable, insightful and fulfilling. As a type of experience, it seems to offer itself as a testing ground for those who believe that all experience is interpreted as against those who would hold that there is a symbiotic relationship between pre-reflective, uninterpreted experience and reflective interpretation.

Much of course hinges on the definition of interpretation and the cut-off points and limits placed on it. Dewey, Merleau-Ponty and Wollheim, for example, would resist the hegemonic moves of the hermeneuticians to assimilate all to the linguistic, while granting interpretation its vital and central place. Richard Shusterman adopts a similar position when he identifies 'forms of bodily awareness or understanding that are not linguistic in nature and that in fact defy adequate linguistic characterization, though they can somehow be referred to through language.'[5] His examples are like those I gave earlier from René Spitz, the proprioceptive sense of right movement that dancers have, our verticality and direction of gaze, and so on.

Quite how subtle these pre-reflective understandings are in relation to looking at pictures was forcibly borne in on me six years ago when I was extensively paralyzed from the chest down. This rather radical 'natural experiment' revealed many things to me about the enabling and foundational role of the body in experience, and one of them was this. On the wall of my hospital room was an amateur landscape, competently naturalistic in style, of a beach scene in the west of Ireland. I had often walked on similar beaches and had a ready fund of memories and 'cognitive stock' to help me 'enter' the picture. But I could not, and not for any apparent reason to do with the quality of the picture. I also had with me a card of a painting by the sixteenth century Dutch painter Jacob Grimmer called *Summer*. This depicted a fantastical pink castle in the centre of the picture which was set against a dark green wood and was blurrily reflected in a pale green lake. Exotic birds rose and flew against a greeny blue sky, hunters shot unseen duck from a boat, a man with his dog fished in the right foreground, and a small translucent yacht sailed towards the left of the picture. This was like nothing I was familiar with and yet I found it utterly absorbing. Afterwards, as I began to recover somewhat and learned to walk again, I was puzzled by this. Why could I not 'enter' the landscape I knew, but could with great pleasure enclose myself in one that I never could know?

The answer seemed to me to have something to do with a vague feeling for which the word 'disqualified' seemed appropriate. My then almost total paralysis seemed to disqualify me at that time from certain forms of pictorial experience even though it should not seem to matter with pictures since their appeal was to my eyes and these were as good as ever. The painting of the west of Ireland landscape was 'walkable' in Arnheim's sense, but precisely for this reason seemed no longer walkable by me. The Grimmer landscape was imaginary and therefore did not in fact exclude my participation in it since whatever it required of me I could fulfil, unlike the requirements of the other one as I understood them. This, fortunately, rare experience seemed to tell me a number of important things. At that time I suppose I was a Goodmanian, and believed in the ubiquity of symbolic interpretation. Now circumstances were revealing for attentive experience all sorts of continuities and subtle interrelationships. Now I knew more fully what Dewey meant by the eye being the outpost of the self. Now I knew what Merleau-Ponty meant when he spoke of the 'pre-given' meaning of the carnal world, a meaning that I do not constitute. My pre-given meaning had been abruptly ruptured and was reforming itself in subtle ways such as was revealed in my different experiences with both types of landscape picture.

Experiential examples like this strongly suggest that the whole body, with its own understandings and continuities, participates in experiences of looking at pictures or listening to music or reading novels, and that it collaborates in grounding and guiding interpretation which is also an essential part of the overall experience. That is why I spoke of qualitative symbols earlier on in Chapter 2. Pragmatism, like the phenomenology of Merleau-Ponty, is sympathetic to this view and the semiotics of Peirce would seem capable of encompassing it. Psychologies that tackle the high-level complexities of everyday life, including those of art as experience, will find much philosophical support and guidance from pragmatic philosophy. And cultural theorists should, I think, find more of interest in that strand of psychology. As for the fertile significance of aesthetic absorption for psychology, and the ideas of being centred and recentring, let me finish with the promise of a line from Rilke – 'All space becomes a fruit around these kernels.'[6]

NOTES

1. See Peter Coveney, *The Image of Childhood: The Individual and Society: A Study of the Theme in English Literature* (Harmondsworth: Penguin, 1967), p. 87.
2. For an excellent study of both the cultural origins and cultural impact of Dewey's thinking on democracy during his lifetime, and of its contemporary relevance, see Westbrook, 1991. For a critical comment on the ways in which the interests of late capitalist consumerism and liberalism are served by artists continually differentiating from each other and the market-led expansion of aesthetic life see Shusterman, 1992, Chapter 9.
3. Benjamin, 1979, p. 236.
4. Ibid., pp. 242–3.
5. Shusterman, 1992, p. 127. See his Chapters 4 and 5 for a discussion of these issues in relation to pragmatism.
6. See Rainer Maria Rilke, *Poems 1906–26*, trans. J. B. Leishman (London: The Hogarth Press, 1968), p. 87.

REFERENCES

Alexander, Thomas M. (1987) *John Dewey's Theory of Art, Experience and Nature: The Horizons of Feeling,* Albany, NY: State University of New York Press.

Allport, Gordon W. (1955) *Becoming: Basic Considerations for a Psychology of Personality,* New Haven: Yale University Press.

Allport, Gordon W. (1971) 'Dewey's individual and social psychology', in Paul A. Schilpp (ed.) *The Philosophy of John Dewey,* 2nd edn, La Salle, Illinois: Open Court.

Ames, Van Meter (1953) 'John Dewey as aesthetician', *Journal of Aesthetics and Art Criticism,* XII, 2 (Dec), 145–68.

Ames, Van Meter (1954) 'Zen and pragmatism', Philosophy East and West, IV, 1, 19–33.

Arnheim, Rudolf (1966) *Toward a Psychology of Art,* Berkeley: University of California Press.

Arnheim, Rudolf (1969) *Visual Thinking,* Berkeley: University of California Press.

Arnheim, Rudolf (1974) *Art and Visual Perception: A Psychology of the Creative Eye,* Berkeley: University of California Press.

Arnheim, Rudolf (1982) *The Power of the Center: A Study of Composition in the Visual Arts,* Berkeley: University of California Press.

Arnheim, Rudolf (1986) *New Essays on the Psychology of Art,* Berkeley: University of California Press.

Aschenbrenner, K. and Isenberg, A. (eds.) (1965) *Aesthetic Theories: Studies in the Philosophy of Art,* Englewood Cliffs, NJ: Prentice Hall.

Ashton, Dore (ed.) (1972) *Picasso on Art: A Selection of Views,* New York: Viking.

Baldwin, J. M. (1911) *Thought and Things,* vol. 3, London: George Allen.

Bandura, Albert (1985) *Social Foundations of Thought and Action,* Englewood Cliffs, NJ: Prentice Hall.

Barnes, Albert C. (1927) *The Art in Painting,* London: Jonathan Cape.

Barnes, Albert C. and De Mazia, Violette (1933) *The Art of Henri Matisse,* London: Charles Scribner's Sons.

189

Barrett, Cyril (ed.) (1965) *Collected Papers in Aesthetics*, Oxford: Basil Blackwell.

Barzun, Jacques (1984) *A Stroll with William James*, Chicago: University of Chicago Press.

Basho (1981) *The Narrow Road to the Deep North and Other Travel Sketches*, trans. Nobuyuki Yuasa, Harmondsworth: Penguin.

Beardsley, Monroe (1966) *Aesthetics from Classical Greece to the Present*, Alabama: University of Alabama Press.

Beardsley, Monroe (1969) 'Aesthetic experience regained', in M. J. Wreen and D. M. Callen (eds) *The Aesthetic Point of View*, Ithaca, NY: Cornell University Press, 77–92.

Bee, Helen (1989) *The Developing Child*, 5th edn, New York: Harper & Row.

Benjamin, Walter (1979) *Illuminations*, trans. Harry Zohn, ed. Hannah Arendt, Glasgow: Fontana/Collins.

Benson, Ciarán (1986) 'Art and language in middle childhood: a question of translation', *Word & Image*, 2, 2, (April–June), 123–40.

Benson, Ciarán (1989a) 'Aesthetics, development and cognitive science', *The Irish Journal of Psychology: Special Cognitive Science Edition*, 10, 2, 247–60.

Benson, Ciarán (1989b) 'Art and the ordinary: reflections on art, non-artists and policy-making in Ireland', in Ciarán Benson (ed.) *Art and the Ordinary: The ACE Report*, Dublin: ACE/The Arts Council, 13–33.

Benson, Ciarán (1991–2) 'Critical notice: J. E. Tiles' *Dewey*', *Philosophical Studies (Ireland)*, XXXIII, 302–7.

Berger, John (1980a) *The Success and Failure of Picasso*, New York: Pantheon Books.

Berger, John (1980b) *About Looking*, London: Writers and Readers Publishing Cooperative.

Berger, John and Mohr, Jean (1989) *Another Way of Telling*, Cambridge: Granta Books.

Bergson, Henri (1911) *Creative Evolution*, New York, p. 145.

Bettleheim, Bruno (1982) *The Uses of Enchantment*, Harmondsworth: Peregrine, 1982.

Bettleheim, Bruno (1985) *Freud and Man's Soul*, London: Fontana.

Bhaskar, Roy (ed.) (1990) *Harré and His Critics: Essays in Honour of Rom Harré with His Commentary on Them*, Oxford: Basil Blackwell.

Blyth, R. H. (1976) *Games Zen Masters Play*, New York: Mentor.

Blyth, R. H. (1981) *Haiku*, 4 vols., Tokyo: The Hokuseido Press.

Bonarius, H., Holland, R. and Rosenberg, S. (eds.) (1981) *Personal Construct Psychology: Recent Advances in Theory and Practice*, London: Macmillan.

Booth, Wayne (1961) *The Rhetoric of Fiction*, Chicago: University of Chicago Press.

Brentano, Franz (1973) *Psychology from an Empirical Standpoint*, ed. Oscar Kraus, English ed. Linda L. McAlister, London: Routledge & Kegan Paul.

Brion-Guerry, Liliane (1977) 'The elusive goal', in *Cézanne: The Late Work*, New York: The Museum of Modern Art.

Brown, Richard H. (1977) *A Poetic for Sociology: Toward a Logic of Discovery for the Human Sciences*, Cambridge: Cambridge University Press.

Bryson, Norman (1983) *Vision and Painting: The Logic of the Gaze*, London: Macmillan.

Bryson, Norman, Holly, Michael Ann, and Moxey, Keith (eds.) (1991) *Visual Theory: Painting and Interpretation*, Oxford: Polity Press.

Bruner, Jerome (1977) 'Language and experience', in R. S. Peters (ed.) *John Dewey Reconsidered*, London: Routledge & Kegan Paul.

Bruner, Jerome (1986) *Actual Minds, Possible Worlds*, Cambridge, Mass.: Harvard University Press.

Bruner, Jerome (1990) *Acts of Meaning*, Cambridge, Mass.: Harvard University Press.

Bullough, Edward (1957) '"Psychical distance" as a factor in art and an aesthetic principle', in Elizabeth M. Wilkinson (ed.) *Aesthetics: Lectures and Essays by Edward Bullough*, Cambridge: Cambridge University Press.

Burkitt, Ian (1991) *Social Selves: Theories of the Social Formation of Personality*, London: Sage Publications.

Burnett, Joe E (1989) 'The relation of Dewey's aesthetics to his overall philosophy', *Journal of Aesthetic Education*, 23, 3, 51–2.

Cassirer, Ernst (1923–9) *Die Philosophie der Symbolischen Formen*, 3 vols, Berlin: Bruno Cassirer.

Clark, Kenneth (1960) *Looking at Pictures*, London: John Murray.

Colapietro, Vincent M. (1989) *Peirce's Approach to the Self: A Semiotic Approach to the Self*, Albany, NY: State University of New York Press.

Cox, M. V. (1986) *The Child's Point of View: The Development of Cognition and Language*, Hemel Hempstead: Harvester Wheatsheaf.

Croce, Benedetto (1948) 'On the aesthetics of Dewey', *Journal of Aesthetics and Art Criticism*, VI, 3 (March), 203–9.

Crystal, David (1989) *The Cambridge Encyclopedia of Language*, Cambridge: Cambridge University Press.

Davis, M. and Wallbridge, D. (1983) *Boundary and Space: An Introduction to the Work of D. W. Winnicott*, Harmondsworth: Penguin.

Deledalle, Gérard (1967) *L'Idée d'experience dans la philosophie de John Dewey*, Paris: Presses Universitaires de France.

Dennett, Daniel (1988) 'Why everyone is a novelist', *Times Literary Supplement* (Sept. 16–22).

Dennett, Daniel (1989) 'The origin of selves', *Cogito*, 3, 3, 163–73.

Dennett, Daniel (1991) *Consciousness Explained*, London: Allen Lane, The Penguin Press.

Deutsch, Werner (ed.) (1981) *The Child's Construction of Language*, London: Academic Press.

De Villiers, P. A. and de Villiers, J. G. (1979) *Early Language*, London: Fontana.

Dewey, John (1922) *Human Nature and Conduct*, New York: Henry Holt.

Dewey, John (1930) 'Qualitative thought', *The Symposium: A Critical Review*, 1 (1930), 5–32.

Dewey, John (1931) *Philosophy and Civilization*, New York: Minton Balch & Co.

Dewey, John (1935) 'Peirce's theory of quality', *Journal of Philosophy*, XXXII, 26 (Dec.), 701–8.

Dewey, John (1938) *Logic: The Theory of Inquiry*, London: George Allen & Unwin.

Dewey, John (1940) 'The vanishing subject in the psychology of James', *Journal of Philosophy*, XXXVII, 22 (Oct), 589–99.

Dewey, John (1946) 'Peirce's theory of linguistic signs, thought and meaning', *Journal of Philosophy*, XLIII, 4 (Feb.), 85–95.

Dewey, John (1950) 'Aesthetic experience as a primary phase and as an artistic development', *Journal of Aesthetics and Art Criticism*, IX, (Sept.), 56–8.

Dewey, John (1958) *Art as Experience*, New York: Capricorn Books, G. P. Putnam's Sons. Also vol. 10 of *John Dewey: The Later Works, 1925–1953*, ed. Jo Ann Boydston, Carbondale : Southern Illinois University Press, 1987.

Dewey, John (1971a) 'Experience, knowledge and value', in Paul A. Schilpp (ed.) *The Philosophy of John Dewey*, 2nd edn, La Salle, Illinois: Open Court.

Dewey, John (1971b) *Experience and Nature*, 2nd edn, La Salle, Illinois: Open Court.

Dewey, John (1981a) 'From absolutism to experimentalism', in John J. McDermott (ed.) *The Philosophy of John Dewey*, Chicago: University of Chicago Press, 1–13.

Dewey, John (1981b) 'Kant and philosophic method', in John J. McDermott (ed.) *The Philosophy of John Dewey*, Chicago: University of Chicago Press, 13–24.

Dewey, John (1981c) 'The need for a recovery of philosophy', in John J. McDermott (ed.) *The Philosophy of John Dewey*, Chicago: University of Chicago Press, 58–97.

Dewey, John (1981d) 'The reflex arc concept in psychology', in John M. McDermott (ed.) *The Philosophy of John Dewey*, Chicago: University of Chicago Press, 136–148.

Dewey, John (1981e) 'The influence of Darwinism on philosophy', in John J. McDermott (ed.) *The Philosophy of John Dewey*, Chicago: University of Chicago Press, 31–41.

Dickie, George (1964) 'The myth of the aesthetic attitude', *American Philosophical Quarterly*, 1, 56–66.

Dickie, George (1965) 'Beardsley's phantom aesthetic experience', *Journal of Philosophy*, 62, 129–36.

Eagleton, Terry (1990) *The Ideology of the Aesthetic*, Oxford: Basil Blackwell.

Eagleton, Terry and Fuller, Peter (1983) 'The question of value: a discussion', *New Left Review*, 142, (November–December), 81.

Eco, Umberto (1977) *A Theory of Semiotics*, London: Macmillan.

Eco, Umberto (1979) *The Role of the Reader*, Bloomington: Indiana University Press.

Edman, Irwin (1967) 'Dewey and art', in Sidney Hook (ed.) *John Dewey: Philosopher of Science and Freedom*, New York: Barnes & Noble.

Ehrenzweig, Anton (1967) *The Hidden Order of Art: A Study in the Psychology of Artistic Imagination*, London: Weidenfeld & Nicolson.

Eliot, T. S. (1969) *The Complete Poems*, London: Faber & Faber.

Erikson, Erik (1968) *Identity: Youth and Crisis*, London: Faber & Faber.

Fancher, R. E. (1979) *Pioneers of Psychology*, London: W. W. Norton.

Ferenczi, Sandor (1952) *First Contributions to Psychoanalysis*, New York: Brunner/Mazel.

Fish, Stanley E. (1980a) 'Literature in the reader: affective stylistics', in Jane P. Tompkins (ed.) *Reader-Response Criticism: From Formalism to Post-structuralism*, Baltimore: Johns Hopkins University Press, 70–100.

Fish, Stanley E. (1980b) 'Interpreting the *Variorum*', in Jane P. Tompkins (ed.) *Reader-Response Criticism: From Formalism to Post-structuralism*, Baltimore: Johns Hopkins University Press, 164–184.

Fish, Stanley E. (1980c) *Is There a Text in This Class? The Authority of Interpretive Communities*, Cambridge, Mass.: Harvard University Press.

Fisher, John (1989) 'Some remarks on what happened to John Dewey', *Journal of Aesthetic Education*, 23, 3 (Fall), 54–60.

Flam, Jack D. (1978) *Matisse on Art*, Oxford: Phaidon Press.

Flarsheim, Alfred (1978) 'Discussion of Antony Flew', in Simon A. Grolnick and Leonard Barkin (eds.) *Between Reality and Fantasy: Transitional Objects and Phenomena*, New York: Jason Aronson, 505–10.

Flew, Antony (1978) 'Transitional objects and transitional phenomena: comments and interpretations', in Simon A. Grolnick and Leonard Barkin (eds.) *Between Reality and Fantasy: Transitional Objects and Phenomena*, New York: Jason Aronson, 485–501.

Flew, Antony (1984) *A Dictionary of Philosophy*, London: Pan.

Freud, Ernst L. (ed.) (1975) *The Letters of Sigmund Freud*, New York: Basic Books.

Freud, Sigmund (1984) 'The ego and the id', in vol. 11 of *The Pelican Freud Library* (gen. ed. Albert Dickson), *On Metapsychology: The Theory of Psychoanalysis*, ed. Angela Richards, Harmondsworth: Penguin, 339–401.

Freud, Sigmund (1985a) *Civilization and its Discontents, vol. 12 of The Pelican Freud Library*, ed. Albert Dickson, Harmondsworth: Penguin.

Freud, Sigmund (1985b) *Art and Literature*, vol. 14 of *The Pelican Freud Library*, ed. Albert Dickson, Harmondsworth: Penguin.

Fried, Michael (1980) *Absorption and Theatricality: Painting and Beholder in the Age of Diderot*, Berkeley: University of California Press.

Friedman, Norman (1955) 'Point of view in fiction: the development of a critical concept', *PMLA*, LXX, 1160–84.

Frith, Uta (1989) 'A new look at language and communication in autism', *British Journal of Disorders of Communication*, 24, 123–50.

Fuller, Peter (1980) *Art and Psychoanalysis*, London: Writers and Readers Publishing Cooperative.

Gadamer, Hans-Georg (1975) *Truth and Method*, London: Sheed & Ward.

Gadamer, Hans-Georg (1976) *Philosophical Hermeneutics*, London: University of California Press.

Gadamer, Hans-Georg (1986) *The Relevance of the Beautiful and Other*

Essays, trans. Nicholas Walker, ed. Robert Bernasconi, Cambridge: Cambridge University Press.

Gauss, Charles E. (1960) 'Some reflections on John Dewey's aesthetics', *Journal of Aesthetics and Art Criticism*, XIX (Winter), 127–32.

Genette, Gerard (1980) *Narrative Discourse*, Ithaca, NY: Cornell University Press.

Gibson, J. J. (1966) *The Senses Considered as Perceptual Systems*, Boston, Mass.: Houghton Mifflin.

Gibson, J. J. (1979) *The Ecological Approach to Visual Perception*. Boston, Mass.: Houghton Mifflin.

Glover, Jonathan (1989) *I: The Philosophy and Psychology of Personal Identity*, London: Penguin.

Gombrich, E. H. (1977) *Art and Illusion: A Study in the Psychology of Pictorial Representation*, London: Phaidon Press.

Goodman, Nelson (1976) *Languages of Art: An Approach to a Theory of Symbols*, Indianapolis: Hackett Publishing Co.

Goodman, Nelson (1978) *Ways of Worldmaking*, Hemel Hempstead: Harvester Wheatsheaf.

Goodman, Nelson (1984) *Of Mind and Other Matters*, Cambridge, Mass.: Harvard University Press.

Goodman, Nelson and Elgin, Catherine Z. (1988) *Reconceptions in Philosophy and Other Arts and Sciences*, Indianapolis/Cambridge: Hackett Publishing Co.

Gotshalk, D. W. (1964) 'On Dewey's aesthetics', *Journal of Aesthetics and Art Criticism*, XXIII (Fall), 131–8.

Gregory, R. L. (1966) *Eye and Brain*, London: Weidenfeld & Nicolson.

Gregory, R. L. (ed.) (1987) *The Oxford Companion to the Mind*, Oxford: Oxford University Press, s. v. 'Perception as hypotheses' by R. L. Gregory.

Grolnick, Simon A. and Barkin, Leonard (eds.) (1978) *Between Reality and Fantasy: Transitional Objects and Phenomena*, New York: Jason Aronson.

Haezrahi, Pepita (1954) *The Contemplative Activity*, London: George Allen & Unwin.

Hanfling, Oswald (ed.) (1992) *Philosophical Aesthetics: An Introduction;* Oxford: Blackwell Publishers in association with the Open University.

Harding, D. W. (1962) 'Psychological processes in the reading of fiction', *British Journal of Aesthetics*, 2 (April), 133–47.

Harré, Rom (1983) *Personal Being: A Theory for Individual Psychology*, Oxford: Basil Blackwell.

Harré, Rom (ed.) (1986) *The Social Construction of Emotions*, Oxford: Basil Blackwell.

Harré, Rom (1991) *Physical Being: A Theory for a Corporeal Psychology*, Oxford: Basil Blackwell.

Harré, Rom and Lamb, Roger (eds.) (1986a) *The Dictionary of Developmental and Educational Psychology*, Oxford: Basil Blackwell.

Harré, Rom and Lamb, Roger (eds.) (1986b) *The Dictionary of Personality and Social Psychology*, Oxford: Basil Blackwell.

Heider, Fritz (1958) *The Psychology of Interpersonal Relations*, New York: Wiley.

Herrigel, Eugen (1953) *Zen in the Art of Archery*, London: Routledge & Kegan Paul.

Hollis, Martin (1977) 'The self in action', in R. S. Peters (ed.) *John Dewey Reconsidered*, London: Routledge & Kegan Paul.

Hook, Sidney (ed.) (1967) *John Dewey: Philosopher of Science and Freedom*, New York: Barnes & Noble.

Hume, David (1969) *A Treatise of Human Nature*, Harmondsworth: Penguin.

Husserl, Edmund (1970) *Logical Investigations*, 2 vols., trans. J. N. Findlay, London: Routledge & Kegan Paul.

Iser, Wolfgang (1974) *The Implied Reader: Patterns of Communication in Prose Fiction from Bunyan to Beckett*, Baltimore: Johns Hopkins University Press.

Iser, Wolfgang (1978) *The Act of Reading: A Theory of Aesthetic Response*, London: Routledge & Kegan Paul.

Jackson, Frank (1990) 'Epiphenomenal qualia', in William G. Lycan (ed.) *Mind and Cognition: A Reader*, Oxford: Basil Blackwell.

James, William (1904) 'Does "consciousness" exist?', *Journal of Philosophy, Psychology and Scientific Methods*, 1, 18 (Sept.). Reprinted in John J. McDermott (ed.) (1968) *The Writings of William James*, New York: Random House, 169–83.

James, William (1908) *The Varieties of Religious Experience: A Study in Human Nature*, London: Longmans, Green & Co.

James, William (1912) *Essays in Radical Empiricism*, London: Longmans, Green & Co.

James, William (1950) *The Principles of Psychology*, 2 vols., New York: Dover Publications.

Jauss, Hans Robert (1982) *Toward an Aesthetic of Reception*, trans. Timothy Bahti, Hemel Hempstead: Harvester Wheatsheaf.

Kadish, Mortimer R. (1981) 'John Dewey and the theory of aesthetic practice', in Stephen M. Cahn (ed.) *New Studies in the Philosophy of John Dewey*, Hanover, New Hampshire: University Press of New England.

Kafka, Franz (1971) *Metamorphosis and Other Stories*, trans. Willa and Edwin Muir, Harmondsworth: Penguin.

Kaminsky, Jack (1957) 'Dewey's concept of "an" experience', *Philosophy and Phenomenological Research*, XVII (March), 316–30.

Kant, Immanuel (1952) *Critique of Judgement*, trans. J. C. Meredith, Oxford: Oxford University Press.

Kaye, Kenneth (1982) *The Mental and Social Life of Babies*, Chicago: University of Chicago Press.

Kearney, Richard (1986) *Modern Movements in European Philosophy*, Manchester: Manchester University Press.

Kenny, Anthony (1973) *Wittgenstein*, Harmondsworth: Penguin.

Klein, Melanie, Heimann, Paula and Money-Kyrle, R. E. (eds.) (1955) *New Directions in Psycho-Analysis*, London: Tavistock.

Kris, Ernst (1952) *Psychoanalytic Explorations in Art*, New York: International Universities Press.

Kristeva, Julia (1980) *Desire in Language*, New York: Columbia University Press.

Kruks, Sonia (1990) *Situation and Human Existence*, Scranton, Pennsylvania: Unwin Hyman.

Kubovy, Michael (1988) *The Psychology of Perspective and Renaissance Art*, Cambridge: Cambridge University Press.

Langer, Susanne K. (1953) *Feeling and Form*, New York: Charles Scribner's Sons.

Langer, Susanne K. (1967) *Mind: An Essay on Human Feeling*, vol. 1, Baltimore: Johns Hopkins University Press.

Langer, Susanne K. (1971) *Philosophy in a New Key: A Study in the Symbolism of Reason, Rite and Art*, Cambridge, Mass.: Harvard University Press.

Laplanche, J. and Pontalis, J.-B. (1980) *The language of Psycho-Analysis*, trans. Donald Nicholson-Smith, London: The Hogarth Press and the Institute of Psycho-Analysis.

Lee, Vernon (1913) *The Beautiful*, Cambridge: Cambridge University Press.

Levin, Janet (1990) 'Could love be like a heatwave? Physicalism and the subjective character of experience', in William G. Lycan (ed.) *Mind and Cognition: A Reader*, Oxford: Basil Blackwell.

Lind, Richard W. (1988) 'Aesthetic "sympathy" and expressive qualities', in Michael M. Mitias (ed.) *Aesthetic Quality and Aesthetic Experience*, Amsterdam: Rodopi.

Lipps, Theodor (1965) 'Empathy and aesthetic pleasure', in K. Aschenbrenner and A. Isenberg (eds.) *Aesthetic Theories: Studies in the Philosophy of Art*, Englewood Cliffs, NJ: Prentice Hall.

Lord, Catherine (1988) 'Intentionality and realization in aesthetic experience', in Michael M. Mitias (ed.) *Aesthetic Quality and Aesthetic Experience*, Amsterdam: Rodopi.

Lorenzer, Alfred and Orban, Peter (1978) 'Transitional objects and phenomena: socialization and symbolization', in Simon A. Grolnick and Leonard Barkin (eds.) *Between Reality and Fantasy: Transitional Objects and Phenomena*, New York: Jason Aronson, 479.

Lycan, William G. (ed.) (1990) *Mind and Cognition: A Reader*, Oxford: Basil Blackwell.

McClatchy, J. D. (1990) *Poets on Painters: Essays on the Art of Painting by Twentieth-Century Poets*, Los Angeles: University of California Press.

McDermott, John J. (ed.) (1968) *The Writings of William James*, New York: Random House.

McDermott, John J. (ed.) (1981) *The Philosophy of John Dewey*, Chicago: University of Chicago Press.

MacIntyre, Alasdair (1985) *After Virtue: A Study in Moral Theory*, London: Duckworth.

Mahler, Margaret S. (1969) *On Human Symbiosis and the Vicissitudes of Individuation*, vol. 1, London: The Hogarth Press.

Malins, Frederick (1980) *Understanding Paintings: The Elements of Composition*, Oxford: Phaidon Press.

Maurer, D. and Maurer, C. (1990) *The World of the Newborn*, London: Penguin.

Mead, G. H. (1933) *Mind, Self and Society*, Chicago: University of Chicago Press.

Mead, G. H. (1938) *The Philosophy of the Act*, Chicago: University of Chicago Press.

Mead, G. H. (1972) *Movements of Thought in the Nineteenth Century*, ed. Merritt H. Moore, Chicago: University of Chicago Press.

Merleau-Ponty, M. (1964a) *Sense and Nonsense*, trans. Hubert L. Dreyfus and Patricia A. Dreyfus, USA: Northwestern University Press.

Merleau-Ponty, M. (1964b) *The Primacy of Perception*, ed. James M. Edie, USA: Northwestern University Press.

Merleau-Ponty, M. (1964c) *Signs*, trans. Richard C. McCleary, USA: Northwestern University Press.

Merleau-Ponty, M. (1974) *The Prose of the World*, ed. Claude Lefort, trans. John O'Neill, London: Heinemann.

Merleau-Ponty, M. (1981) *Phenomenology of Perception*, trans. Colin Smith, London: Routledge & Kegan Paul.

Merton, Thomas (1965) *The Way of Chuang Tzu*, London: Unwin Books.

Merton, Thomas (1976) *Thomas Merton on Zen*, London: Sheldon Press.

Michaels, Walter Benn (1980) 'The interpreter's self: Peirce on the Cartesian "subject"', in Jane P. Tompkins (ed.) *Reader-Response Criticism: From Formalism to Post-Structuralism*, Baltimore: Johns Hopkins University Press. Originally published in *The Georgia Review*, 31 (Summer 1977), 383–402.

Millar, David L. (1980) *George Herbert Mead: Self, Language and the World*, Chicago: University of Chicago Press.

Milner, Marion (1981) *On Not Being Able to Paint*, London: Heinemann.

Mitias, Michael (1982) 'What makes an experience aesthetic?', *Journal of Aesthetics and Art Criticism*, XLI, 2 (Winter), 157–69.

Mitias, Michael (1988a) *What Makes Experience Aesthetic?* Amsterdam: Rodopi.

Mitias, Michael (ed.) (1988b) *Aesthetic Quality and Aesthetic Experience*, Amsterdam: Rodopi.

Morris, Bertrand (1970) 'Dewey's theory of art', in Jo Ann Boydston (ed.) *Guide to the Works of John Dewey*, Carbondale: Southern Illinois University Press.

Morris, Charles (1939) 'Science, art and technology', *The Kenyon Review*, 1, 409–23.

Morris, Charles (1939–40) 'Esthetics and the theory of signs', *Journal of Unified Science [Erkenntnis]*, VIII, 131–50.

Morris, Charles (1964) *Signification and Significance*, Cambridge, Mass.: The MIT Press.

Mühlhäusler, Peter and Harré, Rom (1990) *Pronouns and People: The Linguistic Construction of Social and Personal Identity*, Oxford: Basil Blackwell.

Myers, Gerald E. (1986) *William James: His Life and Thought*, New Haven: Yale University Press.

Nagel, Thomas (1979) *Mortal Questions*, Cambridge: Cambridge University Press.

Nagel, Thomas (1986) *The View from Nowhere*, Oxford: Oxford University Press.

Nell, Victor (1988) *Lost in a Book: The Psychology of Reading for Pleasure*, New Haven: Yale University Press.

Nemirow, Laurence (1990) 'Physicalism and the cognitive role of acquaintance', in William G. Lycan (ed.) *Mind and Cognition: A Reader*, Oxford: Basil Blackwell.

O'Hare, David (1981) 'Cognition, categorisation and aesthetic responses', in H. Bonarius, R. Holland and S. Rosenberg (eds.) *Personal Construct Psychology: Recent Advances in Theory and Practice*, London: Macmillan.

Ong, Walter (1975) 'The writer's audience is always a fiction', *PMLA*, 90 (January), 9–21.

Osborne, Harold (1970) *The Art of Appreciation*, London: Oxford University Press.

Parsons, Michael J. (1980) 'James Mark Baldwin and the aesthetic development of the individual', *Journal of Aesthetic Education*, 14, 1, 31–50.

Parsons, Michael J. (1987) *How We Understand Art: A Cognitive Developmental Account of Aesthetic Experience*, Cambridge: Cambridge University Press.

Pepper, Stephen C. (1939) 'Some questions on Dewey's aesthetics', in Paul A. Schilpp (ed.) *The Philosophy of John Dewey*, Illinois: Open Court, 369–90.

Pepper, Stephen C. (1953) 'The concept of fusion in Dewey's aesthetic theory', *Journal of Aesthetics and Art Criticism*, XII (Dec), 169–76.

Perry, John (1979) 'The problem of the essential indexical', *NOUS*, 13, 1 (March), 3–21.

Peters, R. S. (ed.) (1977) *John Dewey Reconsidered*, London: Routledge & Kegan Paul.

Piaget, Jean (1974) *The Child and Reality*, trans. Arnold Rosin, London: Frederick Muller.

Poulet, Georges (1980) 'Criticism and the experience of interiority', in Jane P. Tompkins (ed.) *Reader-Response Criticism: From Formalism to Post-Structuralism*, Baltimore: Johns Hopkins University Press.

Price, Kingsley (1979) 'What makes an experience aesthetic?', *British Journal of Aesthetics*, 19, 2, 131–43.

Quinton, Anthony (1977) 'Inquiry, thought and action. John Dewey's theory of knowledge', in R. S. Peters (ed.) *John Dewey Reconsidered*, London: Routledge & Kegan Paul.

Rader, Melvin (ed.) (1979) *A Modern Book of Aesthetics*, 5th edn, London: Holt, Rinehart & Winston.

Reid, Louis Arnaud (1969) *Meaning in the Arts*, London: George Allen & Unwin.

Rimmon-Kenan, Shlomith (1983) *Narrative Fiction: Contemporary Poetics*, London: Methuen.

Rogers, Carl (1951) *Client-Centred Therapy*, Boston: Houghton Mifflin.
Rorty, Richard (1982) *Consequences of Pragmatism*, Hemel Hempstead: Harvester Wheatsheaf.
Roy, Claude (1972) 'L'Amour de la peinture', in Dore Ashton (ed.) *Picasso on Art: A Selection of Views*, New York: Viking.
Sachs, Oliver (1984) *A Leg to Stand On*, London: Picador.
Sachs, Oliver (1989) *Seeing Voices: A Journey into the World of the Deaf*, Berkeley: University of California Press.
Scaife, M. and Bruner, J. S. (1975) 'The capacity for joint visual attention in the infant', *Nature*, 253, 266.
Scheffler, Israel (1974) *Four Pragmatists: A Critical Introduction to Peirce, James, Mead and Dewey*, London: Routledge & Kegan Paul.
Scheffler, Israel (1986) *Inquiries: Philosophical Studies of Language, Science and Learning*, Indianapolis: Hackett Publishing Co.
Schilpp, Paul A. (ed.) (1971) *The Philosophy of John Dewey*, 2nd edn, La Salle, Illinois: Open Court.
Scruton, Roger (1989) *Kant*, Oxford: Oxford University Press.
Searle, John (1983) *Intentionality: Essays on the Philosophy of Mind*, Cambridge: Cambridge University Press.
Sebeok, Thomas A. (1986) *I Think I am a Verb: More Contributions to the Doctrine of Signs*, London: Plenum Press.
Segal, Hanna (1955) 'A psycho-analytical approach to aesthetics', in Melanie Klein, Paula Heimann and R. E. Money-Kyrle (eds.) *New Directions in Psycho-Analysis*, London: Tavistock.
Shearer, E. A. (1935a) 'Dewey's esthetic theory I: the earlier theory', *Journal of Philosophy*, XXXII, 23, 617–27.
Shearer, E. A. (1935b) 'Dewey's esthetic theory II: the present theory', *Journal of Philosophy*, XXXII, 24, 650–64.
Shusterman, Richard (1986a) 'Deconstruction and analysis: confrontation and convergence', *British Journal of Aesthetics*, 26, 311–27.
Shusterman, Richard (1986b) 'Analytic aesthetics, literary theory and deconstruction', *Monist*, 69, 22–38.
Shusterman, Richard (1989a) 'Why Dewey Now?', *Journal of Aesthetic Education*, 23, 3 (Fall), 60–7.
Shusterman, Richard (ed.) (1989b) *Analytic Aesthetics*, Oxford: Basil Blackwell.
Shusterman, Richard (1992) *Pragmatist Aesthetics: Living Beauty, Rethinking Art*, Oxford: Basil Blackwell.
Shweder, Richard (1990) 'Cultural psychology: what is it?', in James W. Stigler, Richard A. Shweder and Gilbert Herdt (eds) *Cultural Psychology: Essays on Comparative Human Development*, Cambridge: Cambridge University Press.
Smith, R. A. (1988) *The Journal of Aesthetic Education: Special Issue: Art, Mind and Education*, 22, 1 (March).
Solzhenitsyn, Alexander (1972) *'One Word of Truth . . .': The Nobel Speech on Literature 1970*, London: The Bodley Head.
Spitz, Ellen (1985) *Art and Psyche*, New Haven: Yale University Press.

Spitz, René (1965) *The First Year of Life: A Psychoanalytic Study of Normal and Deviant Development of Object Relations*, New York: International Universities Press.

Steiner, George (1969) *Language and Silence*, Harmondsworth: Pelican.

Stern, Daniel (1985) *The Interpersonal World of the Infant*, New York: Basic Books.

Stevens, Richard (1974) *James and Husserl: The Foundations of Meaning*, The Hague: Martinus Nijhoff.

Stevens, Wallace (1972) *The Palm at the End of the Mind: Selected Poems and a Play*, ed. Holly Stevens, New York: Vintage Books.

Suzuki, D. T. (1954) 'Zen and pragmatism – a reply', *Philosophy East and West*, IV, 2, 167–74.

Suzuki, D. T. (1957) *Mysticism Christian and Buddhist*, London: George Allen & Unwin.

Suzuki, D. T. (1970) *Zen and Japanese Culture*, Princeton, NJ: Princeton University.

Tanz, C. (1980) *Studies in the Acquisition of Deictic Terms*, Cambridge: Cambridge University Press.

Taylor, Charles (1989) *Sources of the Self: The Making of the Modern Identity*, Cambridge, Mass.: Harvard University Press.

Thayer, H. S. (1968) *Meaning and Action: A Critical History of Pragmatism*, New York: The Bobbs-Merrill Co.

Thomas, Glyn and Silk, Angele M. J. (1990) *An Introduction to the Psychology of Children's Drawings*, Hemel Hempstead: Harvester Wheatsheaf.

Tiles, J. E. (1990) *Dewey*, London: Routledge.

Tompkins, Jane P. (ed.) (1980) *Reader-Response Criticism: From Formalism to Post-Structuralism*, Baltimore: Johns Hopkins University Press.

Trevarthen, Colwyn (1987a, 1987b) 'Brain development' and 'Mind in infancy', in R. L. Gregory (ed.) *The Oxford Companion to the Mind*, Oxford: Oxford University Press.

Vollard, Ambroise (1978) *Recollections of a Picture Dealer*, New York: Hacker Art Books.

Walton, Kendall (1976) 'Points of view in narrative and depictive representation', *NOUS*, 10, 1 (March), 49–61.

Wertsch, James V. (ed.) (1985) *Culture, Communication and Cognition: Vygotskian Perspectives*, Cambridge: Cambridge University Press.

Westbrook, Robert B. (1991) *John Dewey and American Democracy*, New York: Cornell University Press.

Whitman, Walt (1960) *Leaves of Grass: The First (1855) Edition*, ed. Malcolm Cowley, London: Secker & Warburg.

Wilkinson, Elizabeth M. (ed.) (1957) *Aesthetics: Lectures and Essays by Edward Bullough*, Cambridge: Cambridge University Press.

Williams, Raymond (1981) *Keywords: A Vocabulary of Culture and Society*, London: Fontana/Croom Helm.

Wilson, Jenny (1991) *The Lakeland Poets: An Illustrated Collection*, London: Weidenfeld & Nicolson.

Winnicott, Donald W. (1974) *Playing and Reality*, Harmondsworth: Penguin.

Wispé, Lauren (1991) *The Psychology of Sympathy*, New York: Plenum Publishers.

Wittgenstein, Ludwig (1958) *Philosophical Investigations*, trans. G. E. M. Anscombe, Oxford: Basil Blackwell.

Wittgenstein, Ludwig (1970) *Lectures and Conversations on Aesthetics, Psychology and Religious Belief*, ed. C. Barrett. Oxford: Basil Blackwell.

Wollheim, Richard (1974) *On Art and the Mind*, Cambridge, Mass.: Harvard University Press.

Wollheim, Richard (1980) *Art and its Objects*, 2nd edn, Cambridge: Cambridge University Press.

Wollheim, Richard (1984) *The Thread of Life*, Cambridge: Cambridge University Press.

Wollheim, Richard (1987) *Painting as an Art*, London: Thames & Hudson.

Worringer, Wilhelm (1953) *Abstraction and Empathy*, New York: International Universities Press.

Wreen, M. J. and Callen, D. M. (eds.) (1982) *The Aesthetic Point of View*, Ithaca, NY: Cornell University Press.

Wright, Elizabeth (1984) *Psychoanalytic Criticism: Theory in Practice*, London: Methuen.

Yeats, W. B. (1970) *Selected Poems*, ed. A. Norman Jeffares, London: Macmillan.

Yourgrau, Palle (ed.) (1990) *Demonstratives*, Oxford: Oxford University Press.

Zeltner, P. M. (1975) *John Dewey's Aesthetic Philosophy*, Amsterdam: R. R. Bruner.

Zink, Sidney (1943) 'The concept of continuity in Dewey's theory of esthetics', *Philosophical Review*, LI, 392–400.

INDEX

absent-minded, 184
absorption, etymological
    derivation, 2
action, immediate, 98
actor, becomes character, 11
acts, voluntary and involuntary,
    135
aesthetic, use of word in book, 8
aesthetic experience, 5
    concept of, 11–20
    control of development, 160
    direct, 19–20
    enabling and foundational role
        of body, 186–7
    immediate non-cognitive, 18–19
    of art, 6–8, 20–7
    reading compared with looking
        at pictures, 166–7
    scrutiny and recollection, 97
    Western vernacular concept of,
        13
Albers, J., 171
Allport, G., 19
American Sign Language, 133
analyic aesthetics, contrast with
    Deweyan aesthetics, 21–2
analytical philosophy, 39
anger, 29, 37
Anscombe, 93
architecture, 184
Aristotle, 43, 44

Arnheim, R., 3, 113, 128, 145,
    167–8, 171, 178, 179, 180
art,
    aesthetic experiences, 6–8, 20–7
    medium, 33
    restoration powers, Dewey,
        66–7, 101
    see also pictures
art theories,
    historical influences, 22
    socio-economic influences, 22 ·
artistic, use of word in book, 8
artistic media, Dewey, 31
artists' psychodynamics, 52
association as basis for transferred
    values, 37
associated living, 182
autobiography, 126, 136–7
awareness, 5

babies, *see* infants
Bandura, A., 123
Barnes, A. C., 33–4, 38, 48, 49
Barzun, J., 13
Beardsley, M., 5, 11, 23
Beckett, S., 79, 113
Benjamin, W., 2, 183–4
Berger, J., 49, 150
Bettleheim, B., 109
biological clocks, 127